SHAKY

SHAKY

THE BIOGRAPHY OF SHAKIN' STEVENS

MICHAEL HEATLEY

MICHAEL O'MARA BOOKS LIMITED

First published in Great Britain in 2005 by
Michael O'Mara Books Limited
9 Lion Yard, Tremadoc Road
London sw4 7nq

Copyright © Michael Heatley 2005

The right of Michael Heatley to be identified as the author
of this work has been asserted by him in accordance with the
Copyrights, Designs and Patents Act 1988.

A CIP catalogue record for this book is available
from the British Library

ISBN 1-84317-177-5

1 3 5 7 9 10 8 6 4 2

www.mombooks.com

Designed and typeset by Martin Bristow

Printed and bound in Great Britain by Clays Ltd, St Ives plc

CONTENTS

Acknowledgements

Many people agreed to assist in our researches for this book, whether or not they wanted crediting. With apologies for any omissions, I'd like to thank the following for their responses: Paul Barrett, Rockin' Louie (Robert Llewellyn), David Roberts, Ian Gomm, Adrian Angove, Patrick Humphries, Clive Selwood, Sean Tyla, Donny Marchand, Alan Clayson, Brian Hodgson, Mike Hurst, B. J. Cole, Tony Hall, Geraint Watkins, Albert Lee, Barry Plummer, Chris Wyles, Gavin Povey, Les Davidson, Pete Wingfield, Don Reedman, Steve Taylor, Darrel Higham, Rod Argent, David Smith, Danny Brittain, Ben Waters, Sue Carlin, Mark Jones, Iain Fergus, Iain McNay, Ben Darnton, Angie at Fumble on the Web, Norman Jopling, Will Birch, Steve Tallamy, Sam Szczepanski and Suresh Tolat.

My team of researchers did me proud, too: many thanks to Gaynor Edwards, Pete Feenstra, Deke Leonard, Alan Kinsman, John Tobler, Spencer Leigh, Geoffrey Davis and Jon Kutner.

Shaky has many brilliant websites dedicated to his music. Particularly recommended are:

www.forevershakin.co.uk
www.shakin.co.uk
www.tonyrivers.com
www.rockabillyhall.com
www.shakinstevens.com (official site)

As well as the Shaky websites, many different publications were consulted, including *New Musical Express*, *Melody Maker*, *Record Mirror*, *Look In*, *Smash Hits*, *Number 1*, *Record Collector*, *The Sun*, *Glasgow Herald* and *Daily Record*.

Thanks and gratitude to Nephele Headland for holding it all together, and to Diana Briscoe for compiling the discography.

Last but not least, thanks to Lindsay Davies at Michael O'Mara for the inspiration and Helen Cumberbatch for the perspiration – both of which Shaky also exudes!

PHOTOGRAPH ACKNOWLEDGEMENTS

PAGES 1–5: Paul Barrett Rock 'n' Roll Enterprises;
PAGE 6: © popperfoto.com (*above*), Empics (*below*);
PAGE 7: ITV/Rex Features (*both*);
PAGE 8: Gered Mankowitz/Redferns;
PAGE 9: Andre Csillag/Rex Features (*above*),
BBC Photo Library/Redferns (*below*);
PAGE 10: Photonews Scotland/Rex Features (*above*),
Nils Jorgensen/Rex Features (*below*);
PAGE 11: Mirrorpix.com (above),
BBC Photo Library/Redferns (*below*);
PAGE 12: TopFoto/UPPA (*above*),
Andre Csillag/Rex Features (*below*);
PAGE 13: Rowan Griffiths/Rex Features (*above*),
Alpha Press (*below*);
PAGE 14: DPA/Empics (*above*),
Ray Tang/Rex Features (*below*);
PAGE 15: Mark Allan/Alpha Press (*above*),
Getty Images/Jim Dyson (*below*);
PAGE 16: Getty Images/Dave Hogan.

INTRODUCTION

ONE MORE TIME: 2005

TALK TO ANY RESURGENT POP STAR about their comeback and the stock answer will be 'I've never been away'. In an era of gold radio, *Top of the Pops 2* and *I Love The 1980s*-style nostalgia TV shows, there's now little reason for stars of yester-year not to 'bop till they drop'. Many, however, have to settle for making a living from playing smaller venues, topping up their bank balance with appearances on the 'holiday-camp circuit', where like-minded music-lovers gather out of season to roll back the years and indulge in a nostalgia-fest for the 1950s, 1960s, 1970s or even 1980s.

Perhaps it's because he had to wait a decade for stardom, travelling the length and breadth of the country fronting the rock 'n' roll band The Sunsets, that Shakin' Stevens has never had to follow that path. Instead, and ably abetted by some shrewd management, the officially accredited Most Successful Chart Act of the 1980s has retained his status as a headlining live attraction.

Though record success later dipped at home as new acts took the limelight, he carefully concentrated his efforts on European markets, especially in Scandinavia, where his following remained strongest and he was able to fill 8,000-seater venues. And, having topped the charts in Denmark in 2004 with a collection of his greatest recorded moments, he reproduced his early successes by taking a CD and DVD release to the UK Top Five – in fact, rarely has a resurgence been so widely acclaimed.

But it hasn't been an easy ride to fame and fortune. Long before the apprenticeship with The Sunsets, Shaky had had to carve out a career for himself despite leaving school with no qualifications and no prospects. The youngest of eleven children born to a working-class couple in a downmarket Cardiff suburb, he'd scrabbled to make a living by taking jobs from window cleaner through milkman to upholsterer. Yet never did his dedication to rock 'n' roll waver. Indeed it was his love for the music that saw him through the hard times, leaving wife and family at home for most of the year as he toured continental Europe to little financial reward, building up his stagecraft and surfing the disappointment of record deals that failed to earn him more than a token sum.

He'd never bent to fad or fashion, even when such big breaks as supporting The Rolling Stones in their prestigious 1969 gigs had come to nothing. It never occurred to him to wear flares, grow his hair or 'go hippie' – his way was the only way, and if it took the world time to catch up then that was the way it would have to be, which is of course what made the taste of success, when it came, all the sweeter.

Thus, when Shakin' Stevens pitched up on reality TV talent show *Hit Me Baby One More Time* in the spring of 2005, he was far from being a washed-up star launching himself in one last desperate attempt to grab the national limelight. In truth, Stevens's appearance was the last brick in a carefully constructed campaign that would see his hits compilation *The Collection* return him to the spotlight in Britain.

The product he was promoting was a CD and DVD package that essentially reprised the years between 1980 and 1992 that, for the first half of the 1980s at least, had seen him dominate the UK singles chart over the hipper likes of Adam Ant and Duran Duran. As *Guinness World Records British Hit Singles & Albums* editor David Roberts explains, the basis for his title of most successful act of the decade is in terms of weeks registered on the chart, rather than sales figures, ensuring the title is indisputable. 'We love to carve up the stats in our database,' says Roberts, 'and one Monday we thought we would find the most successful chart acts of each decade. We came up with Elton John for the 1970s and The Beatles, not surprisingly, for the 1960s. We were amazed when we did the same job on the 1980s, crunched in all the numbers and who should pop up but Shakin' Stevens!

'He was presented with the Most Successful Chart Act of the 1980s award, which is based on something that, unlike sales figures, can't be hyped. The one thing you can't disagree with is the number of weeks that somebody spent on the UK chart, and he spent more weeks on the UK chart than any other artist in the 1980s.

'He was churning out all those Number Ones and appealing to a female audience, which was very much what the 1980s were about – but not his type of music. I think that it's like anything: things come back in circles in very regular fashion and rock 'n' roll had been dormant for so long. It only needed someone with a bit of charisma who could carry a song like Elvis used to do, to remind people of how good Elvis was – and Shaky was that man.'

The big break for Shakin' Stevens had come in 1977 when he was selected to portray the middle-period Elvis in a stage show of the rock 'n' roll legend's life, which was produced by impresario Jack Good in London, just months after the King's untimely death. Shaky not only honed his stagecraft when performing night after night to packed houses, he also caught the eye of the record-company bosses and a manager who would help him make the long-awaited jump to international stardom. He also starred in Jack Good's TV programmes

Oh Boy! and *Let's Rock*, experience that would again prove invaluable in projecting himself into the living rooms of the nation and boosting his singles to the top of the 1980s charts. And as *Hit Me Baby One More Time* would prove, it was a knack he would not lose.

Just as the infant medium of television made the original Elvis a star in the mid-1950s – albeit cutting him off at the waist – small-screen exposure would be crucial in returning Shakin' Stevens to the hearts of his fans. Hence his exposure to the public vote. 'If you have a release,' he reasoned, during an interview on LBC, 'you need to promote it, and you need to let people know it's out there or they're not going to buy it. I wouldn't have done *Hit Me Baby* if I didn't have a release . . . With respect to the other contestants we are all winners anyway, but . . . to me it was . . . a kind of a pride thing . . . They were pleased to get me on their show, so we both got a lot out of it.'

Hit Me Baby One More Time followed the interactive formula of recent series *Reborn In The USA*, where the likes of Tony Hadley (Spandau Ballet) and Peter Cox (Go West) had been bussed from coast to coast with a number of lesser stars, the public voting someone off the bus at each stop via their telephone. Just as those two vocal talents had seemed a class apart from the competition, so Shaky and Carol Decker, formerly of 1980s hitmakers T'Pau, seemed light years ahead of the likes of Tiffany, Chesney Hawkes, Shalamar, Hue and Cry and boy band 911.

It was hard to believe the man strutting and hip-swivelling as to the manner born was now fifty-seven, but youthful good looks had long been a trademark. As Ian Gomm of the band Brinsley Schwarz, who rubbed shoulders with Shaky on the college circuit in the 1970s, says, 'He looks unnaturally young now, but back then he looked *ridiculously* young.' As for dying his hair, the natural brunette had been doing that since his youth.

Yet what the public saw was not the total package. The Shakin' Stevens whom his fans know is an extrovert whose only intention is to rock 'n' roll. Yet the man born Michael Barratt is a considerably more complex individual who, having enjoyed a wild youth and lived the rock 'n' roll life to the full as frontman of The Sunsets from 1969 to 1977, was later preserved from its worst excesses by a string of decisive and influential managers. Not unlike Elvis Presley, whose interests were also looked after by a strong-willed mentor, it was sometimes the case that Shaky was insulated from normal everyday life in order to keep the focus firmly on his all-important career.

A rocked-up version of 'Trouble', first recorded by punky US girl singer Pink, which had been a Top Ten UK hit for her in 2003, was the song on which Shaky's comeback hopes were pinned. He was not known for covering contemporary songs, but a keen eye for unearthing authentic rock 'n' roll material and giving it an 'edge' was a key part of his successful formula. The man who helped him in that quest was bassist and producer Stuart Colman, and the fact that he was back on board after more or less two decades' absence confirmed that Shakin' Stevens meant business.

British Hit Singles & Albums editor David Roberts feels that it's this dangerous 'edge' that helped Shaky cross boundaries – females wanted him, males wanted to be like him. 'There were one or two other [rock 'n' roll acts] like Showaddywaddy who had a good female fan base, but Shaky's fan base crossed over. He's one of these artists who, where the charts are concerned, had super success because he was able to satisfy the demands of two different fan bases.'

It must also be noted that, though he had been more or less invisible in Britain in the past decade, his European fan base – the same one that had let him play the same venues in the 1980s as The Rolling Stones, and Spandau Ballet – had remained faithful. The 2004 Langelands Festival had given him the opportunity to play to 25,000 people and many more on television, proof that he was far from a spent force.

The challenge now was to reconnect with his British fans while hoping to impress a few thousand who perhaps hadn't even been born in his chart heyday. And that was where *Hit Me Baby One More Time* came in. Having strolled through his heat with little 'Trouble', for Shakin Stevens it would be up to the nation to set the seal on his comeback. But then he'd never been away . . .

1

How Green Was
My Valley: 1948–68

THE YEAR OF 1948 DAWNED as the third full year of post-war
peace. Yet it also marked twelve months in which Indian
spiritual leader Mohandas K. Gandhi was assassinated, Czechoslovakia fell under Communist rule and Berlin was blockaded
by Russia. It peaked controversially with the formation of the
state of Israel and ended with the *Kinsey Report*, a publication
summarizing the sex lives of over 5,000 American males. In
between all this London had hosted the Olympics, making
1948 a landmark year for many people.

Not least the Barratt family, of Marcross Road, Cardiff.
Their three-bedroomed house was already well populated, but
the arrival of Michael in March of that year brought the
number of children who'd passed through its doors to eleven.
Six brothers – Jackie, Kenneth, Jimmy, Freddie, Roy and Leslie
– and four sisters – Nancy, Aileen, Joyce and Muriel – had
preceded the new arrival, but so spread out were the children

of Jack and May that only a certain number were ever in residence at the same time.

The Barratt family had started to expand in the early 1920s, with Michael the last addition. 'We were kinda split into two,' he said of the Barratt tribe in a 2005 radio interview, 'and I came at the back of the family with my brother Leslie who's two years older than myself . . . my eldest brother must be late seventies, eighty-odd. So by the time I came along all my brothers and sisters were married and saw for [*sic*]. My mother had me when she was . . . forty-three, so quite late really. My parents aren't with me now, but they were from a generation where my dad was in the First World War, and I never saw my mum with her natural hair, it was always grey.

'People say that it must have been hell to have been brought up with so many brothers and sisters. But what they don't realize is that we really were two families. Half of our family were grown up, married and living away from home by the time that I came on the scene. I basically grew up with Mum and Dad and Roy, Muriel and Leslie. Leslie was just a couple of years older than me so that when I was attending junior school, he was at senior school.'

Michael's formative years in Cardiff brought many happy memories. And many of them were musical. 'There were lots of records played at home,' he remembers, 'from Al Jolson to Hoagy Carmichael. I grew up in a house full of noise, and I suppose, since there always seemed to be music in our house, that was one reason why I was introduced early to rock 'n' roll. A definite influence too, was my big brother, Roy, who had a collection of 1950s records. Roy also used to take me to the cinema when I was a youngster. All that certainly made a considerable impression.'

Television was a relative novelty in those days, and the young Michael was rapidly hooked. 'On the rare occasions I wasn't listening to music, I liked watching TV – I liked programmes with a hero of some kind – like the cowboy series

Hopalong Cassidy, *Robin Hood*, or *Champion the Wonder Horse*.'
When the gogglebox wasn't keeping him indoors, Mike used
the streets as his playground. 'I was an outdoor sort of lad. I
used to like nothing better than to kick a ball around, and
when we went on family holidays to Porthcawl I used to lark
around on the sand dunes with my brothers.'

He loved his family dearly, and he regrets his father didn't
live to see his success. 'He liked to sing [to] himself in our
house . . . show us a Welshman who can't sing!' As with so
many of his generation, father Jack – actually born in Bradford
– had been sent down the mines but had escaped to work in
the building trade. Life underground was never, happily, an
option the youngest of the family had to entertain. 'I'm certain
about one thing . . . I was never going to go to work at the
mines, like my dad had done. He'd got out of that as fast as he
could, and there was no way that I wanted to be a miner.'

In a 1984 magazine interview, Shaky revealed that Welshness
was actually at a premium in his locality: 'Where I come from
you could take or leave the Welsh thing. When I was growing
up they didn't have the [road] signs in Welsh everywhere or
many people speaking Welsh. The Cardiff area isn't a Welsh
community like the Rhondda. [In fact] the Welsh used to look
on Cardiff as Sin City. It had two picture houses and one
nightclub.'

It was to one of those cinemas that brother Roy took
Michael for an early shot of rock. 'He definitely influenced me
the most. He used to take me out to see rock 'n' roll films and
play discs such as the Big Bopper's "Chantilly Lace" – all of
which set me on the path to a lifetime of rock 'n' roll.' The
process had become even more marked in 1956, when Mike
was given an Elvis guitar for his birthday. Of course, it was a
plastic toy and not the real thing, but for a kid that age in love
with music it was beyond price.

Michael's best pal outside the family was next-door-
neighbour Dave Dutton. The pair soon tuned in to a diet of

rock 'n' roll music from the exotically American likes of Elvis, Little Richard and Eddie Cochran. Mike and Dave started their educational life at Windsor Clyde School, graduating to Central and, later, Hywell Dda. Neither made the top stream, preferring to channel their energies into more pleasurable activities. 'I wasn't terribly interested in books, I suppose,' Shaky reflected years later. 'I enjoyed games and being in the fresh air.' Music was playing an increasing part in his life but, while the kind of tuition he was receiving at school was of limited use, his teacher, a Miss Cox, wasn't totally unsupportive. 'Son,' she said to him, 'you're going to annoy an awful lot of people, but keep going. You'll make it in the end.'

Michael's whole life had changed when he discovered music. 'Though I'm ashamed to admit it,' he later confessed, 'I used to play truant from school to listen to records for hours in a neighbour's house.' Nevertheless, a classroom was where the future Shakin' Stevens made his first performance in front of an audience, standing up to sing 'Rock Around The Clock'. This had become a major hit single in Britain for Bill Haley and the Comets when it was used as the theme music for the 1955 film *The Blackboard Jungle,* so it seems reasonable to assume that Michael was at primary school at the time.

Elvis Presley was, of course, another major figure to influence the budding singer in those formative years, and not just thanks to that plastic guitar. Little can the youngster have realized that he would be playing the King in a stage production some two decades later, in the show that would catapult him to fame in his own right. Not that Michael was alone in his passion. He was indulged by mum May to the extent that the family acquired a well-worn upright piano, though it eventually gave up the ghost as a result of the youngster's enthusiastic pounding, and also because it was regularly moved from one room of the small council house to the other to make space for the Barratt tribe.

Dreams of piano-thumping stardom in the wake of Jerry

Lee Lewis and Little Richard would be superseded by his emergence as a singer – amazing since, like so many teenagers then and now, he was painfully shy. It's been said that at the beginning of his career he even used to stand with his back to the audience, but this seems unlikely, since earlier stories have him winning first prize in a fancy-dress competition at his primary school (into which Miss Cox had entered him) by dressing up as a gum-chewing rock 'n' roller (though he was made to remove the gum!).

Much has been made of the fact that the music of Michael Barratt's infancy was in fact the raw material with which he later found worldwide fame. He was six years old, for instance, when Rosemary Clooney took the original version of 'This Ole House' to the UK Number One spot, while two years later 'Green Door' reached the Top Ten in the hands of Frankie Vaughan. But the singer denied the former song even made an impression on him in the 1950s. 'The very first time I ever heard it was just before Christmas 1980,' reveals Shaky. 'I was visiting a friend who has this collection of old records. He pulled out "This Ole House" and played it for me. I was amazed that no one had released a cover version since 1954 and I just knew that I had to record the song.'

But then Rosemary Clooney has rarely been a hip name to drop. Big Joe Turner, whose 'Shake, Rattle and Roll' was issued in Britain in 1954, was another matter. 'Bill Haley, Elvis, Billy Swan have covered it. It's a song many groups have done on stage,' he confirmed on LBC in 2005. 'I first heard this a very long time ago and I was just messing with the radio tuning to different stations. [When] I heard this track I couldn't believe my ears. The snare [drum] was like someone beating a big, round cabbage with a stick! Fantastic brass, the phrasing on his voice was tremendous and I was bowled over. I had to get some vinyl of this man and it's always stuck in my memory.'

Parental approval was sporadic, but Michael wouldn't be put off. 'My father was very encouraging in my musical career, but my mum wasn't so keen at first. When I left school and told her I wanted to be a singer, her first reaction was, "Do what your other brothers and sisters did – get a proper job!" I used to sing in school and I could see the pleasure people would get. That's what I wanted to do . . . perform.'

Another youthful landmark was reached when he heard Bruce Chanel's 'Hey Baby' in 1962. 'I heard his record growing up,' Shaky revealed in a radio interview, 'and it was very catchy and a very unusual voice. I was particularly attracted by the sound of the harmonica . . . it's just a great record, one that will stay around for a long time. The guy who played the harmonica was called Delbert McClinton, a famous country artist. And the story goes that John Lennon [copied it] . . . if you hear "Love Me Do" you'll hear exactly the same sound.'

'Love Me Do' was, of course, The Beatles' debut hit – a first sign that the musical climate was changing, the raw rock of the 1950s giving way first to Merseybeat and, later in the decade, to more sophisticated fare. The music Michael Barratt grew up with was The Beatles and The Rolling Stones, whose covers of Chuck Berry and Bo Diddley inspired little response. 'But rock 'n' roll records, things like Carl Perkins doing "Honey Don't", gave me a quiver up the backbone. It wasn't in my era, but it did so much for me, and a lot of other people as well – Mick Jagger and John Lennon, for starters. When The Beatles heard Larry Williams singing "Dizzy Miss Lizzy", they recorded it! These were explosive records. They did have an effect on me and I'm sure they had an effect on many superstar groups that are still kicking today. I couldn't believe what I was hearing. I thought, "That's for me," and I wanted to try to capture the excitement that I got from those records.'

Although music was to develop at a rapid pace in the 1960s, not everyone was prepared to let go of the past so readily, and an underground rock 'n' roll scene developed. Cardiff's contribution was a band called The Backbeats, whose lead singer Rockin' Louie (real name Robert Llewellyn) became the youngster's role model. So keen was Shaky on these be-quiffed musical throwbacks that he was sometimes even allowed up on stage to sing with the band.

The first time Shaky and Louie met was in a pub in Ely, Cardiff, before a Backbeats gig at the Resurrection Hall. 'We used to play there every Sunday,' Louie explains, 'and because it was a religious place there was no drinking in there. So, while the roadie was busy setting up the gear, I had to walk at least a mile to the nearest pub. And Shaky was in there. He must have been fourteen, he wasn't old enough to be in a pub. He asked me for my autograph. I was just about to order a drink, and it was full of people so I had to push in because I had to get back. I was trying not to cause trouble by pushing in too obviously, so I was leaning over shoulders. He told me then that he used to come and see The Backbeats every Sunday. He was a fan.'

The Backbeats manager Paul Barrett (no relation) was to become a second pivotal figure in the youngster's career. But at that point, in the mid-1960s, his school years coming to an end and no qualifications attained, it was a question of earning a living. And rock 'n' roll was unlikely to provide that, much as Michael might have wished otherwise.

'When it was time to leave school I didn't really know what I wanted to do. But I had a lot of different jobs, doing everything from cleaning windows – which I wasn't very good at – to learning how to upholster furniture. I was also a driver's mate, which was my first job. I was paid three pounds a week for that before tax deductions. I had several jobs . . . I couldn't keep one down 'cos I would sing in the evening.'

The bands he fronted in the mid-1960s included The Velvets, The Bandits and The Olympics. The latter came by its handle because the drummer had an Olympic kit, but it was later re-christened The Cossacks when another band called The Olympics made itself known. Appropriately, the group members briefly decked themselves out in Russian shirts – but, however exotically dressed Mike and his friends became, the music never deviated from rock 'n' roll.

The Cossacks became The Denims, a moniker that at least allowed for a certain licence in the dressing-up stakes. Funnily enough, it was an image Mike liked so much, he's never changed it. He did, however, break away from The Denims for a spell to try life with a band called The Big Five, who had better equipment. But the crunch came when they asked him to sing chart material by the likes of The Small Faces who, at the time, were riding high with songs like 'Whatcha Gonna Do About It?' and 'Sha-La-La-La-Lee'. None of this passed muster with Mike Barratt the rock 'n' roll purist, who promptly returned to his pals, the three Daves: Dutton, Watkins and Home.

Though the band wasn't destined to last, The Denims did make it as far as the Two Is coffee bar in London, where, so legend had it, the skiffle craze had given birth to British rock 'n' roll back in the late 1950s. By the mid-1960s, it had reverted to being a rather seedy watering hole in London's Soho, but it's said that Ray Davies of The Kinks was among the audience present to see them. So was the manager of Them, a rough and ready band from Belfast with Van Morrison as singer. He apparently offered The Denims work on the continent supporting his charges, 'if you play R&B and get rid of your singer', but in the 'all for one, one for all' spirit of the times, the three remaining Denims turned their back on the offer, forgiving if not forgetting Mike's earlier dalliance with The Big Five.

Mike Barratt was good looking enough to attract a female fan following – but he had already met the love of his life at the tender age of fourteen. Local girl Carole Dunn was a petite brunette who clearly saw more in the young man than merely a hip-swivelling singer. She and Dave Dutton's wife-to-be, Pam, were known to chase away would-be teenage temptresses who dared to set their sights on their men, but there was little need for Carole to be insecure – he was clearly as besotted with her as she was with him.

The Denims' fortunes declined rapidly after their visit to London around 1965 – in fact, they started declining the moment they came off the stage to discover their van had been towed away by the capital's traffic police! Once back home in Cardiff, they were finding it hard to get proper paying gigs, having to settle for cabaret or backing female singers at local hops. Rock 'n' roll was in the doldrums, and The Denims with it.

Other ways to bring in the readies had to be pursued, and the group's van was one means of doing so. Mike and Dave used it to run a window-cleaning firm, which proved just as unsuccessful as their musical ventures. The van was also the venue for many of the band members' amorous adventures, as was the custom of the time.

The Denims finally hung up their jean jackets after a disastrous gig at the Victoria Ballroom backing up-and-coming singer Patti Flynn – rock singer and future producer Dave Edmunds was also on the bill – and Mike Barratt was left band-less. He had other things on his mind, however, and on 7 October 1967 waved his bachelor days goodbye when he walked up the aisle of St David's Church in Ely with Carole. (At the time of his marriage, the certificate reveals, Mike was a milkman.)

At the age of nineteen, the pair set up home together for the first time in the third floor of a disused office block in Cardiff's Westgate Street – a central location, and hardly suburban. It would nevertheless be home for the next few years before the area was finally redeveloped.

Rock 'n' roll and Mike Barratt finally reconnected in 1968 when he formed The Rebels and hit the working-men's club circuit around Cardiff. A year of at least moderate success ensued. Two great steps forward came when Mike was persuaded to abandon the acoustic guitar he clutched as more or less a stage prop and concentrate on working the crowd as a frontman. A new, better PA system was also acquired and, armed with extra amp-age and burning confidence, the lead singer of The Rebels set about refining his stage act. It was amazing the transformation that took place once he set foot on any stage, however humble. The quiet Welsh teenager who needed a couple of drinks to get talking in company came alive instantly, making a connection with his audience with no hesitation whatsoever.

The most important person he managed to impress, certainly in relation to his future prospects, was Paul 'Legs' Barrett, manager of the previously mentioned Backbeats. Their paths had probably been fated to cross again, since the older man had founded a popular second-hand record shop that served as a meeting place for Cardiff's rock 'n' roll fraternity. This led to his setting up occasional gigs, and it was at the behest of two rock 'n' roll fans that he first came to see his future protégé perform. The venue for this historic meeting was the social club of the Public Works Department in Grangetown, Cardiff.

'The first time I met Shaky,' Barrett recalled in 2005, 'would be in the early 1960s, when The Backbeats band that I managed from Penarth played at the Church of the Resurrection in Ely, Cardiff every Sunday night. It was that funny time just before The Beatles. The band were playing pure rock 'n' roll and that got a big following. And various fans, young kids from the audience were encouraged to get up and sing because everybody played very long sets in those days, and one of the kids who used to get up and sing was Shaky. We called him "Rockin' Louie 2" because he jumped around a bit like Rockin' Louie, the singer with The Backbeats. And that was it. He didn't make much impression. Years later, I got a record shop in Penarth – which would be in the Summer of Love, 1967 – called the House of Wax, and Mal Clint and Rompin' Russ Allsop told me I ought to go to Cardiff to see this little rock 'n' roll group playing in Grangetown.

'I went along and was impressed with Shaky straight away. I thought the kid was really good. He was a good-looking young kid, singing 1950s stuff. His voice was in the right style. It was good enough, but the band really didn't make it. They were pretty dire. I can't remember if he approached me or I him, but I eventually became the manager.'

Paul Barrett's offer to manage Mike Barratt – note the different spellings – came with certain conditions attached. He had to change his name, change his band and sharpen up his image. The official story behind the name was that it came from a local eccentric whose job was road-sweeping. He'd occasionally act out his own rock 'n' roll fantasies using the broom handle as a mic stand, and when it came to choosing a new identity Mike Barratt simply borrowed an already existing one. In 1982, in Australia, Shaky provided an alternative explanation on a TV chat show: 'It actually came from leaving school; there was a bunch of kids in the street and we used to play baseball and annoy the neighbours. And there was this boy called Steven Vanderwalker and we used to use this piece of wood for a bat and when it was his turn to bat he used to say, "Ladies and gentlemen, this is Shakin' Stevens." The name stuck and I used it. He couldn't sing, but now he's an accountant and I'm Shakin' Stevens!'

He'd explain the reason for the change years later during a TV interview. 'There's a newscaster on telly called Michael Barratt, isn't there? So it didn't have any ring to it, really. I really wanted a rock 'n' roll name, so I decided to change it. Shakin' Stevens is an unusual name, I suppose. It's a bit like you wouldn't be christened Shakin' just like you wouldn't be christened Rocky, so I suppose Rock Hudson had the same trouble as well. I think if I had my time over again I'd pick a name that you could be christened with.' Despite this minor regret, he would eventually insist on being addressed by his stage name, whether 'in character' or not.

Mike Barratt's last job found him commuting from Cardiff

to Bridgend. 'I used to do upholstering up there at a place called Christie Tylers and they used to have a radio,' he revealed during a 2005 radio show. 'To hear a radio while you're working is fantastic! I became an upholsterer by day and a singer by night.'

His father, initially unimpressed, would eventually come around to his son's chosen career. 'When I was doing all the usual clubs and things my dad was so proud of me that he would carry my picture everywhere with him. He would take the photograph out and tell people, "That's my son, he's a singer." I owe so much to my dad. You could say that it was his love of the music of Al Jolson and J. H. Elliot, the soft-shoe shuffle star, that actually got me interested in all this. If he was around today I'm sure that he'd be over the moon at everything that's happened.'

2

SUNRISE . . . SUNSETS: 1969–76

THE FORMATION OF SHAKIN' STEVENS AND THE SUNSETS in January 1969 began a rock 'n' roll apprenticeship that would be served, as with so many others, playing a stream of one-night stands in Britain's pubs, clubs and colleges. Many miles would be clocked up on the then-infant motorway system – and though it was a tough school, the stagecraft Shaky learned there would stand him in good stead thereafter: 'That was when I paid my dues. We travelled thousands of miles all over the country. It was when I discovered what rock 'n' roll is all about.'

The band's first 'gig' was in Aberystwyth's Kings Hall and earned them six pounds each after expenses, but their fame (and petrol money) soon expanded beyond the south Wales region. 'We'd leave Cardiff around 6 a.m. in this battered old van and drive up to, say, Aberdeen,' Shaky recalled. 'We'd rush from the van into a tiny dressing room, wash, change and do our stuff on stage. Then, after the gig, we'd wonder where we could sleep that night. Usually it was in the back of the van – we certainly didn't have the money for hotels.'

The singer still hadn't totally conquered his stage fright, though. There would apparently be times where manager Paul Barrett would have to elongate his introduction to around the quarter-hour mark as Shaky gathered his nerves and prepared to go on. These moments on stage, sometimes even mouthing the words into a microphone with the sound turned down, were the realization of a dream for Paul, who freely admits that he can't sing a note in tune.

This was eventually turned into part of the stage act, a routine that centred upon a clock face behind the drum kit. The Sunsets would strike up the opening chords to a number of songs, ranging backwards in time from, for example, 'Hey Joe' by The Jimi Hendrix Experience to Adam Faith's 'What Do You Want?', until the 'dawn of rock 'n' roll' was reached. At this point, they would break into the opening bars of 'Train Kept A-Rollin'', the cue for Shaky to bound onto the stage and kick off the performance proper.

'Shaky didn't have very much confidence at the start,' Paul Barrett reflects. 'He used to drink to psyche himself up. I mean, he was a young kid . . . also it [Shaky's music] was against every trend that was going on, and this was before Showaddywaddy . . . before everybody started going rock 'n' roll again . . . it was totally out of step with everything. When he played his guitar he used to stand with his legs together and I told him to stand with his legs apart. He's not articulate now, he certainly wasn't then. He was unsure of himself, so what we tried to do was represent the entire 1950s, so we had a vocal group medley for the first fifteen minutes. We'd open up – bang, bang, bang – fifteen minutes relentless non-stop, each number segueing into the next. I would introduce it, and do the bass-voice interjections in "At The Hop"; and I couldn't sing a damn but I'd stay on stage and say, "Don't talk back", "I'm a juvenile delinquent", things like that.'

An interested observer on the scene was one Adrian Angove, born a year after Shaky in 1949. He played his first gig at Penarth Labour Club, 'age fifteen and as nervous as hell', with his band The Firstborn, a purist 1950s rock 'n' roll band complete with bootlace ties, teddy-boy drape jackets and brothel-creeper shoes. Then known as 'Rockin' Merve', he remembers 'piling into the Batmobile, an ancient, crumbling Bedford van (the one with the sliding passenger doors) with Legs, Louie, Shaky, and half a dozen other rocker types and travelling to Culverhouse Cross to see Dave Edmunds' Raiders play in a small church hall. We were all pretty pissed on cheap sherry, so I cannot remember much else about that night, but The Raiders were good as always.'

The picture he paints of Shaky is of 'a naïve and painfully shy individual who never did anything outrageous – he was an innocent abroad. Paul "Legs" Barrett ran an entertainment agency called Jack D. Ripper – "don't rip nobody off" – and he guided Shaky's career very carefully.

'Shaky would sit quietly in the corner of the dressing room, sipping a soft drink, until it was time to hit the stage. He would do all the moves that Legs had taught him, say all the words that Legs had told him to say between numbers and, straight after leaving the stage, Legs would throw a coat over his shoulders and whisk him away from the venue, leaving the band to clear up and pack away.'

Clearly, the man who would wow thousands of teenage girls (and their mothers) a decade later was still learning his craft. One of the key venues at which he cut his performing teeth was the Northcote Arms in Southall, west London, a mecca for the capital's rock 'n' roll cognoscenti thanks to a rock 'n' roll promoter called Harry Holland. His gigs in the back room attracted a clientele from miles around, and it was inevitable that Shakin' Stevens and the Sunsets would eventually play there. Their first gig at the venue was on 31 July 1969, a date that happened to coincide with The Rolling Stones' legendary free Hyde Park gig. This was not of great interest to the Northcote's patrons, but did enable the band to subsidize their travel costs by hiring a coach and charging Welsh Stones fans for a luxury one-way ride up the M4.

Such savings were crucial, for, as Shaky recalls, The Sunsets 'just managed to get by and no more. The meals we had were the cheapest ones we could get in motorway cafés, we didn't have enough money for much else.' But he never considered a return to the day job. 'There was no reason why I should have considered calling it a day. Singing was what I enjoyed, what I did best, and I realized that. Another thing that kept me going was working in front of an enthusiastic audience. That was great, singing for our audiences gave me a tremendous buzz ... There's really no accurate way for me to put into words just what that feeling is like. I suppose it must be like a shot of electricity, when the audience moves with your music.'

The line-up of The Sunsets changed as Paul Barrett set about creating the perfect band for his frontman. The band members adopted new stage clothing – simple black and white with red drape jackets – while Shaky had a contrasting blue number. But Barrett realized he had to do something about the band's standard of playing. 'The first guitarist we had, Alan Langford, who Shaky called "The Australian", left and a guy from Aberdare called Mike Bibby joined. Nice lad, but he was a limited guitarist. He didn't stay very long.

'Then I got in Rob "Carl" Peterson, a guy who used to play second guitar with The Backbeats. He played a very chunky, driving kind of rhythm/lead – the kind that Dave Edmunds mastered. Then I got Stephen Pryor on bass and Brian "Slapbeat" Williams on drums, who were very influenced, particularly Stephen, by the pop/jazz outfit The Peddlers, to the extent that Steve would bring a stool along, and sit there wearing a black roll-neck sweater. Well, he had to go. That just wasn't going to work doing our kind of rock 'n' roll. So they eventually left.'

The masterstroke was to persuade Robert Llewellyn (better known as frontman Rockin' Louie from The Backbeats) to swap the microphone for a pair of drumsticks. 'Rockin' Louie is an old pal and a great rock 'n' roll drummer. He was on the drums and doing second vocals, and we got in this guy, Steve Percy, from a band called The Skyliners, who was a good bass guitarist. I realized I needed a very strong bass player to go with a guitar player that's playing rhythm as well as lead. He needed plenty of support and balance. Then we got Paul "Duane" Dolan, who's become an extremely good sax player but, at the time, was only just a sax player. He'd come out of an RAF band and was the only sax player we had.'

Pianist Trevor 'The Hawk' Hawkins, a Londoner by birth, approached them at the Northcote and asked to join. He strengthened the band musically, though the number of venues that could offer a piano of any sort, let alone an adequately tuned one, were somewhat thin on the ground. 'Trevor was a full Ted in a red suit and the haircut,' Paul Barrett recalls.

The band's fame spread to high places, and when The Rolling Stones invited them to open for them at London's Savile Theatre in December 1969, The Sunsets seemed on the threshold of megastardom. Mick Jagger had sent a tour manager to check them out and engaged the group as their support act on his recommendation.

One reason for this might have been Paul Barrett's open letter to John Lennon, which received much publicity at the time as the ex-Beatle tried to put his immediate past behind him by returning to the rebel music of his youth. When he appeared at a Canadian rock 'n' roll festival singing the likes of 'Blue Suede Shoes' and 'Dizzy Miss Lizzy', Barrett had a brainwave that would catapult Shakin' Stevens and the Sunsets onto the front page of the music press: 'John Lennon played at the Toronto Peace Festival. He'd left The Beatles, and it was reported that he'd performed 1950s rock 'n' roll. There was a photograph of him in a white suit. So I wrote to the *Melody*

Maker saying that if John Lennon's left his band and he's looking for a new one, and if he's still got the white suit, and he remembers all the words of "At The Hop", we'll give him a job. *Melody Maker* played this up, big headlines – "Shakin' Stevens and the Sunsets offer John Lennon a job" – and the next thing I know The Rolling Stones' office rang us and offered us 14 December 1969 – I was twenty-nine, I remember – to support The Rolling Stones, and off we went.'

Needless to say, it was a night Shakin' Stevens would remember for the rest of his life. 'It was the first time I had played on a stage which had curtains, so that you could make a proper entrance. Before the venues were clubs, bars and colleges, but this was a real stage!' The band transported their modest equipment in old suitcases while the Stones had a retinue of roadies and the best amplification around. But the transition proved too much on the night for Shaky, who was unused to the Stones' PA system. 'All I could hear was my own voice. It was almost impossible to hear the music! I also recall that during our spot, the drummer's snare stand broke and he finished up having to beat his drumsticks off a fire bucket.'

Paul Barrett's abiding memory is Shaky ending the act, as was his habit, with 'Mean Woman Blues', 'which would end up with him climbing on top of the piano and doing all these bumps and grinds. So Shaky tried to jump on to the piano, but while the mic lead was fine for the British Legion clubs we were playing, it wasn't long enough for the Savile Theatre. He had to stand there with one leg stretched out and one leg trying to reach the piano. He could never make it. So, there were a few problems like that.'

Reviews were mixed: John Wells, later to enjoy fame as Denis Thatcher's TV impersonator, was impressed 'when the curtain drew back to reveal a group looking as if they'd stepped straight from the local Palais circa 1958'; music journalist Lon Goddard 'could have done without [a group that] blasted everybody into slumber with [a] dilapidated version of rock 'n' roll standards served in Wimpy Bar fashion. Nobody knows who Shakin' Stevens was, but nobody shook uncontrollably.' The *Melody Maker* said The Sunsets, with their fairly limited equipment, would have been great fun in a small club.

One young man who remembers the show vividly was future *Melody Maker* writer Patrick Humphries. He recalls that, while it was a thrill to be two seats down from actor John Gielgud, he had failed to catch one of the promised support acts. 'I really wanted to see Procol Harum, but I got Shakin' Stevens and the Sunsets – I was really pissed off!' Yet he was converted by the sheer power of their performance. 'They were really good! This was before the rock 'n' roll revival, before people like Bolan and Bowie started referencing Gene Vincent and Eddie Cochran. Then, of course, there was *That'll Be The Day* [the 1973 film] and Showaddywaddy in the mid-1970s.

'Shaky was a very obvious Elvis lookalike, and there was a deep intake of breath [from the audience, because this was] not very cool at time. We were all street-fighting men just after Woodstock. I remember the incongruity of seeing a rock 'n' roll revival act at that time. There was another act called The Wild Angels [who were] the only other ones at all rock 'n' roll. And rock 'n' roll – which meant The Wild Angels and Shakin' Stevens and the Sunsets – was invariably uncool.'

Amusingly, those self-same Wild Angels had attempted to pull a 'fast one' and turned up with their equipment at the stage door, claiming The Sunsets had broken down and they'd been nominated to replace them. Unfortunately for them, Shaky and crew were already on the premises.

Paul Barrett didn't rate it a particularly memorable performance by The Sunsets, 'not helped by the fact that the Stones didn't get the audience they wanted. It was all the London cool – very cool. I remember Jagger throwing rose petals at the audience from a bowl, and when that didn't get a reaction, he threw the bowl at them. I thought, "Nice one, Mick." The Stones all looked as if their craggy heads were too big for their bodies. It was like they had the Easter Island heads with the bodies of David Cassidy. All Mick Jagger said to me was . . . he sung me the introduction to "High School Confidential", and I thought, "Well, maybe he's not so bad, after all."'

Unfortunately for Shakin' Stevens and the Sunsets, the show proved to be a false dawn. The Stones, shell-shocked by a year in which Brian Jones had died, and the fact that just days before the Savile Theatre show an audience member had been murdered by a Hell's Angels biker during their appearance at Altamont in San Francisco, were taking a break and concentrating on movie careers and a new record label. The link was always fated to be a one-off, though the Stones would occasionally enter and leave the stage to rock 'n' roll music by the likes of Eddie Cochran in the future.

The following year saw The Sunsets find an unlikely champion in John Peel. The Radio One DJ was normally to be found on air playing cutting-edge progressive rock acts on his *Perfumed Garden* show. But as manager and long-time friend Clive Selwood recalls, 'John was always a basic rock 'n' roller – that was his roots, as with so many of us.' Indeed, Peel had caught the legendary pairing of Eddie Cochran and Gene Vincent at the Liverpool Empire in April 1960, just days before the car crash that took Cochran's life and left Vincent with a disfiguring limp. (Coincidentally, Clive Selwood had been involved with the tour organization.) Both men have since separately highlighted the moment Cochran swivelled 180 degrees to face his audience on the Empire stage, singing the first line of Ray Charles' 'Hallelujah I Love Her So', as the most exciting in all their years of witnessing rock shows.

Peel and Selwood had founded their own record label, Dandelion, the only unifying thread running through its roster being that all the acts featured enjoyed Peel's patronage. A notable early single was a re-cut of 'Be-Bop-A-Lula' by Gene Vincent, by then merely months from a premature death.

Vincent's one and only album featured members of The Byrds and Steppenwolf, but the budget was never there to expose this quality music to a wider public. 'When you can't afford full-page ads in the music press,' Peel told *Record Collector* in 1994, 'artists become very resentful . . . there's no faster way of losing friends.'

Paul Barrett had already approached John Peel about recording for his Dandelion label, and enticed him to the Northcote Arms. Enjoying what he experienced, Peel went into print in his regular *Disc* magazine column. 'If you talk of a "rock 'n' roll revival" in south Wales,' he wrote, 'the chances are good that no one will understand you – as far as they're concerned it's never been away. Shakin' Stevens and the Sunsets come from Swansea [*sic*] and they look and sound just right. Shakin' Stevens sings and plays guitar that's not plugged into anything and only has three strings anyway. He sings well too and it's good to hear the band get away from "Summertime Blues" and "Good Golly Miss Molly". They do some Johnny Burnette numbers and Jack Scott's classic "Leroy", and Paul, who's their manager and really part of the act too, said they were working up "Nothin' Shakin'", which is good news.

'Rockin' Louie plays drums and I stood by the wall and talked to him about rock and he's really into it, and friendly too. Not into rock because it's fashionable or quaint or anything like that, but because that's what Rockin' Louie is all about. The bass player wore a silver lamé jacket and the lead guitar stormed into his solos in such a way that you just knew he wasn't going to play any bad notes. Do you feel that confident about your own trendy guitar hero? The pianist was, I was told, a newcomer to the group – in fact he's only been with them for a year, which tells you something else about Shakin' Stevens and the Sunsets. They're going to record soon and they'll be doing things that you've not heard time and time again. They don't see the point in recording rock classics when the originals are available on the LP if you want them.

'The audience was as interesting as the band. There were many rockers and a few teddy boys. It was good to see those long drapecoats, string ties and drainpipe trousers. The atmosphere was rowdy and yet there was no menace in the air ... It was a good evening.'

The next logical step was for Shakin' Stevens and the Sunsets to cut an album for Dandelion – 'I had nothing much to do with it,' says Selwood – but though they recorded an album with Peel producing, the material was never released. 'The tapes disappeared! Of course, since then Shaky has become popular – he met Stuart Colman and he turned it all around. Shaky's aware of it and we are having an on-off conversation through a third party, and so I hope that this [album] will come out sometime, be released in some way or another. We didn't even get to the artwork stage. CBS have copies in their vaults but will only release it to me, as Dandelion's past owner.'

At that time, Shaky admitted, 'We looked like we'd landed from another planet, but we were doing what we believed in, what we enjoyed. [Peel] must have thought, "These guys are so wacky I gotta record them," so we did some recording for the Dandelion label. We didn't do the standards, we did some obscure stuff like "Flying Saucers Rock 'n' Roll," stuff like that. We made the album, but it didn't come out. We didn't go with it in the end.'

Paul Barrett recalls that Peel's original suggestion was a 'split album' release. 'He wanted us to record one side of an album which would be shared with this other band, Lee Tracy and the Tributes. But when we went in the studio for John, he wanted to do a full album with Shaky and the Sunsets. But I wasn't particularly pleased with the results. I thought John really didn't differentiate between what was good and what wasn't quite good enough. He wasn't critical enough. Just the fact that they were doing songs he liked, that seemed to be enough. Also, the fact that people like [Liverpool poet] Adrian Henri were there.

It was a little bit like, "Oh, look at that man in the red suit, oh, look at that man's haircut." I thought, "We're novelty appeal, here," and I felt a bit uncomfortable with that.'

As Rockin' Louie remembers it today, 'Peel wanted to put us on a ten-inch and we didn't like that. You know, quaint rock 'n' roll band. We thought of ourselves as "now", although we were doing Fifties music in 1968. So we didn't like that quaint business. It was a novelty thing. We didn't feel like a novelty. We thought it was a way of life.

'Then Dave Edmunds drove past the Drope [a Cardiff music venue] and heard us rehearsing. Came in, started talking to Legs while we were performing, and I was singing "I Hear You Knockin'", the Smiley Lewis song. And Dave Edmunds heard it and thought he was listening to The Backbeats. There's Rockin' Louie, there's Carl Peterson on guitar, there's Duane on sax. That's The Backbeats.'

Paul Barrett takes up the story. 'We went back to Wales and did a couple of sides with Edmunds up at Rockfield [recording studios], and when we heard the playbacks they were so much better. A decision had to be made so I said we'd better go with Dave, and that was that. Dave said we had a release on Parlophone. It certainly marred . . . my relationship with John Peel, and that lasted all his life, unfortunately. But I still think I made the right decision for the band.'

Edmunds was a south Wales legend; his band The Raiders was the first Mike Barratt had ever seen. So when Edmunds heard The Sunsets' music coming out of the Drope, it was fate bringing things full circle. 'We were rehearsing in this hall near where I lived and who should drive past but Dave Edmunds?' remembered Shaky. 'He pulled up in his car and said, "I really love the sound you're doing – I'd like to record you." We thought Dandelion, and then we thought Parlophone – The Beatles, a big label – so we kind of thought we're going to be really successful!'

Edmunds had created hits such as the guitar tour de force

'Sabre Dance', which won him a deal with Gordon Mills, who at that time was manager to Tom Jones and Engelbert Humperdinck. 'Dave said they'd given him a great deal on Parlophone,' explains Louie. 'So we said, "Okay, we'll go with you instead of John Peel." So we did the same songs we'd been rehearsing for John Peel. Then we went into the studio.'

That was Rockfield Studios in Monmouth, south Wales. Paul Barrett, for his part, believed the band had been overawed by the plush surroundings of the 'Peel session' studio in London's New Bond Street, and had played poorly as a result. Rockfield was unlikely to have the same effect, so they showed up and gave it a whirl. Things must have gone well because the next thing they knew they were recording an album.

The band were untrained in the art of putting music on recording tape, and things appear to have taken an inordinate length of time – largely because, unlike most groups, they hadn't rehearsed and routined an album before going into the expensive studio confines. Twenty-three years later, when the album had been reissued several times in the wake of Shaky's solo success, a lawsuit concerning this recording was to put The Sunsets on one side, and Shaky and Edmunds on the other.

As Shaky had suggested, an album to be released via the mighty EMI, home of major bands from The Beatles to The Shadows, suggested the chance of a breakthrough. The unusual title, *A Legend*, came from the horror novel *I Am Legend* written by Richard Matheson and first published in 1954. 'Well,' Paul Barrett explains, 'all rock 'n' rollers are legendary. We are legend. We are not just us, but we are all rock 'n' rollers and rock 'n' roll. But the title became *A Legend*.'

The line-up on the album featured Llewellyn, Hawkins, Percy and Peterson, augmented by second guitarist Roger McKew, a twenty-seven-year-old classically trained pianist and cellist from London, who switched to the guitar because all his friends had one. Roger was a member of beat combo The Quiet Five and had turned to session work in 1966. The spring of 1970 had seen him join Neil Innes's short-lived post-Bonzos band, The World. After spells with Joe Brown, Lonnie Donegan and others, McKew would crop up again in the Shakin' Stevens story, featuring on his breakthrough hits and remaining in the ranks throughout the 1980s. Here, though, he was strictly a session musician, thickening up the guitar sound.

The songs varied in style from rockabilly favourites like Billy Lee Riley's 'Flying Saucers Rock 'n' Roll' (a 'Peel session' remnant), Jack Scott's 'Leroy', The Rock 'n' Roll Trio's 'Train Kept A-Rollin'' and Johnny Burnette's 'Believe What You Say', to more varied fare. The latter included Jerry Byrne's 'Lights Out', a brace of Chuck Berry on 'Thirty Days' and 'School Day', and just one original, 'Hawkins' Mood', from pianist Trevor Hawkins.

Dave Edmunds' authentic production was full of echo, which tended to obscure the less accurate moments of musicianship and, in the words of one reviewer, added 'the aural equivalent of sepia-tinting on a Victorian photograph'. According to Paul 'Legs' Barrett, however, Edmunds apparently didn't rate Shaky as a singer. 'I think it was because his mindset was that these guys were The Backbeats and he really didn't take to Shaky. I'm not trying to be derogatory to Shaky, but Shaky was only a kid, he was much younger than the rest of us, he was under a lot of pressure in the studio, and it looked like his group was going to be taken away from him. So I said to Edmunds that it was his group – it's Shakin' Stevens and the Sunsets. I love Rockin' Louie – he's still my best friend – but Louie can't front this band. Shaky's the frontman. It could never have worked with an older guy. I knew Louie had a better voice, but it was Shaky's band, and that's the way it was going to be.'

Louie explains that the original plan had been somewhat different. 'We put all the backing tracks down and Edmunds said, "Go on, Lou. Go out and do the vocals." But Shaky went out. And I could see . . . he was talking in the studio to Legs . . .

and Legs explained that, "No, Shakin' Stevens and the Sunsets isn't the new name for Rockin' Louie and the Backbeats. Shakin' Stevens and the Sunsets is a new band and Shaky's the singer, but Louie's gonna sing the black-orientated rock 'n' roll like Little Richard or Fats Domino songs, and Shaky's gonna sing the white rock 'n' roll like Ricky Nelson and Elvis." So Dave Edmunds was a bit confused by all that. But that's what went down.

'Legs wanted it to be me doing six numbers and Shaky doing six numbers. We were in the toilet and Shaky was crying, literally crying, saying, "If I allow this to go ahead, what will my family think? What'll my family think with Louie singing?" It startled me. We didn't even know his family in those days. We'd only just started backing him. It resolved itself by me being cool, just backing off. Me saying, "Don't worry about it, Shaky. It was just an idea that Legs had, more like a Johnny Otis show, rather than just a band. Two singers." In the original concept, that was the idea.'

The lead track of the first Sunsets single was to be their revival of Big Al Downing's 'Down On The Farm', but there was just one problem – it wasn't Shaky on lead vocals but Rockin' Louie, the choice that had caused much consternation in the studio. Seemingly for the sake of diplomacy, the disc was flipped and 'Spirit Of Woodstock', an original song written by Paul Barrett, made the A-side. Barrett recalls the song's message as a clarion call: 'The spirit of rock 'n' roll is still alive and we're all rock 'n' rollers. But Edmunds didn't like it. He wanted it to be the old rock 'n' roll.'

Looking back in 1986, Shaky pronounced 'Spirit Of Woodstock' 'perfect for the time. It was all about "they slept in bags down the grassy slopes of highways" – a rock 'n' roll song with lyrics that summed up the Woodstock festival and the live music of the 1960s. I was doing a lot of college and university gigs then and felt pretty close to that whole scene.' A modicum of radio play came from the likes of Emperor Rosko, who also flipped the disc and aired 'Down On The Farm'. But sales of the single and *A Legend* album were disappointing, and EMI dropped the band.

Ironically, one of the tracks featured on the album was 'I Hear You Knockin'', a song that, in The Sunsets' repertoire, was sung by Rockin' Louie rather than Shaky. Edmunds re-recorded it himself and turned it into a 1970 chart-topping single. '"I Hear You Knockin'" had been released over here by Georgia Gibbs, a pop version,' explains Barrett. 'But the version we did was [based on] the pure New Orleans rock 'n' roll of Smiley Lewis. We'd heard the record in the early 1960s in Newport, in a teddy boy's house, a man called "Breathless" Danny Coffey and, of course, Edmunds liked the song.

'He borrowed part of "Let's Work Together" by Wilbert Harrison, and he got Micky Gee to do the arrangement – I'm pretty sure, though Edmunds wouldn't admit it, that Micky Gee played lead guitar on it. But EMI didn't like the recording, they thought it was too rough, and they turned it down. So Edmunds went to MAM, and it sold five million copies. EMI immediately dropped Edmunds' Rockpile Productions, and I believe he had to make some settlement with them.'

Shaky's recollection was similar. 'Dave heard that track and loved it so much he wrote the words down. He'd never heard it before . . . He had the big record and the big success and the album we did, *A Legend*, failed dismally.' The main difference, says Louie, was that Edmunds' version was 'guitar-orientated rather than sax and piano. And he did it well. The next time we went up to Rockfield he said, "Lou, come and listen to this," and he played me what became the Dave Edmunds single. So we heard it before it became a hit.'

Understandably, Paul Barrett sees The Sunsets as victims of the piece: 'We had a single out on EMI, the band were hot and we were on the university circuit and everything was going fine. We had an album out on Parlophone [an EMI label], we had a single on Parlophone, and then Parlophone went cold

[after] they fell out with Edmunds over "I Hear You Knockin'".
I'm sure this is what happened.'

Undeterred by the loss of their record deal, The Sunsets
returned to the live circuit and found their music much in
demand on mainland Europe. British work, which tended to
be more poorly rewarded, often entailed opening the show for
rock 'n' roll legends of the past, many of whom would find it
an uncomfortable experience to follow a band of such live
calibre. A 1970 tour supporting Chuck Berry was cancelled, but
the following year found them opening for Gene Vincent, then
nearing the end of both his life and career.

The Sunsets were well accepted by 'authentic' rock 'n'
rollers, Shaky would recall. 'We were the leaders of the pack in
those days. The Teds were very particular about what you did –
especially your appearance. It could get a little heavy for
members of certain groups with longer hair. Me, I've always
dressed this way because I like it.

'We always stuck to our guns. We rehearsed in back sheds,
then began playing seedy clubs and church halls. We spent our
lives driving up and down motorways, sleeping in vans and
often having to wait for the AA to rescue us. At a few places
the audience would hiss and boo, tell us we were old hat or
throw the odd beer can, but mostly we attracted a loyal
following of genuine rock 'n' rollers.'

He would also later admit to 'looning about on stage', also
conceding that he 'used to go too far': 'In the early days I used
to wreck the place. I've torn down curtains, pulled over lights,
fallen off things and injured myself – all by accident just to
keep things exciting.'

Yet Shaky wasn't always as keen to vary the musical content
of the set – in fact, according to Rockin' Louie, when he or
Paul Barrett would put forward suggestions for new songs,
'Shaky would go totally comatose. Because somebody else had
used their initiative – he'd just sit back and look at you. "So,
what do you think, Shaky? It's a good idea, I think. Don't you?"

"Well, yeah. I like the number." "Well, there's every reason to learn it, then. Me and Legs think so. How about you?" We'd get fed up and bored with having to father him, really.

'Then, a full eighteen months later, he might say, "I've written a list of songs to learn." And we'd look at it, and it would be the same songs! We'd go, "You cheeky bastard! Shaky, don't you realize that me and Legs spent hours nagging about these songs?" He either couldn't remember or he was lying. He used to say, "Well, I like it. I played it last night. I like that song. I wanna learn it." And that's how it went. It was exhausting.'

The set list was usually Legs' prerogative – though, Louie recalls, 'Shaky used to ponder over what Legs had written down. And he'd criticize after a bit of hesitancy. And that's what I used to hate. All that hesitancy. The painfully slow decision-making would get you on edge, it was like pulling teeth. He'd put you through the mill, and it wasn't until he got on the stage that he came into his own, when he'd cut loose. And that's why it appeared so hysterical, the very fact that he wasn't great at communicating off stage. Then people would be clapping, which he got off on. You could see the transition, the change. It was incredible. He'd give his all.' Any amount of offstage frustration was worth suffering, it seems, for the end product.

One of The Sunsets' 1970 dates was as support to pop act Harmony Grass, still cashing in on the success of the previous year's hit single 'Move In A Little Closer Baby', at Aberystwyth University – and this was where the paths of Shaky and future backing vocalist/harmony arranger Tony Rivers first crossed. The pair would not encounter each other again until 1982, and it would seem that the future star made little impression on Rivers at the time. 'I don't really remember watching Shaky do his show,' Rivers confessed years later, 'but now I wish I had.'

The university gig circuit, funded with public money, hardly meant playing to the rock 'n' roll elite – but it did pay. Sean Tyla of pub-rockers Ducks Deluxe rubbed shoulders with The

Sunsets several times during those years, as disparate bands could often find themselves sharing a stage. 'It was good fun, the college circuit, with a catholic mix of music for the audience. You could have all kinds of acts on the same bill. Unfortunately the whole scene was dead by 1980 when the agencies had the social secretaries under their wing.'

Tyla particularly recalls a gig at Harlech University when they shared the same bill. 'It was Shaky, The Tyla Gang and The Troggs. We flipped a coin to see who would headline and The Troggs won. We were happy, as our next gig was in Dundee and we wanted to get away! Shaky was all right, a pretty polite kind of a bloke. He was definitely a non-star person, in fact the whole band were nice to talk to and easy to be with.'

Ian Gomm from Brinsley Schwarz recalls he 'used to encounter him all the time on the college circuit. Shaky was always value for money, but the thing that held The Sunsets back was that they were playing exclusively old songs. They were like a throwback to the *6.5 Special* [a 1950s rock 'n' roll TV show] – more exciting than Lonnie Donegan and more credible than Wayne Fontana and the Mindbenders. Legs Barrett, their manager, was the driving force. He motivated them: "Get in this dressing room, get on the stage ..."'

More than that, Barrett was part of a show that he'd planned down to the last detail: 'I'd introduce the band and if we were playing support gigs I'd get their attention. I'd say, "This is a space and time machine." And I'd say at universities, "It's great to be at your high-school hop tonight." So I got their attention and then the band would start playing. That carried on as a necessity for about two years, perhaps three. But after that, Shaky was into his stride, he'd got his stagecraft under his belt.

'I think it's important for bands trying to get to a higher [level, to have an] edge ... have someone to introduce them, and, when they finish, they have someone to walk on and say, "Thank you, ladies and gentlemen, that was rock 'n' roll. That was Shakin' Stevens," and off they'd go. Sometimes they didn't milk it for an encore. So there was always a beginning and an end to each performance. If you were supporting people, they'd say, "What the hell was all that about? How do we follow that?" We'd just done a whole damn show. One thing I was particularly keen on was if we started with something, with a climax in the middle, then we'd build up again to a finale. It was a show – that's why we did it.'

Rockin' Louie also took note of Shaky's unique and essentially natural 'edge': 'He was very nervous, so he had a few drinks before going on, but it didn't take a lot to give him that edge. It was just a couple of drinks. He never took drugs. But a couple of drinks and after about forty-five minutes he was ready to go on. Then you could see what the fans [in his solo years] must have hooked up on.'

Despite Paul Barrett's showmanship and Shaky's burgeoning stagecraft, the success or failure of dates opening for progressive rockers like Juicy Lucy and Stone the Crows tended to rest on the open-mindedness of the headliners' fans. The band themselves had a 'can do' approach, fostered largely by Barrett, and were happy to play anywhere with anyone – despite their jealously guarded claims to authenticity. Another gig at Aberystwyth University with Stone the Crows was memorable for the fact that the Scots' rockers' equipment van failed to arrive. On being offered the use of The Sunsets' gear, the Crows' road manager, despite being beside himself with frustration, retorted that 'We wouldn't even rehearse on that rubbish!'

Shaky recalls doing 'about a thousand miles a week in the van. There's three this side of you and four on the other, going from Cardiff to Aberdeen – you can imagine what that was like! You start off and read music papers and then the nationals; once that's done, it's time to pick on each other or stare out of the window. You stop at a greasy spoon, then forever onward.'

Having encountered two potential Svengalis in the very different forms of John Peel and Dave Edmunds, and fallen out with both of them, The Sunsets tried for third time lucky in 1971 in the shape of US record producer Donny Marchand, a man who had a track record that included time as a staff writer with Acuff-Rose in Nashville and having his songs recorded by the likes of Eddie Floyd and Wilson Pickett. The link was forged through a *Battle Of The Bands* compilation album instigated by B&C Records, an indie label that already had one of The Sunsets' rivals, The Wild Angels, on its roster. The concept, instigated by teddy boy writer Waxie Maxie and promoted in his column in pop weekly *Record Mirror,* was intended to raise the profile of authentic rock 'n' roll, which would assist The Wild Angels and maybe hook a new band or two for the label in the process.

The Sunsets travelled to London's Morgan Studios in Willesden to record their contribution, having first politely asked Dave Edmunds for permission. 'We did "All By Myself", the old Fats Domino number,' Paul Barrett recalls, and while Barrett has less than fond memories of the man who produced it, Marchand himself was much taken by the band. 'In those days I had a deal with Morgan, so basically recorded everybody there,' he explains. 'I would hang out in the lounge bar and Waxie Maxie would send me these groups. It was funny, as Morgan was a popular studio and you would have some pretty well-known stars there as well as session guys, producers and wannabes – that lounge and eating area was a really cool place. Then in the door would walk some group either in motorcycle gear or drape jackets! The deal was that everybody would have one track except for Gene Vincent, who was having two. At this point, I didn't know who the hell this group Shakin' Stevens and the Sunsets were.

'So in they came. The album was probably the worst I made in my life, but you can't make a silk purse out of a sow's ear. The groups would say, "We want to do this song," and if somebody had been in before and done it I'd tell them to pick another. Every song on that album was the choice of the artist.

It was a funny for me not to have much input with regard to the material but I knew these songs, "Good Golly Miss Molly", "Lucille", things like that, and it was quite logical for it to be done that way. When they went around to their gigs this is what they played for their fans, so I didn't see I had to interfere.

'The Wild Angels album I'd just done for B&C had done well – I was surprised, because it was just old rock 'n' roll. You can't do that with a new group in America, because, apart from The Fabulous Thunderbirds and one or two others with something different about them, you've got to be the original. Rehashing Jerry Lee Lewis and Little Richard songs just doesn't sell there.

'Shakin' Stevens and the Sunsets were the best out of all the bunch I did – and that included Gene Vincent, because he was well past his day and was very high on dry Martinis and morphine; it was a bit sad. So I thought maybe these guys can sell records. I asked Paul Barrett if the boys had a deal and he said, "No". Would they be interested in doing a two-album deal with me and I'll see if I can get a record deal? He went to the table, came back in two minutes and said, "Yes".

'We agreed that if I didn't get them a record deal within three months we would rip it up, so they wouldn't be tied for ever. Also, it was only for two albums and they weren't tied to me, so we drew up a contract.' Marchand then managed to get CBS interested – surprising, since the label had recently declined the band's direct approaches. 'I went to a guy called Dave Margerrison; he now manages Chris de Burgh, but in those days he was A&R at CBS. He knew of them because these guys seemed to gig an awful lot. Dave agreed to a deal and we cut their first album, which was originally called *I'm No JD*, for CBS at Morgan. I think my budget was £800. I told them to put it out budget-price because of Wild Angels being budget price on B&C and they'd sell more records, but they wouldn't listen to me. I think we sold 1,000 copies.'

By this time pianist Mike 'Ace' Skudder had replaced Trevor Hawkins, who had been left stranded when he made the move to Cardiff on the basis of a planned Chuck Berry tour only to find it cancelled. (Paul Barrett: 'It just got impossible for him with a mortgage and touring abroad. He went back to London and eventually emigrated to Australia.') Skudder, a stocky black Bristolian, joined in his stead.

It was an unlikely combination, as illustrated by Paul Barrett's tale of an all-nighter at Strathclyde University on which the band shared the bill with Afro-rockers Osibisa. 'All the bands were told to stay in the dressing room – don't mingle with the students. It would be dangerous out there; drink would be brought in to us. So we were sat there with Ace, our piano player, a big black guy, at a table having a drink, when Osibisa came in with their robes and their assegais – they got all this stuff. When they saw Ace, they said, "What now? There's a brother there. Come with us now, man." And Ace, who's from Bristol, answered them, "Oh, arr, I got me pint now, arr." Osibisa just cracked up. They couldn't handle a black man speaking like Long John Silver.

'But Ace was a hell of a good piano player. And a great gymnast. He used to do somersaults off the stage. That's pretty unique, isn't it? He did cartwheels. I remember one time, he did a cartwheel and he caught a girl in the audience right under her jaw with his foot. Knocked her out, like that. Unfortunately, that was the same night when Shaky did a Gene Vincent, pulled up the mic and the stand came off, hit him across the head and knocked him out as well! We killed them dead, that night.'

Another personnel change saw slap bassist George Chick succeed Steve Percy after an incident when a full bottle of whisky was broken on Shaky's head. There was no doubt that a bass player was easier to replace than a lead singer – he had to go.

Rockin' Louie remembers the incident well. 'We did a *Radio One Club* for the first time in Hereford. It was the first time we were interviewed on the radio, and afterwards Steve was euphoric. Me and Legs just thought, "Ah well, that's good exposure."

'Shaky was quietly chuffed. But Steve made the mistake of saying, "This is great, Mike." It was the first time he'd said Mike instead of Shaky. And Shaky went absolutely mad, saying, "Only my mam can call me by that name. Nobody else is allowed to call me Mike like that." Me and Legs just looked at each other, dumbstruck.

'When we got back to Penarth, where we were all living in those days, Steve went across the road and bought a bottle of whisky from the off licence, came back over, had a big row with his girlfriend downstairs and walked upstairs to Legs' flat. He broke the bottle over the first head he saw . . . and it happened to be Shaky's. Steve said, "Sorry." Then he said, "No, I'm not. That's for insulting me when I called you Mike, and you said, 'Nobody's allowed to call me Mike.'" Shaky didn't go down on the floor. It must have hit him on a very hard area. He was holding his head, but he didn't collapse.'

Percy's replacement, George Chick, was a real showman. A veteran of the Cardiff scene, he was not just a bass player but an extrovert who came alive on stage. His antics would push the less than confident Shaky into upping his own performance, and the results of this friendly 'competition' were evident for all to see.

But Carl Peterson was soon to follow Steve Percy out of the exit door. His wish to leave rock 'n' roll behind and tune into the 1970s saw him quit during the recording of the second album. Paul Barrett: 'Carl, unfortunately, had decided to progress musically – as far as we were concerned it was digress – at the wrong time. He decided to do other things.'

Cardiff session man Micky Gee was given the call and featured on six tracks on *I'm No JD*. He played a few gigs with The Sunsets after the sessions, but, as Paul Barrett explains, really didn't fit on the live gigs. 'At that time, in '71, the band had turned into a powerhouse rock 'n' roll band, with sax, piano, drums, bass and guitar. So what could you do, other than lay it on the line? It didn't work so well when you did that rockabilly picking. So you'd have Micky picking away and, behind him, mayhem. Micky quit because he said he couldn't stand everybody smoking No. 6 [cigarettes] in the van. That was the straw that broke his back, if not the camel's.' It wouldn't be the last time he featured in the Shakin' Stevens story, however.

The photo that appeared on the album cover was that of Peterson's permanent replacement, Willie Blackmore. 'We called Willie "Slowhand,"' says Barrett. 'I know that's a nickname for Clapton, but he looked a bit like Eric Clapton. He was a good guitarist, but he was never that powerful or driving a player.'

The album's title, *I'm No JD*, derived from the song 'I'm Not A Juvenile Delinquent', first popularized by Frankie Lymon and the Teenagers. (While JD is clearly an abbreviation of Juvenile Delinquent, the record company actually thought it was DJ backwards!) Manager Barrett exercised his lungs on 'Super Star', while dedications on the album included Alan Freed, Marilyn Monroe, recent 'convert' John Lennon and Jerry Lee Lewis, further underlining The Sunsets' claim to be the real rock 'n' roll deal.

The Sunsets were allotted the standard three hours per track in the recording studio. Donny Marchand remembers being more careful when he recorded them second time round than on *Battle Of The Bands*. 'I took my time a little more but did it the same way – in my mind it was rock 'n' roll and I was trying to do it as originally as it was cut. I did things like put up ambience mics and used normal separation boards [wooden boards used to isolate sounds produced by different instruments].

'Rock 'n' roll musicians are looser than session players – not a lot of musical theory and stuff but they know what they're playing and play pretty well for what they were doing. In authentic rock 'n' roll you have to be a little rough around the edges, that's the difference between my albums and Stuart Colman producing them, he was using people like Albert Lee . . . great guys but a totally different sound. Rock 'n' roll guys don't always start and stop together, which is what makes it rock 'n' roll and that's what I shot for. These guys played frequently in pubs and clubs, and were able to give me a take in three or four times. Once that was down with a guitar overdub or whatever the guys wanted, then they would go have a beer and I'd take Shaky, put him in a booth and say, "Start singing."

'Michael – in those days, because he wasn't a star – was quite easy to work with. When I did The Wild Angels their lead singer, Mal Grey, had very little studio experience when I recorded him, and he was difficult to get to do something. When I put the ambience mics up he immediately said, "I ain't going to like that." I told him I'd play the tracks back for him to decide if he wanted it on or not . . . I still don't think he quite understood. But Shaky was different; he didn't try to pretend he had all this great experience. I think he owes me and Dave Edmunds a lot, but he was workable. He wasn't a guy who immediately said, "I think we ought to do this or that," he'd always try. The other thing he was good at in those days was performing in front of a mic. Too many people, the moment they stand in front of a mic in a studio, they start to freeze and sing differently.

'I tell people that if you can put your heart in it and imagine you're standing in front of a thousand rockers who love it, that's how to sing a song. Shaky did follow that kind of direction, he was a quick learner, easy to work with.' The same couldn't be said, in Marchand's opinion, of Paul Barrett. 'He was one of those guys who liked to feel he was more than just a manager, but part of the creative process. He wasn't a big pain in the arse to me, but I think that was because he didn't know what he was doing either . . . He liked to do a vocal or background vocal now or then. To me, if there was room in the record and it made everybody happy I couldn't care less.'

Marchand also produced the following year's *Rockin' And Shakin'*. 'By that time I'd become friends with the guys who ran a subsidiary of Polydor called Contour, and they were very interested to get the boys to do an album, but their budget was even less [than CBS's]. We did it in a studio just south of Clapham Common [Majestic Studios] and that was it. I really never saw the boys after that; everybody went their own way.'

Paul Barrett looks back on *Rockin' And Shakin'* as 'the worst record I've ever made, a dreadful record. When we cut it we had eight hours to put down the backing tracks and Shaky did the guide vocals, and then we expected to do the overdubs, and we were told, "That's a wrap." We said, "What do you mean, that's a wrap?" And that was it. Actually, it went on to become a gold record, because when Shaky became a star, certain records were reissued. *I'm No JD* and *Rockin' And Shakin'* were both reissued in the early Eighties on Hallmark, and both sold in excess of 270,000 copies each, because it took 270,000 copies to get a gold record in those days. So Shaky got the gold records. I know, I've got the silvers. Unfortunately, we didn't get the money.'

The choice of songs, producer Marchand remembers, was down to The Sunsets. 'I had no argument about it, because this is the kind of stuff they did. I had one or two songs that I played to them, which were rockers, but they just wanted to do the well-known standard stuff. I thought that was a mistake, [that they should] do something original and maybe get a hit single. There was one track on *Rockin' And Shakin'* called 'White Lightning' that I tried like mad to get released as a single – I thought it could have been a hit.'

Given that record sales would put him on the musical map in the next decade, it's hardly surprising that Shaky regards this aspect of his early career with no great affection: 'We made some albums but nothing happened to them 'cos there was no good promotion, no marketing. They were put out, but nothing really happened to them. We really didn't fit into the rest of the music that was around, but we did what we believed in and we kept going. We were very much a live band and we didn't take much care with the production side. We'd just pop in, do the record, pop out again and back on the road.'

Yet their status as a dynamite live act endured, even though they could not translate this into record sales – a fact underlined when they were voted the Top Live Band of 1972 by readers of *New Musical Express*. George Harrison's biographer Alan Clayson had caught Shakin' Stevens and the Sunsets when they headlined the Freshers' Ball at Reading University the previous year. The fact that they were out of step with prevailing 'progressive' trends was underlined by the support band – though, despite their prog-minded tendencies, they nevertheless finished off with a self-conscious rock 'n' roll medley.

But, says Clayson, 'This was brushed aside like matchsticks when Stevens and his ensemble took the stage. Yet there was no grand entrance after their larger-than-life manager thanked us for letting his charges play "at your high school hop". Later, he'd come on again to conduct an onstage raffle for one of their LPs. He was observed too, wandering the dance floor gulping at a bottle of Southern Comfort.

'The main attraction started casually with light rockabilly – "Honey Don't", "Woman Love", you get the drift – with Stevens coyly strumming an acoustic guitar. Then he abandoned it, and there was a sudden explosion with something like "Tutti Frutti" or "Roll Over Beethoven". From then on, the audience – perhaps tacitly sick of post-Woodstock drip-rock, heavy metal and technoflash – were eating out of Stevens' palm, though his continuity was almost monosyllabic, restricted mostly to "Thanks very much" and "We'd like to do a number by . . ."

'A contingent of non-student Teds – possibly smuggled in by the group – invaded the stage at several points, most conspicuously during "White Lightning" and the "Hound Dog" finale, which was prefaced by a teasing vignette of waltz-time "Que Sera Sera", and concluded with Stevens streaming with visible sweat, and in a state of knee-dropping near-collapse. An earlier highlight had been when he took a breather, and The Sunsets had had the unmitigated audacity to pile into [the instrumental] "Nut Rocker".

'Overall, Shakin' Stevens and the Sunsets were fun – and they earned every penny of their fee – but they were also, as far as I was concerned anyway, food for deep thought. Certainly, I was never to miss a performance whenever they appeared locally over the next three years.'

Shaky regarded such college audiences as a challenge. 'A chap came round once to show me his jeans,' he remembers. 'He'd frayed the bottoms and put patches all over the place. He said he was freaking out and that this was the scene to get into. I told him he'd ruined a perfectly good pair of jeans! It wasn't my scene anyway. So I carried on wearing the clothes that I liked and carried on playing the music that I liked. It was always rock 'n' roll. Even when we used to do gigs with the freaks sitting cross-legged on the floor saying that they'd seen God. Mind you, by the end of the show they were on their feet dancing!'

Guinness World Records British Hit Singles & Albums guru David Roberts, then a schoolboy, was tempted to experience Shakin' Stevens and the Sunsets live after he saw a 1974 show advertised in *New Musical Express* or *Melody Maker*. 'I wanted to go through the card, see all the people that were different. And he was doing rock 'n' roll, which was actually quite rare at the time, but doing it very well. And that was my first introduction to Shakin' Stevens.

'He wasn't particularly wild. I remember thinking the key thing about it was they were an incredible act in the same way as Dr Feelgood. The music press used to dictate what was fashionable and what wasn't fashionable a hell of a lot more than they do now. I was very impressionable. If somebody had sold out you were almost told not to follow their career any more. "This album is the pits, don't buy him, he's sold out." But some of them moved on to great things, and I suppose Shaky was one of those people.'

A 1972 gig at the Ocean Club in Cardiff saw Shaky cross paths with Brian Hodgson, who would write a 1981 single, 'Shooting Gallery', for him and perform with Matchbox as bass player. Both had come to see Marty Wilde, whose backing musicians Billy Bremner and Pete Baron were friends. 'Shaky had come down to see the show and I spoke to him later,' Hodgson recalls. 'In fact I lent him his bus fare home that night . . .'

But it was away from home shores that Shakin' Stevens and the Sunsets would find greatest acceptance. The seeds were sown by a 1972 tour of Sweden, their first trip abroad, which established a following in Scandinavia that persists to this day. Having survived a first gig in the unpromisingly titled town of Bastard, Shaky and the Sunsets had some wild times in the Land of the Midnight Sun. Highlights included a TV show in which they once again encountered Afro-rockers Osibisa (and their assegais!) and a recording session for a rock 'n' roll sampler album called *Rock Rivalerna*. This, as ever, yielded no financial rewards, but helped boost the band's reputation and ensure they would forever be welcomed back.

The year of 1972 brought yet more personnel changes, with guitarist Ian Lawrence replacing Willie Blackmore, who had not taken to the touring life. 'Ian was from that Cardiff school of lead/rhythm,' Paul Barrett remembers, 'and could really do those Chuck Berry drives. He used to try to sneak a wah-wah pedal on stage, so I had to confiscate it. He was really upset because he didn't have a nickname like everybody else. He was tall, thin and emaciated, and looked like a vampire, so I suggested "Bobby Drac". He was appalled. He hated it!'

A bigger addition, certainly in showmanship terms, was saxophonist Tony 'Twizzle' Britnall. The story is still told in rock 'n' roll circles of a 'legendary night' at the Greenford Hotel in London, when he used lighter fluid to give the impression of breathing fire. When this spilled onto the floor and set light to the piano, Shaky jumped onto it and grabbed a light fitting, swinging over the crowd like Tarzan. The fitting then fused, the sparks from it allegedly setting light to a teddy boy's quiff!

Following the Swedish experience, The Sunsets next set their sights on Holland, where they were promoted by Cyril Van Der Hemel. Though the Dutchman's terms were tough, Barrett felt the band were going nowhere in Britain and wanted to open up broader horizons. The year of 1973 saw no fewer than seven months taken up in touring the Netherlands, and by 1974 the group were big enough to play successive nights at the Paradiso, a major rock venue in Amsterdam. (Having supported Shaky many times over the years in Penarth, Adrian Angove once more found himself opening for The Sunsets with his pop/rock outfit Ingroville.)

It was something of a triumph against the odds, the power of primeval rock 'n' roll making a connection with the stoned audience at the most basic of levels. 'You know what it's like at the Paradiso,' Shaky would explain, 'they're all there with their kaftans and their dope. They're all paralysed. We did the whole show and they loved it. So that became a regular gig. We went back there many, many times, and we were treated great. And we did a lot of festivals and civic auditoriums.'

In August 1973, they shared the stage with progressive rockers Argent at a festival in Emmen. Actually, forget 'shared' the stage — the fact was that, while the progressive rockers were on the crest of a wave at home with hits like 'Hold Your Head Up' and 'God Gave Rock 'n' Roll To You', they were forced to accept second billing to local heroes The Sunsets. Whether or not bandleader Rod Argent recalled this when he produced Stevens in 1992 is not known . . .

Shaky later conceded that the mid-1970s were 'probably the hardest times for us. Drugs never really interested me at all, but at one point in the 1970s period, it was "cool, man" and all the audience would sit on the floor, stoned. There were all these progressive bands doing ten- or fifteen-minute solos with their enormous gear. We were more bizarre than they were, with our bright loud jackets, singing away with our little amps, doing three-minute numbers! We always managed to get them to their feet somehow.'

Shaky may have had no time for drugs, but he was still partial to a drink or two and as such, says Paul Barrett, had to be 'managed all the time. You had to keep an eye on him. I was in charge of most things as the manager and I stayed sober long enough to . . . not always!' When Barrett's own self-control wavered, 'I'd put Louie in with Shaky so he could keep an eye on him, because they'd be okay together.'

Paul recalls Shaky being something of an innocent abroad. 'We were at the Paradiso and this guy running the gig was called Tarzan – I was suspicious about this guy's sexuality. He's praising Shaky and telling him how good he is, [saying] "Let's go to a party." And he wanted Shaky to keep his gold suit on. So I said to Shaky, "I'll come along too." But they certainly didn't want me. So we went over to this place, and there were all these guys dressed like Captain America. And Shaky said, "This is great, they're all buying us drinks." I said to him, "Don't you think there's something funny about this place?" "No," he said, "no." "Shaky," I said, "There's no women here." "No," he said, "there's no women here." I said "Shaky, we're gonna go now." And I don't really think he got it. He just said, "They're fans, really. Oh, another drink." He had that naivety, and in some ways that can be kind of attractive. But he got out of there, boy.'

The band's debut Scandinavian tour, a six-week jaunt in September/October 1973, coincided with the Yom Kippur war in the Middle East, a conflict that raised international tension to yellow, if not red, alert, but appeared to have passed over the head of The Sunsets' singer. 'We were in Odense in Denmark,' recalls Louie, 'and one day we got up for breakfast . . . we were drinking till four in the morning . . . and we'd been away for about three weeks, and we saw a headline in a Danish newspaper saying, "Yom Kippur" and "Soviet and US missiles". Shit! What's going on since we've been away? We hadn't had any news. Shaky was non-political . . . totally non-political. The rest of us were very left-wing. Legs is a Communist and I have sympathies that way myself. I said to Legs, "Something's going on", so we found out what it was.

'The missiles were up for the first time since the Cuban missile crisis . . . ready for World War Three. And I'm not even home with my family. Legs and I telephoned home. And after listening to all this, Shaky was very silent, and I realized why. It suddenly hit me. And Legs realized at the same time. He leaned over to me and said, "Louie, we'd better not talk any more," because we were talking about the end of the world, and not about his career. We weren't talking about Shaky, the choice of songs, or whatever.'

The Danish tour was also remarkable for the effect of the local brew known as Elephant beer – one of the strongest ales known to man, and one that reduced the band members to shells of their former selves. According to Paul Barrett, George Chick was found the next morning cradling a half-consumed crate of Elephant on which he'd spent his gig fee . . . swearing blindly he was still owed money for the previous night's performance!

George quit the band at the end of 1973, and his loss was keenly felt. 'He was the guy in the band that everything falls on. Whenever we finished a gig and the roadies had been beaten up or arrested, or gone missing, who carries the equipment? Well, it was always me and George. And who drives the van? Well, it would be George. So I suppose in the end he had had enough.' He was replaced by Malcolm Priest, and was soon joined on the out escalator by Ian Lawrence, whose replacement was a young guitarist, Mike Lloyd-Jones. 'For a time,' Paul Barrett explains, 'we had both in the band, because we were very influenced by John Fogerty and the Blue Ridge Rangers. We were trying to do that country/rock 'n' roll, a sort of extension of rockabilly. Ian actually played steel guitar on quite a few numbers.' (On his departure, Lawrence formed a Welsh country-rock band called 'Southpaw'.)

When they were in Amsterdam, which was often, The Sunsets would use the Hotel Whiteman as a base and usually return there after every gig. 'Legs quite often put me in with Shaky,' Louie recalls. 'Now, he knew that the dope-heads in the band didn't want to be in with Shaky because he didn't participate. He was uncool. So Legs used to say, "Lou, I've got you a nice double bed, but it's in a room with Shaky." And I'd say, "Well, thanks a lot, Legs!"

'The worst thing about it was that there was never any conversation. Zilch. Unless we talked about the gig. We could talk about that. Once I was in there for about a fortnight with him. It was a living nightmare. And I kept saying to Legs, "I'll never forgive you for this." Incredible.'

Back home with a bump, The Sunsets found themselves mixing in high society after film critic Kenneth Tynan's daughter saw the band at Southampton University and persuaded her father to book them for her twenty-first birthday party. Louie takes up the story: 'It was at the Young Vic, and she'd booked Max Wall, Dudley Moore playing piano, and Shakin' Stevens and the Sunsets. So we do the gig and it was the first time Peter Sellers and Liza Minnelli had ever been seen together, and the next day it was in all the Sunday papers – Peter Sellers and Liza Minnelli are an item.

'We do our set, go back into the dressing room, and [Irish writer] Edna O'Brien comes in, and she was highly interested in Shaky. And she kept saying, "You give so much. You give so much in your show. You give so much of yourself for so little reward." The next thing I know, Max Wall is crying in the next dressing room because Frankie Howerd and Eric Morecambe had been booing him when he was on stage. It was just before he became a straight actor. They had him there as a joke, really. I couldn't believe it. I thought they were joking. They were leaning on the edge of the stage, and me and Legs were next to them. They're cursing him out, booing him, cat-calling, the whole shebang. It was incredible. And I thought, "No, they're artists. They can't mean it. They're just having a laugh." No, they weren't. And Max Wall was crying later on in the dressing room.

'That was quite a night. But it ended up with Edna O'Brien in the van, in our transit with us. She took us back to Chelsea, where she lived, and gave us whisky and sandwiches.'

The year 1974 found The Sunsets selected as support act for a Bill Haley tour, but the end of the year brought a residency at London's Hope and Anchor pub in Islington – the head-quarters of the 'pub-rock scene' that would eventually explode into punk. The experience of seeing Shakin' Stevens in a dingy cellar where there was barely enough headroom to swing a mic stand must have been unforgettable. The Torrington, Dingwalls Dancehall and the Greyhound were among the other venues to be graced by The Sunsets' presence.

'They've got a wonderful dressing room down the Hope and Anchor,' Shaky would recall, with more than a hint of irony. 'It's damp and you feel like cattle in there. You finish one half of your set and you come off steaming, with the sweat pouring off you, and there's five of you huddled in this cold, damp, brick dressing room, all trying to change at the same time. There were times we'd change in the corridors!'

Though you can't dine out on respect, the band were well thought of by their fellow musicians. Dr Feelgood were trying to popularize a basic R&B format on the same circuit – and indeed would score an unexpected Number One hit in 1976 with the uncompromising live album *Stupidity*. Their guitar player Wilko Johnson was a big fan of The Sunsets. 'We did a gig with them [once] and they're really a great band,' he revealed at the time. 'They've been going ages and they're real good. They're looked on with contempt by the critics because they're stuck a bit in the teddy-boy circuit. They deserve [respect for] sticking to what they believe in and they're not going to start doing something else just to try to impress the critics or whatever – and I really respect them for it. They come from Wales – and Wales is a real rock 'n' roll place.'

Ironically, of course, the punk wave was followed by a further rockabilly boom, spearheaded by the likes of The Stray Cats, Matchbox and The Meteors. By that time The Sunsets would be long gone. Aside from The Wild Angels and The Houseshakers, the leading rival to The Sunsets' crown in the 1970s had come in the form of fellow Welshmen Crazy Cavan and the Rhythm Rockers, led by Cavan Grogan. Though the bands hadn't always got on with the outfit from nearby Newport, a face-off in a transport café had resulted in mutual respect being established. Crazy Cavan were more of a rockabilly band than out and out rock 'n' rollers, and would win a recording contract with Charly Records in 1976.

Tony 'Twizzle' Britnall quit the ranks in 1974 to join a Dutch group called Long Tall Ernie and the Shakers. For his new compatriots, it was akin to having a hero in their midst, as the group had been formed by two bands who'd supported The Sunsets on their first Paradiso show! Twizzle's departure had an inevitable effect on the balance of power in The Sunsets, because the sax player had been the only real competition to Shaky in the image and showmanship stakes; his departure took a lot of the fire out of the band.

But Shaky had been steadily growing into his frontman role. While Paul Barrett had more or less been the stage announcer in the early days, now Stevens was both the band's mouthpiece and the undisputed star of the show. The once-diffident young man, now in his mid-twenties, was harnessing something inside him to become a memorable performer, as Barrett acknowledges: 'He learned his stagecraft as he went on. What he used to do was a natural hysterical outburst, sometimes a rage. I think sometimes his frustration at not being too articulate drove his performance. I think that edge is what made him a great rock 'n' roller . . . If he just rocked and rolled, he'd be fine. He's got that edge, and you need that edge. You're not sure what they're going to do next. Like Jerry Lee Lewis. They've all got it. And Shaky had that.'

As the sax wasn't to be replaced – Twizzle being considered an impossible act to follow – Shaky now started to play the acoustic guitar on stage again in the style of the early Elvis, though he'd use the cover of a mid-set instrumental to leave the stage and return in a new outfit to finish the set *sans* guitar. (Shaky even recorded a solo single, 'Lonesome Town', which was a chart hit in the Netherlands.)

As Paul Barrett explains, though *I'm No JD* had sold few copies in Britain first time round, 'it did pretty well in Europe, particularly Holland. So we ended up cutting a couple of albums over there. We teamed up with a Dutch label called Dureco and did an album called just *Shakin' Stevens And The Sunsets.* What I wanted to do was call it *Working Class Hero*, after the John Lennon song, because I thought the lyrics of that song were terrific. Apt then, apt today and apt tomorrow.' But Stevens' new-found confidence let him down when it came to the cover shoot. 'There was an Amstel brewery in Amsterdam,' says Barrett, 'and when the whistle blew, hundreds and hundreds of workers all came out of the factory in grey, dull clothes. I had this idea for an album sleeve: Shaky had a gold lamé suit and, dressed in the suit, he'd join them and march out with them. The photographer would take the photographs and that would be the album cover, which was a great concept, I thought . . .' Understandably, perhaps, Shaky declined the opportunity.

While rehearsing in Holland, The Sunsets made many demo recordings of titles including 'Sugaree', 'Tiger' and 'Baby I Don't

Care', which would appear on budget-label compilations in the early 1980s following Shaky's rise to stardom. *Classics* on the Magnum Force label also contained 'Your True Love' and 'Rock-A-Billy Rock', two tracks that the singer recorded in the mid-1970s without The Sunsets and which have never appeared on any release since.

The band continued to record for Dutch label Dureco, cutting *Manhattan Melodrama* in 1975. This was a semi-concept affair conceived by Paul Barrett around the theme of rebellion. 'It was, to me, about the outlaws of the 1930s and the outlaw music of the 1950s. *Manhattan Melodrama* was the title of the film starring Clark Gable that John Dillinger saw before he was gunned down outside the cinema by the FBI, in the back of the head – typical FBI heroes! The concept was if an outlaw like John Dillinger had been around in the 1950s, he might have been a rock 'n' roll singer, not a bank robber. We had a lot of hope for that album.'

As with earlier efforts, however, there just wasn't enough time to do the music justice, though it was some consolation that the group received a £2,000 cash advance – the biggest payment they ever received in their career. Unfortunately, producer Shel Shelvekins did extensive remixing on the album and overdubbed flutes and synthesizers, resulting in a record that lacked the band's customary hard edge. 'We weren't too happy with the production, because it was fairly contemporary,' confirms Barrett, 'but we liked the material and what we did. I don't think the Dutch producer understood what we were talking about and we didn't really have enough time to do the whole concept, so we ended up doing songs. So it wasn't a concept, it was just a series of songs, but it was pretty close.

'The Dutch records came out in Britain on Emerald, which I understand was some subsidiary of Decca via Island. So I think these albums went from Holland to Ireland to the UK. Needless to say, they didn't sell very well.' Armed with these recordings, Barrett did the rounds of British record companies, where he met with a lukewarm response. '[Though] I remember Island Records were interested, I also remember Richard Williams saying that the name – Shakin' Stevens and the Sunsets – would never sell. The name was too silly. It was too 1950s, it wouldn't work. So I said, "What about Eddie and the Hot Rods?"'

Such a dismissive attitude was strange indeed, because record companies were at last becoming aware of the rock 'n' roll gold they had in their vaults. Three volumes of seminal Sun label rockabilly emerged in 1974 on the Philips label, the then owners of that music, while the previously mentioned Charly label, set up in England the following year, bought the rights to the Sun catalogue and started making it available again in many different forms. And fans of live music got their share of 1950s rock too: London's Lyceum found its monthly rock 'n' roll night hugely oversubscribed. So the tide was turning . . . but was it too late for Shaky and his pals?

While record success was proving as elusive as ever, there was no doubting the potency of The Sunsets' live act. After his group Brinsley Schwarz split up, college circuit colleague Ian Gomm encountered Shakin' Stevens again. 'It was 1976 or '77, I was working in a studio in north Wales, and the Sunsets were booked to appear at a barn dance across the valley at a little hamlet called Cefn Coch. And it was literally a dance in a barn: I guess he'd lost direction by then. The dressing room was the front room of a council house next door to the farm with the barn!

'I was employed to tune the piano, and so I negotiated two free tickets for myself and my wife. Shaky gave it his all – I had forgotten how good he was. In fact I went backstage afterwards and offered him some free recording time. Sadly, he didn't take up the offer, or didn't take me seriously, and next thing I heard two weeks later he'd auditioned for the *Elvis* show. He was clearly destined for greater things.

'In fact, The Sunsets had motored up from south Wales for the show, and this hamlet in the hills was so obscure that two

Early days (*left*): At a 1968 gig in his native Cardiff, Shaky leads The Sunsets alongside bassist Steve Pryor.

Relaxing backstage in Cardiff with The Sunsets (*below*): (*from left to right*) Drummer Brian 'Slapbeat' Williams, Shaky, drummer and singer Rockin' Louie (Robert Llewellyn), guitarist Robert 'Carl' Peterson and Steve Pryor.

Man on the mic (*left*): Shaky sings his heart out at a gig in the late 1960s while Mike Bibby accompanies on guitar.

Winding down (*below*): Shaky and Rockin' Louie engage in youthful high jinks after a show in 1968.

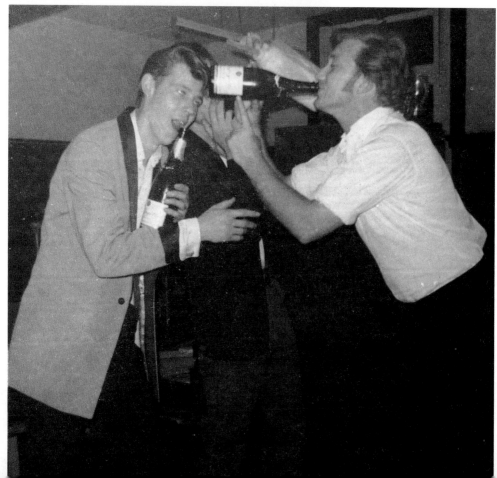

In foreign fields: Shaky and the band pose outside TV studios in Frankfurt, Germany, during the filming of *Hits A Go Go* in 1972. (*From left to right*) Guitarist Ian Lawrence (standing), bassist George Chick and pianist Mike 'Ace' Skudder (both crouching), drummer Rockin' Louie, Shaky, and Boo-Boo the roadie (behind the glass door).

Shakin' Stevens and the Sunsets enjoyed many European tour experiences, and in 1972 the band performed in Sweden. Pictured backstage after one such show: (*back row, left to right*) Ian Lawrence and band manager Paul Barrett; (*middle row, left to right*) George Chick and Rockin' Louie; (*front row, left to right*) former Swedish rock 'n' roll star Jerry Williams, Shaky and Ace Skudder.

Laying down some tracks (*right*): Shaky performs vocals at a 1974 recording session.

Below: The singer adopts a characteristic pose at an early photo shoot in the mid-1970s.

During the 1970s, Shakin' Stevens and the Sunsets became regulars on the college-gig circuit. At a 1975 show, Shaky plays up to the crowd while Rockin' Louie keeps time on drums (*right*). Bassist George Chick and guitarist Mike Lloyd-Jones lend a hand with vocals (*below*).

A change in direction (*above*): In 1977, Shaky was persuaded to audition for a key role in the forthcoming West End show *Elvis – The Musical*. Despite initial reservations, he got the part and shared the limelight alongside US singer P. J. Proby (*middle*) and sixteen-year-old newcomer Timothy Whitnall (*right*).

Left: As the 'middle' Elvis, Shaky portrayed the rock 'n' roll legend during his explosive rise to fame. The show ran from November 1977 until June 1979 at London's Astoria Theatre, and provided the springboard for the launch of Shaky's solo career.

Above: In 1979, Jack Good, producer of *Elvis – The Musical*, brought back a revamped version of his successful 1950s rock 'n' roll show *Oh Boy!* to ITV, on which Shaky was a regular guest. Recorded on Sunday evenings, it gave the singer an opportunity to reach a wider audience on television.

Right: So popular was *Oh Boy!* that a further twenty-six similar shows were commissioned under the title *Let's Rock*, in which Shaky continued to feature prominently.

Success around the corner: After years of hard graft on the road across Britain and Europe, Shaky began his solo career as a rock 'n' roll singer, and was soon rewarded for his patient endeavour and hard work.

of them only just made it before show time. The pianist didn't show at all – so all my work was in vain!'

In all his time on the road with Shaky, Paul Barrett can only recall the singer reading one book. 'It's a paperback by Harlan Ellison called *Rockabilly* that I gave him years ago. I always said, "When you make it, we'll film this, and you can play the guy" . . . But apart from that I don't think Shaky's read any books.' Louie concurs: 'I've never seen him read a book or buy a newspaper.'

Politics and current affairs also left the singer cold according to Barrett. 'I'm a Communist, Louie's a Marxist and all the band were pretty left wing, and we'd start talking politics and you could see Shaky blank out. I'd have to start talking about the set or his career because I felt he didn't have much conversation, or much outside what he did and what really concerned him. He did lots of benefits for the Communist Party, and the people who were fighting against Saddam, but Shaky had no interest in who we were playing for. "Why are they waving all those red flags, Legs?" "It's okay, Shaky, they're cool. They dig it."

'We played in Holland when the Vietnam War was at its height and they had a big thing – Amsterdam Helps Saigon. We did a gig for them and we arrived at this all-night concert hall, the band went on and I'd got them to play this instrumental called "Red Flag Rock", featuring the piano player. It was "The Red Flag" rocked up. And at the end this huge docker guy came running on saying, "Marvellous! Wonderful!" – he vigorously shook Shaky's hand and broke his finger. He was off the road for three weeks. And he went on with a splint for a while. I remember Shaky saying, "Where's Saigon?"'

As the college circuit started to implode, Paul Barrett looked around for other sources of income. The May Balls at Oxford and Cambridge provided rich pickings, as long as the band were prepared to play as a covers outfit, plying music to 'pissed upper-class twits'. They always seemed to hit the stage at around five in the morning, when the bright young things were dimming a little. In 1976, the band were contracted to play seven such events in just five days, resulting in them booking into a truckstop near Cambridge for the duration.

Shaky had become a family man in 1973 with the birth of his first child, Jason; two more were to follow. Though he wasn't around much to experience it, home for the former Mike Barratt and his family was now a maisonette in Fairwater, just outside Ely. They'd moved from their initial home in Westgate Street when it was finally demolished by the council in favour of an office block.

There would be just one more record before The Sunsets split, a 10-inch LP entitled *C'mon Memphis* for the Dutch Dynamite label in 1976. As with so many of Shaky's pre-fame recordings, it has also been endlessly recycled by a number of labels under a variety of titles. The music was recorded on a basic mobile studio and was almost rockabilly-based, even though the group hadn't played with an upright bass for some considerable time.

This had been preceded by a recording of the band's final single, a version of Hank Mizell's rockabilly classic 'Jungle Rock'. Released on Mooncrest, it went nowhere – and, frustratingly, the Mizell original was subsequently reissued, giving the nascent Charly label an unexpected Number Three hit in March 1976. It was the same old story, so near yet so far . . . but the latest piece of bad luck for The Sunsets was finally to lead to their singer's big break.

3

ELVIS – THE
MUSICAL: 1977–9

IN THE AUTUMN OF 1976, a sequence of events that would have a profound effect on Shaky's future career began with a call to Track Records from Phil Bailey, who had produced The Sunsets' version of 'Jungle Rock' not long before. Bailey made his approach with a view to interesting the label in Rock Island Line, a rock 'n' roll band he was managing at the time. His powers of persuasion were clearly good enough to bring Track's Danny Secunda and Mike Shaw to see Rock Island Line on the same bill as The Sunsets at Warwick University. But after the event Track were much more interested in the Welsh headliners than Bailey's charges.

Musically The Sunsets were back to their best, Ian Lawrence having rejoined on steel guitar to add a new texture to their now rockabilly-style music alongside Mike Lloyd-Jones, while George Chick returned in place of Mal Priest. Yet quite why Track should have been interested in either them or indeed

Rock Island Line remains something of a mystery. Track, formerly the label of The Who and The Jimi Hendrix Experience (in the UK, anyway), had no history of dealing with traditional rock 'n' roll acts, and their recent signings had consisted mostly of US punk and garage bands – ideologically similar, perhaps, but stylistically poles apart.

The Warwick University gig proved to be the start of many months of uncertainty, as Track kept Shakin' Stevens and the Sunsets dangling, seemingly unsure of what to do with them. Without making any commitment to a formal contract, Track's first move was to send the band into Gooseberry Studios with Danny Secunda. The sessions proved to be extremely enjoyable, and the results were reckoned to be among the best performances the band had ever recorded. Paul Barrett rates 'Lightning Bar Blues' (originally recorded by Arlo Guthrie back in 1970) and 'Lend Me Your Heart' as some of the best music they ever committed to tape.

Good as the results might have been, Track remained less than enthusiastic, and they were equally unimpressed with the images captured by Adrian Owlett, a professional photographer and friend of the band who had been asked to do a shoot with them around the same time. Despite successfully capturing the essence of the band as it was, neither the music nor the pictures seemed to fit with the label's idea of what The Sunsets ought to be – which again raises the question of why they showed an interest in the first place.

Caught up in the musical mayhem that was unfolding in the final weeks of 1976, Track seemed intent on marketing Shakin' Stevens and the Sunsets as some sort of hybrid punk act, despite their purist rock 'n' roll credentials. Sent back into the studio, this time with Charlie Gillett at the controls, they tried again. The results were, at best, lacklustre, perhaps because Gillett – the eminent broadcaster and writer, whose *The Sound Of The City* is the definitive text on the rise of rock 'n' roll – had no more idea of what Track had in mind than did the label. The band became irritated, tired and disillusioned, as what had looked like a golden opportunity turned slowly to dust.

Worse still, it became increasingly obvious that not only did Track have a totally different image in mind for the band, but also their real interest was primarily in Shaky himself. Their next attempt to dictate the future course of Shaky's career involved producer Mike Hurst, who suggested recording 'Never', an Eddie Cochran song, but who had no intention of using The Sunsets to back Shaky on the recording. Hurst recorded a backing track with session musicians, then got Shaky in to do the vocals. With no firm contract in sight, this proved to be the final straw for Mike Lloyd-Jones, Ian Lawrence and George Chick, who promptly quit to form their own country-rock band, Quarter Moon.

Paul Barrett acted quickly, bringing guitarist Danny Wild and a former roadie in on bass. Christened Colin Hopkins, they called the new bassist 'Johnny Chop' – not because of any oriental connection, but because when he signed his name it came out as C. HOPkins. At first, this new, slimmed-down line-up seemed to offer some hope for the future, and the group were well-received at a number of gigs in pubs and clubs around the capital, but by this time Track clearly had other ideas. Their interest in Shaky, rather than in Shakin' Stevens and the Sunsets, had increased after they'd heard Hurst's recording of 'Never', on which, of course, The Sunsets hadn't performed. In April 1977, the label finally came forward with a contract – but predictably it was for Shaky as a solo act.

With 'Never' slated for release as a single, Track decided to throw their weight behind their latest signing by shooting a promotional video to go with the song. For reasons that no one could have foreseen at the time, this decision proved to be a turning point in Shaky's career.

The shoot took place at the London rock venue Rock Garden in late summer. As the band slogged through countless repetitions of the song for the benefit of the cameras, Fumble, another seasoned rock 'n' roll act were busy setting up for a gig at the venue the same evening. The group had been around in one form or another since 1967, and had played at such legendary venues as the Star Club in Hamburg and the Cavern in Liverpool. In 1972, they had supported Bill Haley on tour in Germany, and the following year they had accompanied David Bowie on his UK and US tours. By the mid-1970s, they could also boast of having served as Chuck Berry's backing band, but on this September afternoon Fumble were on a different high, having just secured the job of house band for *Elvis – The Musical*, a new stage production celebrating the life of Elvis Presley.

Although the show had been conceived by Jack Good some time earlier, Presley's death, just a couple of weeks beforehand, had given renewed impetus to the idea and Good had moved quickly to seize the moment. London's Astoria Theatre, then under the stewardship of Ray Cooney, had been booked, and the relatively unknown Keith Strachan had been chosen as musical director – a demanding role in a production that featured around eighty songs, almost all of them from Presley's repertoire.

Strachan was certainly equal to the task, and has since enjoyed a hugely successful career on both stage and television. His credits include the West End production of *Grease*, the Liverpool Playhouse production of *Imagine*, and national tours with *The Roy Orbison Story* and *Four Steps To Heaven*. He has also written numerous TV themes, the best-known of which is probably that for *Who Wants To Be A Millionaire?*, and composed Cliff Richard's 1988 Christmas chart-topper, 'Mistletoe And Wine'.

With the venue and the MD finalized, Good and Cooney had begun the hunt for the actors who would play the King at three key stages of his life: the early years, those of his explosive rise to fame, and the Las Vegas era. By the afternoon of the

Shakin' Stevens video shoot, two of the three roles had been filled — the young Elvis would be played by Timothy Whitnall, an unknown sixteen-year-old schoolboy from Bury St Edmunds, and the Las Vegas model would be portrayed by P. J. Proby, a genuine American (born James Marcus Smith) who was anxious to use this opportunity to leave behind the notoriety he had achieved in his earlier incarnation as a pants-splitting, ponytailed pop star.

As Shaky and the band worked on the video, Paul Barrett got chatting to Fumble. They were old friends — the rock 'n' roll fraternity was close-knit, and The Sunsets had played alongside Fumble on many a bill over the years. As they talked about the new show, Barrett realized instantly that here was the chance of a lifetime, and after the shoot he made it clear to Shaky that he thought he should audition for the still-vacant 'middle Elvis' role.

Shaky, however, wasn't convinced. On the face of it, it's hard to see quite what he had to lose, since it was clear to everyone around him that his career was going nowhere fast. Shakin' Stevens and the Sunsets were, at best, only modestly successful, and there were no signs that things were about to improve dramatically for any of them, even allowing for the recent contract with Track. 'Never' had sold disappointingly and although the promotional video might still turn it into a hit, there were no guarantees.

Rock 'n' roll was still very much a minority interest, and in reality Shaky had precious little to show for ten years of hard work except a wealth of experience and a handful of unsuccessful record releases. But fronting a rock 'n' roll band was all he knew, and the idea of abandoning the dream for a West End role must have seemed a totally alien concept.

Within The Sunsets' camp, there was a growing feeling that it might just be time to call it a day. Ten years on the road had taken its toll, and the fact that Track had chosen not to offer the band a contract had brought the situation into sharp relief.

Speaking in 2005, Barrett recalled there being an atmosphere of resignation around the group at the time – 'We'd all had enough. It had been ten years and we were all tired. Louie, Shaky and I were the only constants for the entire ten years and everybody else had been around long enough. The band had run its distance, and it wasn't quite as good as it used to be . . . The plan was to come off the road at Christmas '77, and just take local gigs, make demos and send them off to record companies, and try all that, but all get day jobs.'

Barrett, meanwhile, continued to try to persuade the reluctant singer to try out for the show. Convinced that this would be an excellent career move, he arranged for one of Jack Good's team to come to a Sunsets gig at the Greyhound, a well-known rock pub in Fulham Palace Road. The dubious honour fell to Annabel Leventon, the show's assistant director, who was clearly impressed enough by what she saw to approach Shaky after the gig. He, however, was still distinctly cool on the idea, and pointedly ignored her for the remainder of the evening, although Paul kept the door open by telling her to contact him the following week.

Whatever discussions may have followed, there was no immediate outcome, and for the moment The Sunsets continued their normal round of gigging, while Shaky himself remained undecided about what to do for the best. The band, and Ace especially, were broadly in favour – as Barrett had pointed out, The Sunsets could carry on gigging while Shaky was in the stage production, and they would gain the added credibility of a West End star in the band's line-up on his return.

After much persuasion, Shaky went for an audition. Barrett's recollections of the day reveal why the role had been so hard to fill: 'There were plenty of rockabilly kids, a multitude of fat, cheeseburger Elvises, but no King of Rock 'n' Roll Elvises. There was no one from *Jailhouse Rock* to *GI Blues* – there was nobody there. Shaky got up and sang "Teddy Bear" and they wanted him straight away . . . But Shaky turned it down and we got back in the van and we went back to Wales.'

Shaky was a natural for the part – despite his well-known dislike of comparisons between himself and Presley, he had spent his entire professional career, consciously or unconsciously, recreating the spirit of rock 'n' roll that Presley had embodied. He was no straight Elvis impersonator, to be sure, but he was pursuing the same rock 'n' roll dream Elvis had pursued all those years before, and he owed his very nickname to onstage gyrations that had their roots in those early Elvis performances.

Despite this, or perhaps because of it, Shaky still remained unconvinced. He later explained in a *Look In* interview, 'When I first heard about it I didn't want to be part of it – I didn't want to be part of anything that was a send-up.' In fact, Shaky refused to commit to the production until Jack Good himself took time out to reassure him that *Elvis – The Musical* was to be a serious and respectful recreation of the Presley phenomenon. Good persuaded Shaky that he certainly wasn't looking to create a caricature or an impersonation of Elvis Presley on stage, but that he was trying to find the singer who could convey the special magic that Presley conjured up every time he walked out into the spotlight.

Good is one of popular music's outstanding characters, an intelligent man with a deep love of rock 'n' roll that had seen him popularize the genre in the UK through pioneering Fifties shows such as *6.5 Special* and *Oh Boy!* As the 1950s drew to a close, he'd acted as image-maker to both Cliff Richard and Adam Faith, and brought Gene Vincent to the UK, before relocating to the US in the 1960s. While in the States, he'd produced stage musicals, television specials and worked as a promoter, and so he had a wealth of experience to draw on by the time he returned to London to stage *Elvis – The Musical*. He had pedigree, knew what he wanted and who he wanted, and knew exactly how to persuade the reluctant Shaky to agree to the role.

Alongside Jack Good's efforts, Adrian Owlett – in whose Surrey home Shaky sometimes stayed after gigs in the capital – may also have done much to persuade him that this was an opportunity too good to pass up. As they discussed the stage show one night, Owlett gave a brutally honest assessment of Shaky's diminishing future prospects, telling the singer in no uncertain terms that The Sunsets simply weren't making any progress, and that he would be a fool to let this chance slip through his fingers. Moreover, Owlett was prepared to offer Shaky a place to stay until he could find something more permanent.

Paul Barrett is convinced this was a major factor in Shaky accepting the part: 'I suppose, like most of us, he hates change and it was something he wasn't equipped for. And if it hadn't been for a mutual friend living in Walton-on-Thames, who had a big house and said to Shaky, "You can stay with me", I don't think it would have happened. The fact that Shaky had that push . . . it was somebody he knew, and he had a place to stay.'

Finally, after working tirelessly on the singer, Barrett, Owlett and Good heard the news they had been waiting for – Shaky decided to take the part. 'Jack Good and [co-producer] Brian Rix told Legs it was a forgone conclusion that Shaky was going to play one of the three Elvises,' Rockin' Louie recalls. 'We knew that was gonna happen and we were happy with that.' Optimistically, he suggests that Shaky was supposed to rejoin the band again. 'But he never did. He was up there with all the luvvies in London. He just didn't come back. Which was a peculiar thing to do, seeing that we supported him for all those years.'

Shaky, for his part, was happy to put touring behind him – for now, at least. 'I don't regret it,' he revealed in a magazine interview. 'It's good to do it; it's like an apprenticeship. And it was a long apprenticeship. But I've seen it, I've witnessed it, and I can say I've done it! I enjoyed it, but there came a time after five or six years when it was time to think, hang on a sec, we're going round in circles here, doing the same venues all the time.'

Ironically, one of The Sunsets' swansong gigs, at the Rock Garden in May 1977, had been caught by *NME*'s Cliff White who used his write-up to ponder whether British rock 'n' roll had improved since he'd last decided it was 'substandard Eddie Cochran imitators draped in irrelevant clobber'. His conclusion – 'Yeah, I think British rockers are all right' – was reached after seeing a set that included the likes of 'Tear It Up', 'Honey Hush', Charlie Rich's 'Rebound' and 'Lights Out'. A smattering of ballads included the just-released 'Never', Freddy Fender's recent 'Wasted Days And Wasted Nights' and Presley's 'It Hurts Me'. White felt less enthusiastic about covers of 'Johnny B. Goode', 'Sweet Little Sixteen' and 'Great Balls Of Fire', though he approved of Shaky's trim stage version of a drapecoat, contrasting with the band's less authentic sweatshirts and jeans. 'They know what they're about – and that, along with a love of the music, is all it takes to rock 'n' roll. I think I'll come again,' concluded White, little knowing that he wouldn't have the opportunity.

Once the singer had signed on the line as Elvis, Barrett was quick to finalize the deal. Shaky would be paid more than either Whitnall or Proby, an arrangement that hadn't figured in Good and Cooney's original plans, but which was agreed after Barrett pointed out that Shaky was certain to be the star of the show, appearing as he was alongside a total unknown and a faded 1960s balladeer. Rehearsals would begin on 27 October, three days prior to which there was to be the curious matter of a further audition – an entirely bogus affair, as the cast had already been chosen – designed purely as part of the publicity build-up for the show.

The *Daily Mirror*, who had earlier invited readers to fill in a form and send it in if they fancied their chances of playing Elvis in the show, ran banner headlines declaring 'The Great Elvis Hunt Is On!' Whether the newspaper knew of the deception or not is open to conjecture, but prospective Elvises turned up in their hundreds on the day, their stories dutifully recorded by dozens of reporters who had no more idea that the whole thing was a sham than did the candidates themselves. One exception was Shakin' Stevens himself, who had only to go through the motions of auditioning, and by all accounts did so with little enthusiasm. His performance on the day would certainly have fallen far short of securing him the role . . . had he not already been chosen for it.

Shakin' Stevens and the Sunsets signed off with a final gig at the Broom in Woolwich, just two days before rehearsals for the show began. It was a riotous send-off, with conspicuous consumption of alcohol fuelling a spirited evening's entertainment. There were a number of encores, and the exuberant audience clearly didn't want to see them go, but eventually it was over, and a new era in Shaky's life was about to begin. Not only would he have to adjust to life on the West End stage, but he would be doing so without the help and guidance of Paul Barrett, for whom the strain of looking after the singer's affairs had finally become too much.

Although The Sunsets continued in various forms for another eighteen months with Rockin' Louie on vocals, Barrett's association with the band barely survived Shaky's departure, and ended for good after an acrimonious post-gig encounter with the management of the Rock Garden a few weeks later. His relationship with Shaky himself had already become severely strained, and as negotiations for the Elvis role had progressed, the singer seemed increasingly to be relying on Adrian Owlett for support and advice. When Track had finally come up with a contract, Shaky had asked Owlett to check it out; he, in turn, asked his lawyer, Bryan Carter, to do the honours.

Adrian also organized transport to and from the theatre for Shaky for the first few months of the show, as the singer was without his own vehicle temporarily, and he hated using public transport, especially late at night. Once again, Owlett stepped into the breach, selflessly chauffeuring the singer back and forth to the Astoria whenever his other commitments allowed, until Track could be persuaded to provide a car and driver for their man.

Barrett, meanwhile, became steadily more disillusioned with life at Stevens' beck and call. Once the negotiations for *Elvis – The Musical* were complete, he effectively withdrew from his association with the singer, and from statements he made subsequently it seems to have come as a huge relief. He had been there all through the 1970s, throughout the years when no one wanted to know about rock 'n' roll. He had worked tirelessly for The Sunsets' cause and could justly claim to have been instrumental in whatever success they had enjoyed. But when rehearsals for the stage show began, Paul Barrett was conspicuous by his absence. It soon became clear that their relationship had sadly deteriorated, not helped by the fact that Barrett felt he had not been given sufficient credit for helping Shaky to secure his new role as Elvis.

With Paul Barrett out of the picture, Adrian Owlett became Shaky's *de facto* new manager. Owlett quickly realized that his new charge was hopelessly out of step with the theatrical crowd he would now have to mix with, and that the prospect clearly terrified him. Shaky pleaded with Adrian to come to the Astoria with him for the first few days of rehearsals, and, under the circumstances, he felt unable to refuse. They were difficult days, and whenever the opportunity arose, the pair would withdraw to the depths of the auditorium and keep their own company.

It rapidly became obvious that Shaky wanted nothing to do with his co-stars, regarding himself as having nothing in common with young Tim Whitnall, and quickly forming a strong dislike for Jim Proby. (Paul Barrett: 'I think Shaky was slightly in awe of him initially, but he wasn't overly impressed by his behaviour.') The two simply didn't get on, and Proby's erratic behaviour, widely rumoured at the time to be due to drink problems, simply made things worse. He missed several performances before eventually being reportedly sacked from the production in June 1978, to be replaced by Bogdan Kominowski.

Shaky was clearly ill at ease in these unfamiliar surroundings, and equally unsure about the new way of working that a stage production entailed. Unlike his work with The Sunsets, this was a precise art, the songs had to be sung word-perfect, and, as many of them had never featured in The Sunsets' shows, some had to be learned almost from scratch. Like Presley, Shaky was a far from fluent reader, and the prospect of working from a script was another serious concern for him. Owlett spent many hours studying the scripts with the singer, going over and over the lines and the songs until Shaky was comfortable with what was expected of him. Painstaking work, to be sure, but Owlett remained confident that his boy would be the star of the show – and so he proved to be.

Elvis – The Musical opened on 28 November 1977, and went down a storm with both the tabloids and the hundreds of Elvis fans who packed the theatre every night. Like Shaky, the fans were living out their own rock 'n' roll dream – that of being able to see the King live on a British stage – and they clearly loved every minute of it. Shaky finally had the adulation he had always craved, even if it was only for portraying the man whose spirit had always pervaded his performances with The Sunsets. Once he settled into the role, Shaky showed every sign of enjoying himself, and a contemporary review in the *New Musical Express* certainly backed up the idea that Shaky was the show's main attraction. 'Shakin' Stevens acquits himself far more creditably as the middle Presley. He carries the weight of the rock 'n' roll material and obviously cares deeply about what he's doing. Stevens is, after all, a well respected jobbing rocker . . . [who] has clearly studied Presley's moves probably most of his life, and although he doesn't have the agility or build to duplicate Presley's wilder displays, he knows his limitations and works well within them . . . His voice is powerful and experienced, and he seems to be sincerely trying to work into the part, and not just running through an Elvis-ized version of his own stage routine.'

In a 2000 interview on Radio Merseyside, Shaky revealed to Spencer Leigh how Jack Good had played the Elvises off against each other to improve their respective performances. 'He'd go into one dressing room and build one artist up, then go into another and build the other artist up, so it became like a competition. He'd say to each of you, "You're the best", so when you went out there you'd really believe it and give it your all . . . that's how he'd get the best out of everyone involved.' Starring night after night in *Elvis – The Musical*, he told Leigh, gave him some vital hints about stagecraft he'd take into his solo career. 'It taught me a lot, because performing in the clubs in Wales and then in the colleges and universities I was always used to working at eye level. Working in the West End reminded me that there was a circle up there above the stalls, and I learned a useful lesson there.'

Fumble, whose ranks were swelled in the show by a number of session players (not to mention future comedy star Tracey Ullman on backing vocals), also had their contribution recognized, reviews highlighting the demanding nature of the programme for the musicians and the panache with which they carried it off. 'Apart from Shakin' Stevens, the hardest-working people in the show are the augmented Fumble, who are onstage for the whole two or so hours and lay down the backing like the road-hardened professionals they undoubtedly are.' One member of the band took a break during the show's lengthy run – keyboard player Sean Mayes left in March 1978 to play with David Bowie on his world tour promoting *Heroes*, returning to the UK to rejoin the show in December. During his absence, Krysztof Kafka stood in.

While the critics applauded Shaky's interpretation of the Presley magic, there were episodes behind the scenes that shed a rather different light on the singer's character. As Adrian Owlett was to discover during his brief term as Shaky's mentor, the Welshman wasn't always the most sensitive of people, which was something that became immediately apparent as early as the show's opening night.

That evening was a glittering occasion, with celebrities parading in their finery and cameras working overtime to capture the moment, but for Shaky's wife Carole, it proved to be an unfortunate experience. Initially uncertain whether to invite her at all, Shaky had decided otherwise when he was advised that her absence might appear odd to the world at large. To set Shaky's mind at rest, Adrian assured him that he would look after Carole throughout the evening, so Shaky eventually made the call that brought her to London. When Carole arrived at the theatre, however, it was obvious that there had been a misunderstanding. While everyone else was wearing designer gowns and dinner jackets, Carole was dressed in jeans, having been told by her husband to come 'as you are'.

It was a situation that was doubtless embarrassing for her, and one that could certainly have been avoided but for a little more thought on Shaky's part. But this was not the only time that he'd showed a lack of consideration where other people were concerned. Not only had Owlett's offer of a place to stay during rehearsals for the show turned into an indefinite arrangement, but Shaky quickly came to regard his manager's Surrey home as his own, asking friends back after the show and inviting his wife and children down from Cardiff for Christmas without consulting his host first.

To be fair, though, Shaky made a regular weekly contribution to the housekeeping while he was living under Owlett's roof, and in truth Owlett was in no hurry to push him out. The two shared a love of rock 'n' roll – even though they were poles apart in other respects – and although their relationship had its ups and downs, they enjoyed some good times. But occasionally Adrian witnessed moments when Shaky's drinking appeared to get the better of him. As one of the stars of the Elvis musical, Shaky was under considerable pressure and expected to perform to the max every night. There were reports of clashes with Fumble's Des Henley and, on one occasion, Billy Hartman, who had stepped up from the chorus to cover for Tim Whitnall's absence with flu. The enthusiastic reaction of the girls in the audience to the understudy was said to have annoyed Shaky, who felt his thunder had been stolen and that the screams should be reserved for him alone. Tim Whitnall was also said to have received the odd barbed comment from his 'senior' Elvis. If true, however, the experience clearly wasn't too damaging, as Whitnall's subsequent career has seen him in numerous stage productions, musical and dramatic, and involved in a great many TV shows, both as actor and writer. In 1996, he and Proby returned to the West End for a revival of *Elvis – The Musical* at the Prince of Wales Theatre, with Whitnall playing the role Shaky had made his own almost twenty years earlier.

An immediate hit, the original show ran for nineteen months and won the *Evening Standard* award for Best Musical of 1978, as well as gaining a nomination for the Society of West End Theatre Awards (SWET). Playing to about 8,000 people a week throughout its run, the show was, by anybody's standards, a critical and commercial success. Offstage, however, things were not going quite so well.

Neither of Shaky's first two releases on Track – the singles 'Never' and 'Somebody Touched Me' – had made an impression on the charts (though the latter was a Top Forty hit in Australia), but the label sensed that things might change now their new signing had landed a prestigious West End role. Looking to capitalize on the publicity the role would generate, Track promptly sent Shaky into the studio to record an album of material for a projected Christmas release. Backing came from sax player Alan Holmes, drummer Tony Newman and bass guitarist Dick Thomas – all veteran members of British session band Sounds Incorporated – with the addition of guitarist Phil Palmer; Sunsets piano-player Ace Skudder was also invited.

The album was recorded 'live to tape' in one day at Island Studios, in the next studio to Bob Marley – conversations at the coffee machine must have been interesting! Shaky recalled that it 'was like one big party, the studio was full of people, food and booze'. Shaky's vocals were somewhat harder-edged than before, and the end results were, once again, encouraging.

The resulting album, simply entitled *Shakin' Stevens*, was released in the UK on 7 April 1978. (It was known elsewhere in Europe as *Play Loud*.) A number of unreleased Track recordings surfaced in 1983 on EMI's budget Music For Pleasure label entitled *The Track Years*. Former manager Paul Barrett has suggested that Shaky recorded 'Green Door' – the song that would give him his second chart-topper in 1981 – during his time with Track, but this has never been conclusively proved.

Some twenty-five years later, Sanctuary Records acquired the rights to this material and, in summer 2005, was due to release a first compilation of Track music, but the project was postponed. The proposed title, *Got A Lot O'Livin' To Do*, was due to be issued on the Castle label, and its featured songs would have come from *Shakin' Stevens/Play Loud* and *The Track Years* albums, along with a few bonus tracks. Talks were ongoing with the singer's management to follow up with the unreleased material, the prospect of which excited the Shaky cyber-community more than a projected album of new material.

But in the late 1970s, all was far from well in the Track Records camp. After Chris Stamp, one of the label's proprietors, was successful in pursuing a lawsuit against The Who, one of the label's financial backers, he withdrew his stake in the company and Track folded soon after. It was a sad end to a frustrating period in Shaky's recording career, since the material he'd recorded for Track ranked among his best, but the company's liquidation meant that the recordings soon became unavailable, and remained so for many years.

So Shakin' Stevens was once again without a recording contract, and effectively without a manager, since Adrian Owlett was really only helping out whenever other commitments allowed. Nor was it long before Owlett had come to the conclusion that it was time for Shaky to move out of his home and find a place of his own.

By now, Shaky was spending less and less time with his family in Cardiff, and Owlett felt sure that he was missing the vital steadying influence that Carole and the children had on him. Not only that, but Shaky had just seen his weekly wage in the show rise from £150 to £500, thanks to the negotiating skills of Mike Hurst, who had re-entered the Shakin' Stevens story after coming to see the show in April 1978. In the dressing room after the performance, Hurst and Stevens had got talking about business, and Hurst asked what was in the pipeline now that Track had gone to the wall. When Shaky answered, 'Nothing,' Hurst expressed an interest in managing him, still convinced that the singer had a bright future.

'He was over the moon with the money,' Hurst now recalls, 'and, just as importantly, the fact that I was handling his affairs. The show was doing very well, and little over two weeks later, I visited Brian Rix again and doubled Shaky's money to £1,000 a week. He was very happy, and the theatre got a great show, night after night.'

Within days, Hurst and his business partner Chris Brough had offered Stevens a management deal, and, after consulting the ever-faithful Owlett, he signed on 16 May. Offstage, Track Records having disappeared, Shaky was a free agent once again, a situation a manager as astute as Mike Hurst wasn't to let persist for too long. 'While the show was going exceptionally well, and Shaky was getting great publicity, I was aware of the fact that he had no record deal. So I went to see a mate of mine, Dan Loggins at CBS, who also ran Epic Records. I sat down with him and asked, "Ever hear the *Elvis* show?" He said he's heard of it and it sounded pretty cool. I asked, "Well, do you know Shakin' Stevens?" He paused, thought about it and said, "Yeah . . . "

'But when I followed up by asking about his interest in signing him up, his reply was, "Nah, not for Epic." So I persuaded him to come and see the show, and his response was, "Wow, we've got to sign him!" And that is how Shakin' Stevens started his career with Epic Records. I thought Shaky was always a great performer, and basically Elvis was God to him. I think it was just waiting to happen for him, once he was given the chance.'

The revised salary for *Elvis* would allow Shaky to move his family out of their council maisonette in Cardiff and into something altogether more genteel. But like so many things about Shaky's life, the purchase was far from straightforward. It involved a mortgage, a top-up loan and the final £2,500 in the form of a personal loan from Adrian Owlett himself, but the deal was eventually done, and the family moved in during the summer of 1978. In a few short weeks, Shaky's life had been transformed – he had a manager, a recording deal and a home of his own with his family. Once again, things were looking up.

A former member of The Springfields, when they counted British soul diva Dusty Springfield among their number, Mike Hurst had cut his teeth as a producer in the 1960s with the likes of Cat Stevens and Manfred Mann. Success had continued in the 1970s with Showaddywaddy, a group with two of everything – guitar, bass, drums and vocals – from Leicester, who'd enjoyed a lengthy run on the TV talent show *New Faces*. Not only did they win their programme, they came second in the all-winners final and were snapped up by Bell Records to become labelmates to the likes of David Cassidy (with whom they'd tour), Gary Glitter and The Bay City Rollers.

Hurst had enjoyed a string of hits with Showaddywaddy by the time he took on Shakin' Stevens, yet as the producer reveals, 'They were actually a bit jealous of my relationship with him!' Hurst saw Stevens as a potential teen idol in the David Cassidy mould, someone to tempt 'a whole new teenybopper audience who hadn't heard the likes of "Pretty Little Angel Eyes", "Under The Moon Of Love" etc.

'As regards the question of why Shaky became successful and the bigger question of why rock 'n' roll found a new audience, I think it was because of the music of the time. If you consider that, say, punk was a step too far for many record buyers, and that parallel to that there were rock bands such as ELO, Queen, 10cc, then rock 'n' roll somehow slotted in the middle of the two. Onstage Shaky was always fantastic and he was also TV friendly, even if he didn't have much to say offstage. He had a great saying about the whole scene, which used to crack me up . . . "See Mike, it's so old, it's new!" And in many respects he was right.'

It was true – the likes of Gary Glitter, Mud and The Rubettes had all looked backwards to move forwards musically, even if they were marketed as glam-rockers. The success of the 1973 movie *That'll Be The Day* – starring David Essex as a 1950s fairground worker who dreams of becoming a rock 'n' roll star (Dave Edmunds served as musical director) – had further underlined the potential of good old rock 'n' roll to entertain a new generation. Showaddywaddy had tapped into this in '74 . . . could it now be Shaky's turn?

Work began on a new album, with Hurst operating in exactly the same way as he had when recording Shaky for Track – backing tracks were constructed with session musicians and then the singer was brought in to add the vocals. The process continued for a marathon fourteen months, due to Shaky's lack of availability during his theatre work. Whereas Track had found the results of this process to their liking, CBS were distinctly unimpressed, feeling the recordings were not commercial enough, despite the choice of more pop-oriented material that Shaky was normally associated with – which is, ostensibly, what CBS were looking for.

Former Spencer Davis group bassist Muff Winwood, brother of Steve, was the head of A&R at CBS subsidiary label Epic, and Hurst recalls him as one stumbling block to Shaky's progress. 'In his inimitable Brummie accent, he'd simply say, "I don't really see this at all." We ended up making three great singles, but nothing really happened. We recorded a version of "Spooky" [a US pop hit in 1968 for The Classics IV] that I think was really, really good, and Epic put it out, but again it wasn't successful. It wasn't until Shaky came up with the idea of doing a rock 'n' roll album and thought about including some obscure tracks that things started to happen.'

The problem seemed to lie with Shaky's vocal delivery – the songs might have been more pop-oriented, but the vocals were still decidedly rock 'n' roll, with more than a hint of Elvis Presley creeping in. Moreover, Hurst recalls, 'Shaky did have a star mentality going on in the studio, to the point that he wouldn't show up until the basic tracks had already been recorded . . . and this was before the hits started! This was when I was producing him, before Stuart [Colman] came on board. But he was funny in lots of ways. On one session we had recorded about four tracks, and when it came time for Shaky to go into the control room, I watched as he started to swallow hard – in fact I thought he was going to have a fit at one stage.

'It turned out he was okay. But he then suddenly gasped, "Ooooohhhh Gaaaad." I shouted, "Shaky, are you ill?" He shouted out, "This is in the wrong key, you gave me the wrong key to sing in." I said, "But that's what you wanted." He said, "Yes, but I sing it in that key in my bathroom to get the rock 'n' roll echo." [Laughs] He was always like that – very straightforward with things, but often unable to immediately communicate the problem.'

The three singles issued via Epic – 'Treat Her Right', Jody Reynolds' 'Endless Sleep', and 'Spooky' – were released at the end of 1978 and the beginning of 1979, and have since become very collectable.

The CBS contract ended, Adrian Owlett came to Shaky's rescue yet again by persuading them that he was worth another shot, and securing a three-month extension to his existing deal. There were clear indications that there would be no more releases unless Shaky came up with the goods, however, and so Owlett was faced with the task of finding something special to make CBS sit up and take notice.

He decided that Mike Hurst still represented their best bet, and approached him with a shortlist of half a dozen songs that he'd decided might do the trick. Buck Owens' song 'Hot Dog' seemed favourite, but after their earlier studio spat, Hurst was reluctant to get involved with Shaky again. Owlett managed to get him to agree to produce the track, but Hurst insisted that was all he was going to do — Owlett would have to organize everything else, including the backing musicians. He came up trumps, and the rest, as they say, is history — Shaky finally had a hit on his hands, and CBS duly snapped him up for the most successful period of his career.

Meanwhile, back in January 1979, with *Elvis — The Musical* still playing to packed houses, Jack Good was busily working on his next major project, a revamped version of his successful 1950s rock 'n' roll TV show *Oh Boy!* The idea was to hold the show on Sunday evenings, the one night of the week that *Elvis — The Musical* wasn't being performed. Good was full of admiration for Shaky, describing him as 'one of the most exciting rock performers around', so it came as no surprise that he wanted the singer to be one of the regular attractions on the revived TV programme. Rehearsals for the broadcasts took place during the day on Saturdays and Sundays, and Good's rock 'n' roll credentials ensured that there was a regular stream of big-name stars on parade.

One such was Joe Brown, whose career already spanned more than two decades, and whose appearance on the show indirectly had a massive effect on Shaky's future career. When Brown appeared on *Oh Boy!* he was allocated space in Shaky's dressing room for the duration of rehearsals, a move that Adrian Owlett, who had remained in close contact with Shaky, realized was likely to be a cause of intense irritation to the singer. But Owlett, a big fan of Brown, decided this was the perfect opportunity to meet his childhood hero, so he made his way up to Shaky's dressing room to find the man whose career he'd followed with interest for so many years. There was also the small matter of ensuring that Shaky behaved himself in the face of this perceived slight, but Owlett's primary consideration was getting to talk to Joe Brown.

Shaky offered little to the enthusiastic discussion that followed, especially when it was suggested that rock 'n' roll had become overtly commercial since the 'good old days', and that Shaky's modern-day version of the genre was less than authentic. The frosty atmosphere that was rapidly developing was abruptly shattered by the arrival of Joe Brown's manager, however – an imposing woman by the name of Freya Miller. Although she didn't take to Shaky on first meeting, Miller would later become the single most important influence on his life, and the hugely successful partnership they later forged stemmed from this chance meeting early in 1979.

Oh Boy! was screened by ITV, and proved popular enough for a follow-up series of twenty-six shows to be commissioned under the name *Let's Rock*. Again, Shaky was a mainstay of the show, which ran through the summer of 1979, and spanned the period of uncertainty that surrounded the difficulties at CBS and the final curtain going down on the first run of *Elvis – The Musical*. *Let's Rock* was shown on both sides of the Atlantic, and did much to raise the profile of both rock 'n' roll in general and Shaky in particular.

'The shows were recorded at ATV's Elstree Studios, where they make *The Muppets*, and they ran for about twenty-six minutes each,' Shaky later recalled in *Look In* magazine. 'It was very hard work recording them, because although they are not long on the air, we used to start work at nine in the morning and work through until nine at night on each one. It was a tough schedule, but I enjoyed it – I enjoy television work because it seems so natural.' He would show the same assured confidence many times over on the video set in future years.

The years of hard work were beginning to pay off, but there was a downside – like so many people for whom success comes after years of graft, Shaky now found himself attacked by the critics. He was denounced as a second-rate Elvis impersonator and subjected to a storm of quite vitriolic abuse in some sections of the press. In the light of these vicious snipes it's perhaps easier to understand why he remains so defensive to this day. 'Shakin' Stevens is Shakin' Stevens,' he later stated in an interview with writer Martyn Leese. 'I don't look like Elvis and I haven't moulded myself on him. I think about the Elvis tag a lot, but Jack Good was not looking for an impersonator, he wanted someone who could put across the feel.' The next sentence of the interview would be much repeated over the years by incredulous fans, even though it was clearly said for effect at the time. 'To be honest, I was never much of an Elvis fan myself. I respected him a lot and, let's face it, he was the launching pad for everything that's happened in pop music. I look upon Elvis as a great entertainer and I respect him for what he did for music. That is why I turned down the part at first. It was only when I became convinced that the musical was going to be a tribute, not a send-up, that I agreed to appear in it.'

To this day, Shaky remains immensely wary of the press, and aggressively defends his integrity as an artist in his own right. He consistently and vehemently rejects any comparisons with Elvis, and hates to hear people say that he is selling nostalgia or that he is part of a rock 'n' roll revival. Whatever accusations his critics may have levelled at him in the wake of his stint as the 'middle Elvis', Shakin' Stevens would have the last laugh as a new decade dawned.

4

FIRST HITS: 1978–80

THE ARRIVAL OF PUNK caused a major wood-shedding in the music business. A lot of acts had been living on their reputations for some time, and the arrival of such career-lengthening ploys as the triple concept album (Yes) and double live album (Peter Frampton, Deep Purple, etc) suggested a shake-up was overdue. For the first time since British youth started skiffling, using home-made tea-chest basses and acoustic guitars to mimic American rock 'n' rollers, a new generation was realizing that it could make exciting music without having to study the subject at length.

Punk, while thumbing its nose at the established order, was also making that connection, harking back to the young, pure days of rock 'n' roll for its inspiration. Hence, Billy Idol of Generation X could be heard singing about Elvis in his 'King Rocker' and seen wearing a Presley T-shirt. Ian Dury, too old to be a punk but happy to jump on the bandwagon, paid heartfelt tribute to a rock legend with 'Sweet Gene Vincent', and Elvis Costello – visually, anyway – brought Buddy Holly back to life in all his knock-kneed glory.

It seems punk had an unlikely fan in Shakin' Stevens. 'I think that music became too serious when The Beatles started to go psychedelic in the late 1960s, and things were blown out of proportion,' he reflected. 'People sat down to listen to music as if it was classical, and treated it far too reverently. Then disco came along, and instead the dancing became serious! The good thing about the arrival of punk was that it took things back to the basics again, and now the music scene is very healthy because we have a vast selection of styles and sounds, which gives everyone the opportunity of going into a second-hand shop, and buying a cheap guitar, learning a few chords quickly and going out to have a bash themselves.

'Every record buyer is a frustrated performer, I'm sure. We've all stood in front of mirrors miming to our favourite records at some time or other. Now that music has become fun again, people can enjoy themselves as performers and listeners.'

The end of *Elvis – The Musical*'s West End run came in June 1979, and with publicity for their boy still running high, CBS had high hopes as, with Mike Hurst remaining at the helm, Shaky headed for Eden Studios to lay down what would become his first CBS/Epic album, *Take One!* One musical ace in Stevens' hand was the presence of guitarist Albert Lee, who had been in Hurst's country-rock outfit, Mike Hurst and the Methods.

There would be many other notable names in the band assembled to back Stevens – in fact, it was nothing if not star-studded in terms of session musicians. Notable among them was Brian 'B. J.' Cole, Britain's best-known steel guitarist, who has since played on innumerable albums by artists from right across the musical spectrum, from Elton John to John Cale. 'Mike Hurst was the original producer,' he recalls, 'but Stuart Colman was brought in, because it wasn't going very well, and Stuart, who was already playing bass, called in lots of his mates like Geraint Watkins, who probably knew Shaky anyway, and me.'

Born in Harrogate, Yorkshire, Colman had first troubled the rock 'n' roll radar as a member of Pinkerton's Assorted Colours in 1966. On the group's demise, he was recruited to promote Tony Macauley and Geoff Stevens' studio project Flying Machine, whose 'Smile A Little Smile For Me' was a surprise US Top Five hit in 1969. He then became a BBC radio broadcaster, and, in his capacity as champion of the cause of authentic rock 'n' roll, he marched on the Houses of Parliament with a deputation in 1976 in an attempt to win it more airtime.

In fact, returning to spinning records rather than making them was a reversion to past form. As Colman explained to journalist Norman Jopling, his first DJ gig had been at Harrogate Town Hall in the pre-Beatles days of 1960. 'I didn't say anything, just played the records,' he admitted. Then, after Pinkerton's Assorted Colours faded and Flying Machine crash-landed, he moved to London in 1971 and played London pubs and clubs as a member of a rock 'n' roll revival band.

Then one night at a party, he found his attention drawn to the DJ – for all the wrong reasons: 'The guy was appalling. No personality, terrible choice of records. I said to a friend that I could do better with one hand tied behind my back. So I got the rock 'n' roll residency at the Castle pub [in Tooting, south London], and it all took off again from there.'

His move onto the national airwaves with BBC Radio One in 1976 had been as a result of a home-made demo tape, and Colman's weekly show *It's Rock 'n' Roll* ran from then until 1980. This was crucial to his later success, as the material aired mixed discs with specially recorded sessions. With rock 'n' roll music an enclosed 'circuit', Colman quickly got to know and work with some of the best in the business, so when the time came to spread his wings and work with Shaky in a production role, he had all the right names in his notebook.

'Shaky was desperate,' he told Jopling, 'and said, "Do you fancy coming and we can do some work together?" By then my confidence was sky-high. I found a great drummer called Howard Tibble through the BBC sessions, a young guy who could really lay down rock 'n' roll. Geraint Watkins was a new-on-the-scene piano player, the very best, and I'd got to know Albert Lee through interviewing him on the Beeb.'

Steel guitarist B. J. Cole confirms Colman's role – in fact, he 'knew Stuart before I knew Shaky. I was aware of Shakin' Stevens and the Sunsets, but I hadn't met Shaky before. I think Shaky decided to work with Stuart because he knew Stuart was seen as a rockabilly expert. Shaky wanted authenticity, which was why I was invited, to play the backing like the early rock 'n' rollers who used steel guitar, like Bill Haley and the Comets, and Tennessee Ernie Ford.

'I'd say Stuart Colman was the Mark Lamarr of his day. I think Shaky had some bad experiences from his Jack Good *Elvis* days, but he trusted Stuart completely, and with Stuart having all but assembled the band, things worked incredibly well. Shaky also knew what he wanted. He felt the music intuitively and sang his parts superbly. Stuart helped from the musical point of view, suggesting songs, arrangements etc, the band had no problem with that, and we had some very exciting sessions. It was a good combination, although we had no idea this would be commercially successful when we started.'

Mike Hurst was still credited as producer on the album sleeve, and, according to B. J. Cole, 'He was certainly there for some of the time in Eden Studios, but definitely not for all of it. Shaky wanted to go back to his roots. I'd worked with many of the other musicians before, like Albert. My first ever proper session in 1968 was for Albert Lee's first solo album, which wasn't released until recently.'

Alongside Lee (lead guitar), Colman (bass), Tibble (drums) Watkins (piano) and Cole was rhythm guitarist Roger McKew and a two-man brass section of Tony 'Too Tall' Hall (tenor sax) and Sid Phillips (baritone sax). The cover of the album featured a head-and-shoulders illustration of Shaky in the style of Elvis, or UK rocker Billy Fury.

Sax-player Hall was also a pal of Colman's: 'I was doing quite a few [BBC] sessions for Stuart and he basically drafted in most of the guys, including me. I don't think the record company was very happy with the first album Shaky had done, and I don't think Shaky liked it that much either. So Stuart took the reins and brought in the rock 'n' rollers. Stuart was responsible for putting a different slant on the whole thing. I think Shaky was open to a new direction and seemed happy to try again.

'For my part I'd seen Shaky years before when I was playing the same circuit as him in the rock 'n' roll clubs. He was fronting The Sunsets, and I was in Earl Sheridan and the Houseshakers. I'd also seen him in Wales a few times, so I knew what to expect. He was good at what he did, but in all honesty we didn't see much of him. Stuart knew what he wanted, we laid it down, and Shaky came in afterwards mostly, but it worked well.'

Geraint Watkins had recorded with Colman before, notably with Welsh rock 'n' roll revivalists Memphis Bend, of whom Micky Gee was a member, but though he'd seen Shaky perform, he had never met him: 'The recording was fine, in fact I thought with the band we had it was really great. But Stuart was a guiding hand. By the time we ripped through the material I thought it was brilliant as it was, but Stuart was very particular. At the time I thought he should have left it as it was, it had a nice raw edge; Shaky had laid down his vocals well and the band had played very well. In retrospect, it was probably all to do with making it palatable to the radio.'

Watkins reveals that, alongside Colman's perfectionism, 'Shaky always knew what he wanted. He was very demonstrative when he needed to be. Shaky might not be the most erudite of people, but with the players we had, and with the feel of the music, it wasn't a problem. Sometimes Shaky would seem like he had a bee in his bonnet, but he knew exactly what was required. He knew what he wanted, and we understood what was required. It was a good combination, as all the players were familiar with where this music came from. If Shaky called for something that, say, Elvis might have done, we would know how to respond.'

The song selected as the first single was 'Hot Dog', and B. J. Cole, who contributed much to the arrangement on a non-pedal steel guitar, admits he was 'chuffed' when Buck Owens, its original performer, did a new recording that borrowed the arrangement: 'He even followed the steel guitar parts!' Cole is happy to acknowledge his own role: 'I helped to put his music into a wider context, in other words bringing in the boogie and western swing genres. The authenticity of the songs was crucial, and when I was working with him Shaky had integrity.'

After 'Hot Dog' had given Stevens a UK singles chart debut in March 1980, albeit at a relatively lowly Number 62, most managers would have thought their ship had come in. But for Mike Hurst the hassle was proving too much: 'By this time Stuart Colman had taken over the production duties, and to be honest I couldn't take the management side any more. I sat on the steps of Soho Square with him, pulled out the contract, and told him I was quitting.

'As an artist he [Shaky] was fantastic, but offstage it could be hard work. He was about thirty-five years old, and I made the decision that if anything I would produce him but not manage him any more. What happened was that Stuart Colman was already starting to produce some of his stuff. I knew a lot of the band, but by this stage I wasn't too upset about finishing my role with Shaky.'

Shaky's friend Adrian Owlett was, almost inevitably, the man entrusted with managing his affairs after Hurst exited the scene, and in his attempts to divest himself of this responsibility he approached and was turned down by most of the major figures in the business – including Cliff Richard's manager Peter Gormley.

The woman who stepped into the breach was the aforementioned Freya Miller, the daughter of cartoonist Roy Ulyett, who had made her name and reputation managing the likes of The New Seekers. No one was there to record the first conversation between Shaky and his new manager, but according to her it went something like this: Shaky to Freya: 'I want someone to manage me who will think Shakin' Stevens twenty-four hours a day.' Freya to Shaky: 'By the time I've finished with you, everyone will be thinking Shakin' Stevens twenty-four hours a day.'

Freya's aim for him was stated loud and clear not long afterwards: 'Shaky is very shy and very quiet. He needed a voice, so I have done the screaming and shouting. I also wanted to make him an untouchable, magical star, which is how he will remain. The fans might hate me for it, but they love him.' The agreement, according to Paul Barrett's 1983 book, was based on 25 per cent of his gross earnings. If true, there was every incentive for Miss Miller to make her charge one of the highest-earning figures in the music business – and this she proceeded to do.

Meanwhile, as 'Hot Dog' hit the charts, the long-forgotten Sunsets' debut *A Legend* was reissued by EMI on their NUT budget label. DJ Roger Scott had been playing the album on Capital Radio, which inspired *Melody Maker's* Richard Williams to investigate further. Incidentally, this was the same Richard Williams who, as an employee of Island Records, had turned down Shakin' Stevens and the Sunsets in 1976 on the grounds of their name! The scales having fallen from his eyes, he compared the music favourably with The Band's *Moondog Matinee*, the album of standards they recorded in 1973, and concluded that 'it seems to sum up, in a most pleasingly unaffected manner, a kind of rock 'n' roll which made a particularly lasting and strong impact in Britain. After all these years, it would be nice to see Shakin' Stevens get a piece of the action.'

The material contained on the new album *Take One!* was credible with a capital C. Opening track 'Lovestruck' came from the repertoire of Jerry McGill and the Topcoats, and had been released on the original Sun label in 1959. Geraint Watkins came to the fore on Conway Twitty's 'Is A Bluebird Blue?', while Smiley Lewis's 'Shame, Shame, Shame' saw the brass section take a bow.

Albert Lee was outstanding on Tennessee Ernie Ford's 'Shotgun Boogie', a song that gave B. J. Cole 'a great thrill, as he's one of my favourite country acts. I played on most of this album, and that was one of the best line-ups of musicians I've ever worked with. We were so hot that the tracks for the album were completed in three days.'

Shaky's Elvis delivery was perfect for Ral Donner's 'I Got Burned'. A Buddy Holly song made the grade too – not a signature tune, but the little-known ballad 'I Guess I Was A Fool'. The tempo cranked up again for Billy Crash Craddock's 'Ah Poor Little Baby' and Chuck Sims' 'Little Pigeon'. As with side one, the final track saw Tony Hall and Sid Phillips earn their money, as the band tackled Thurston Harris's brassy 'Do What You Did'.

The album features 'musical coordination' and remixing by Stuart Colman, whom Albert Lee now credits as the architect of Shaky's success: 'We basically came together because of Stuart. He told me he wanted some good guys to play rock 'n' roll, and I was pleased to see people like B. J. Cole there, who really knew their stuff. So we got to Eden Studios, and I think we did a few sessions. I don't think they were done with one particular album in mind. It was more just the fact we gathered together to see how it all came out. I remember we recorded "Hot Dog" at those sessions, and it went on to be a hit. I couldn't believe that there was this interest in some of the music we all loved.'

Significantly, when the musicians reconvened later in the year to cut a second CBS album, Stuart Colman was the man officially in the production hot seat. Interestingly, he'd been able to prime the pumps by booking Shaky for a session for his own Radio One show, *It's Rock 'n' Roll*. Broadcast in late 1979, this featured 'Is A Bluebird Blue?', 'Lovestruck', 'Apron Strings', 'Shotgun Boogie' and 'Hot Dog'. All but the third track, a Tennessee Ernie Ford cover, would appear on the album.

Geraint Watkins also believes that it was Stuart Colman who brought it all together. 'He set up the first album, and that was followed by a couple of tours. It was a real pleasure to work with both Shaky and such a great band. In truth, even though the sessions went well, I doubt any of us really thought there would be hits with this material. So when "Hot Dog" stayed in the charts for nine weeks, we were gobsmacked. It was a case of "Wow, look at that!"'

Take One! was released in February 1980 but only charted for two weeks, peaking at Number 62 – a particularly disappointing performance, given that 'Hot Dog' had climbed to the Number 24 spot in the singles chart. No further 45s were released as attempted follow-ups to 'Hot Dog', though it would soon become clear that Shaky was more likely to find success with seven-inch plastic, the original 'currency' of rock 'n' roll.

A thirteen-date tour to promote the album in February/March 1980 kicked off at the University of East Anglia and continued in a swathe across southern England, through the un-rock 'n' roll likes of Southsea, Bognor Regis and Poole, before a penultimate date at the London Astoria, scene of Shaky's *Elvis* triumphs, on 16 March. Support came from The Never Never Band. 'We did a few gigs after the [first] recording,' Albert Lee recalls, 'and one of them was the Astoria, which did particularly well. There were also a few gigs outside of London.' B. J. Cole also remembers the capital gig as his live highlight with the band.

Lee's onstage appearance on lead guitar with long hair and a wah-wah pedal was said to have bemused the rock 'n' roll purist section of Shaky's fans. In truth, the tour hadn't been an easy one to put together: the money offered hadn't been up to Freya Miller's expectations, so the original agent doing the booking had been relieved of his duties. His replacement called in a few favours, but the fact the tour started and ended with university gigs was some indication of the confused situation of the time, because the student market wasn't exactly the preferred target audience for Shaky's music.

Live shows at this point were smoking. Albert Lee, despite his 'hippie' image, was delighted to have an excuse to play the music of his youth. 'This was quite a breath of fresh air for me as it wasn't really cool to be into rock 'n' roll at that time. It was like coming full circle for me. Shaky knew exactly what he wanted, even if he didn't always know how to express that. But he was a straight-ahead rock 'n' roller, and once we hit our stride he wasn't hard to please!

'It was a great feeling at the time playing with Shaky and a great band, and of course he'd built up a following by then, particularly with young girls! We also did quite a few TV shows, although often he'd sing to a backing track, but myself, Roger McKew and Geraint did some TV with him.'

Stuart Colman was in charge when the band reconvened in the studio in mid-1980, and, as well as contributing the steel guitar that added authenticity to the sound, B. J. Cole now played a key role in the production side. 'I was certainly involved in the production of a track on the *Marie Marie* album entitled 'Hey Mae', because I'd suggested it. I got it from a compilation album called *Hillbilly Rock* and the track was by Rusty and Doug Kershaw.'

'Hey Mae', which kicked off the action, was indeed so impressive it was lifted as a single. Next up was the self-penned 'Baby If We Touch', featuring the handclaps that were soon to become a Shaky trademark. The first ballad of the set was

'Lonely Blue Boy', featuring brilliant Conway Twitty vocals. 'Make It Right Tonight' and 'Move', two uptempo rockers with Cole and Watkins much in evidence, ended side one.

As noted, there had been a personnel change in the guitar department, as B. J. Cole recounts: 'Albert wasn't on that second album, but we had Micky Gee instead, whom Shaky knew from Cardiff. He had probably the two best rock 'n' roll guitarists in the country in succession, and both worked so well in the context of what Shaky was doing. Micky was more of a rockabilly player than Albert, but was less versatile. I knew him from when he was in a band on United Artists called Memphis Bend, and I was also at UA with Cochise.' Another guitarist, Eddie Jones, was also in evidence, but otherwise it was the same tried-and-tested crew.

The departing Lee, who returned to the States to work with The Everly Brothers, was sad to see the rollercoaster ride end – but certainly wasn't going to lack for work elsewhere. And the malaise he pinpoints was one that would, in time, account for his colleagues too: 'It was an enjoyable time, but eventually I think the star thing crept in, with different dressing rooms and eventually different hotels for Shaky and the band, and that was when things changed.'

Micky Gee's contributions jumped out of the recordings, notably his solo on 'Revenue Man'. Paul Barrett, who'd seen Gee in action during The Sunsets' recording session for *I'm No JD*, believes his contributions have been understated. 'I know that Micky did the arrangements on those songs, and he's never had the credit for that. That's the way it goes, isn't it? I know he did the arrangements because the producer told me he did them for "This Ole House" and "Green Door" . . . it's funny the things you hear later.'

The fact that Stuart Colman had taken the reins from Mike Hurst was not lost on songwriter Brian Hodgson. He had a deal with Warner Chappell Music and had worked with Tony Colton, Albert Lee's associate, in severely underrated band

Heads Hands and Feet. 'Tony and I had written this song called "Shooting Gallery" we thought would be a great song for him. So Ian Reed at Chappells got the song to Shaky's people. Meanwhile, another song plugger knew Shaky's drummer Howard Tibble, and in the end I think he got the song from about half a dozen people.

'Anyway, Shaky recorded it and sang it very well; he is good at what he does and it fitted the song well . . . he had my demo and I got a call from Freya Miller, his manager, who said that Shaky had told her he liked the vocal. So I went to Eden Studios, and they said the song was going to be a single as well as a track on the album.

'I met Stuart Colman, talked to him about the project, and he played the other guy's [Mike Hurst's] stuff. To me there was nothing wrong with the other tracks that Stuart had played on [Colman being a bass player as well as a producer], but Shaky simply wanted my vocals on the song.'

The selected title track for the album, 'Marie Marie', had been a US turntable hit for retro-rockers The Blasters, suggesting that there might be a more contemporary angle this time – but the remainder of the material came from more traditional rock 'n' roll sources. A high-energy take on Little Richard's 'Slippin' And Slidin'' preceded Brian Hodgson's 'Shooting Gallery' and a mid-tempo Conway Twitty song, 'Make Me Know You're Mine', which would have been ideal for Billy Fury in his heyday. 'Two Hearts', from the pens of Jesse Stone and Otis Williams, would be omitted when the album was reissued, while live favourite 'Nobody' was a suitable closer. The cover photo showed Shaky reclining in a moody pose and, in the words of rockabilly expert Shaun Mather, 'looking like a moody rocker who's just had his blue suede shoes stepped on'.

Three singles would be released during the course of the year to attempt to follow up the success of 'Hot Dog'. 'Hey Mae' appeared in May, 'Marie, Marie' in July and 'Shooting

Gallery' to coincide with the album in October. 'Marie Marie' stayed in the German charts for nine months, an early indication of Shaky's future success in mainland Europe. In Britain, it managed to make Number 19 in August 1980 despite the lack of a promotional video (one was belatedly recorded in 1984 for inclusion on the compilation release, *Shakin' Stevens Video Show Volume 1*).

Shaky, who was being billed on posters at the time as 'The Star of *Oh Boy!*', was clearly on his way. The autumn of 1980 brought a special for Anglian Television featuring Messrs Gee, Jones, Colman, Cole, Watkins and Tibble. The repertoire aired included Elvis's 'Big Hunk O'Love' alongside tracks from the forthcoming album and the recent 'Hot Dog'. A Billy Fury cover, 'Don't Knock Upon My Door', was an unusual choice inasmuch as it wouldn't appear on a Shaky album until 1985, but was impressive nonetheless. The special would make for an interesting DVD release, if the footage still exists.

The December tour, which would become a Shakin' Stevens tradition, kicked off at Hemel Hempstead Pavilion and finished at the London Apollo Victoria just over a fortnight later. An earlier capital date saw the band record for a BBC Radio broadcast from the Paris Theatre that, sadly, appears now to have been lost or erased.

In 1980, Shaky experienced his first stand-offs with the press. One such incident came late in the year at the Brighton Dome, where photographer Barry Plummer became incensed at his handling by Freya Miller who, he believed, was being just a little high-handed. 'We had it all arranged – by CBS, I think – but when we got there it was kind of "You can't come and take pictures." There were arguments but I got my way in the end. I know she was a bit funny about people taking pictures of him.'

The print media, too, had their obstacles to overcome. One writer with *TV Times* – at that point the nation's premier television guide, with a readership of six million – was famously informed: 'Shaky never answers personal questions . . . stick to his rise to fame' when she strayed onto the subject of his private life.

But who exactly were his fans, and what did they want to know about him? *Record Collector* advanced this theory in 2005: 'His rock 'n' roll-pop crossover had ensnared a double-generation audience with the vintage rockabilly sounds attracting mothers and fathers while the glossy 1980s production lured their kids.' His official website puts it this way: '[From the] Punk era and into New Wave, Electronic and the New Romantics, Stevens's resulting sound was glossy enough to appeal to those weaned on *Smash Hits*, but one that retained enough of rock's basic energy and excitement to gain the attention of an adult audience who could relate to his music.'

For the star of the show, 'Rock 'n' roll is for everybody, for all ages. My audience is right across the board. From youngsters to married couples to pensioners. I've met an eighteen-month-old baby whose dad tells me that the child likes banging his little toy hammer on the furniture when my songs are playing, and I've met grandmothers who have bought all of my records. I don't think rock 'n' roll is just all that teddy-boy stuff. I don't think you have to dress like a rock 'n' roller to like it.'

It was only rock 'n' roll, but as the 1980s opened it offered a feel-good alternative to the fag-end of punk, gender-benders and synthesizer bands. There was something reassuringly traditional about Shakin' Stevens that appealed to a jaded marketplace. And there was much more to come.

5

THE GOLDEN ERA, PART ONE: 1981–3

IF THE DECADE HAD OPENED BRIGHTLY, then 1981 was to prove a dazzling year for Shakin' Stevens, with not one, not two, but three hit albums to his name. But it was in the singles listings that he'd make his biggest mark, with two chart-toppers, a Number Two and a further Top Ten entry, the first three of which would become signature songs. He was now comfortably in his thirties, though a fact file in teen magazine *Look In* – as well as noting his dislike of cruelty to animals and love of steak and white wine – trimmed three years off his age!

It took exactly a month for his revival of 'This Ole House' (a 1954 UK Number One for Rosemary Clooney) to go from entering the charts to giving Stevens his long-awaited breakthrough, topping the UK chart on 28 March for the first of three weeks. It displaced 'Jealous Guy', Roxy Music's tribute to the recently departed John Lennon, and would itself be succeeded by Eurovision victors Bucks Fizz.

The feel-good song had a surprisingly macabre history. It had been written in the early 1950s by little-known US singer/songwriter Stuart Hamblen. He and a friend were out deer hunting in the sierras when a blizzard struck. Their trail obliterated, they became lost, but eventually found an old prospector's shack with a dog sheltering in the front porch, though with no smoke coming out of the chimney. 'There's a dead man in there,' Hamblen concluded – and indeed, when they entered they found the body of an elderly prospector, who had suffered a fatal heart attack. Hamblen penned another hit, 'It Is No Secret', but had a success with 'This Ole House' first, in 1954.

Shaky had never heard the song previously – 'I was just a kid when it first came out. I may have heard it, but it didn't sink in' – before a cover by US country-rockers NRBQ brought it to his attention as he was going through some records and tapes with Stuart Colman. Well, that's one version of the story, anyway. Another is that Shaky heard Rosemary Clooney's version just before Christmas 1980, 'when I was at the home of a friend, who collects old records. As soon as he put the disc on I knew, right away, that this was something I should record. I was absolutely amazed when I learned that no fresh version had been released since 1954.'

Writer Fred Dellar later analysed the song's widespread appeal: 'The record tapped several audiences. Those who remembered it from the first time around, those who regarded it as a new song, plus the then emerging wave of new rockabillies who perceived it as their kind of material. As his audiences grew bigger and increasingly diverse, the demand for Shakin' Stevens records grew. And Shaky continually rang the changes ...'

'This Ole House' also inspired Shaky's first promotional video, shot in a derelict house in a field near Bury St Edmunds, Suffolk. 'Those people singing along with the track were people we pulled in from a farm next door,' he recalled during a BBC TV interview. 'It was like – okay, you've got the derelict house, what do you do? Just move around with the song, legs on the window, do this, come through the door . . . and that's what it was really.' Though it sounds as if it was developed 'on the hoof', the video set the style for a series of Shaky clips to come, all of which seemed to feature the man doing the splits or jumping over the camera in athletic fashion.

Chart historians might wish to note that this became the sixth song in UK chart history to have become a Number One in two different versions. Shaky felt 'it had a nice kinda rhythm to it, a nice snare in it, very earthy and organic. It was really, really good. We did our own arrangement, but I really thought it had something.' When he later met Hank Marvin at a *Guinness World Records* function, The Shadows guitarist told him, 'That song came out at the right time.' And Shaky, of course, agreed. 'He was right – that was the record that opened things up for me internationally. It was fresh and what was needed.' Shaky was working on a television show in Madrid when he took the telephone call that told him he had finally made the big time. 'I was speechless,' he recalls. 'It was the best moment of my life!'

Someone else to whom it came as a big surprise was one-time Sunsets producer Donny Marchand. Having returned to his native America, he was now back in Britain, though out of the music business. 'I was working in a DIY shop selling toilet bowls – and you can't get any closer to the bottom than that!' One day he ran into the boss of EMI Music, who remembered him, asked if he was still writing songs and offered him a job as a staff writer.

'I went in [to the office] once a week, when the girls were just getting ready to go home. I was waiting in the reception and *Top of the Pops* was on. [The DJ] said, "At Number One is Shakin' Stevens with 'This Ole House'," and I looked and thought, "Shrieking hell." I was amazed – I knew what he did he could do good, but never thought of that kind of success. I never thought he was going to be [famous] like David Bowie!'

Its success also clearly came as something of a surprise to CBS/Epic, since the song had not been included on Shaky's album *Marie Marie*. Originally released in October, when it reached a lowly Number 56, the long-player had been named after the second hit single of 1980. Now it was to be re-titled to take advantage of the chart-topper. Reissued under this new identity, and with a new sleeve and catalogue number, at the end of March 1981, *This Ole House* shot to Number Two. A spring tour was rapidly assembled to make the most of the success, starting in Birmingham in mid-May and ending in London a month later, with four Irish dates tacked on to the end.

Geraint Watkins remained a musical mainstay, alongside guitarists Gee and McKew. Stuart Colman had bowed out of live performance by this point in favour of Dick Bland, though he continued to play bass on the recordings, while drummer Howard Tibble continued to pound out the all-important rock 'n' roll backbeat.

'I thought the same thing as the rest of the guys,' Watkins reminisces, 'that it was just great playing rock 'n' roll in theatres, and being paid well, and looked after reasonably well. And night after night we played to screaming young girls and mums ... [laughs] It was a great two or three years.'

The audience was very mixed age-wise, a fact Shaky himself noted during an interview in 1984. 'The mums and dads actually lived through the 1950s, they can see me through when they were teenagers, and the younger generation see me as someone they can relate to,' he reasoned. 'I don't try to appeal; I just feel the music is not for one type of person or for one type of dress, it's for everybody. Rock 'n' roll still has teenage appeal, but not exclusively. It's like The Rolling Stones. In the 1960s and 1970s, they were rebellious and all that, but you can even hear the Stones on Radio Two nowadays.'

His hip-swivelling stage act received surprisingly few complaints from Mary Whitehouse and her fellow moral guardians – maybe they were still recovering from Johnny Rotten and his tribe. 'I don't set out to be sexy,' said Shaky at the time, 'but when the beat gets going, my legs and pelvis go wild. I don't get up there to be a sex symbol. That's the way that the music takes me. It's my way of putting over a song.'

The success of *This Ole House* had a swarm of potential songwriters making a beeline for Shaky. One was Pete Waterman – not yet the dancefloor Svengali he would end the decade as thanks to the Stock, Aitken & Waterman production company. He offered 'Pretend' as a potential follow-up, but it was turned down. Using lateral thinking, Waterman then pitched it to Alvin Stardust, with whom he'd worked in the 1970s at Magnet Records. 'I rang him up and he agreed to do it, so I put the money up and we recorded it,' Waterman recalled. The result was a UK Top Three single on Stiff Records and a career rejuvenation for Stardust, a glam-rocker with a rock 'n' roll background. 'I knew that boogie rock 'n' roll could fly across the globe,' said Waterman – a trade secret Shaky was already well aware of, even if this was one hit he missed out on.

While adulation and full houses were uplifting for the spirit of any musician, they couldn't keep the band together. Albert Lee had already departed, and B. J. Cole was the next to go. So why did it end? 'Freya Miller, who was his manager at the time, started getting involved in the creative process,' Cole explained in 2005. 'When managers try to separate the artist from the band, it always falls apart.' He then went on to make an interesting observation about his erstwhile employer: 'People talk about Shaky as the Welsh Elvis, but I think he's more like the Welsh Cliff Richard, and there is absolutely no negativity attached to that. We got on really well, although I haven't seen him for a long time.'

Rather than delve back to the past album, another new track, 'You Drive Me Crazy', was cut as the next single. An original song penned by one Ronnie Harwood, and featuring prominent piano from Geraint Watkins, it was the singer's own favourite of his recordings at that time and entered the UK chart in early May '81, climbing all the way to Number Two. It was unfortunate not to become Shaky's second consecutive chart-topper, but was forced to linger for four weeks behind labelmate Adam and the Ants' immovable 'Stand and Deliver'.

Music-business veteran Jonathan King felt at the time that 'You Drive Me Crazy' had the potential to break into the US country market and cross over from there into pop, but, Shaky recalls, 'Nothing happened . . . a lot of the problem was the radio situation, which is very different to the UK.' The video for the song was, like that for 'This Ole House', shot in a country house, but this one was more haunted than derelict, with all manner of spooks coming out of their closets to join in the light-hearted fun.

All his life, Shaky has had trouble pronouncing certain words, an endearing idiosyncrasy that certainly hasn't held back his career. But it's astounding to note than no one at CBS/Epic noticed he was singing 'cwazy' throughout the song – a fact he cheerfully admitted in 2005. 'Neither I nor the producer realized until it was released,' he smiled. 'But then I recorded "Cry Just A Little Bit" with the same producer and the same thing happened!'

Ronnie Harwood, who rightly won an Ivor Novello award for writing the song, was an unlikely author of a mega-hit. He had been in one of the line-ups of Screamin' Lord Sutch's Savages with veteran Brit-rock drummer Carlo Little, who in turn had worked with Stuart Colman in Hurricane, an early 1970s rock 'n' roll band featuring pianist Freddie 'Fingers' Lee. Harwood believed 'You Drive Me Crazy' would be a sure-fire hit for Shakin' Stevens and it became a million-selling single, though he could never duplicate the feat. (He would, however, pen songs with Shaky for a 1990s Christmas project.)

Record Mirror was to feature Shaky on their cover in June – but having agreed to do so, the magazine spoiled things somewhat by sending sparky reporter Mike Nicholls, a man to whom pure rock 'n' roll was something of an anathema as well as an anachronism, to stir the pot. Nicholls was quick to point out the unwanted presence of Freya Miller in the interview. 'Ms Miller has had a lot to do with Stevens's success as she is only too keen to point out,' he remarked, before comparing the couple to a comedy double act, 'except without the sense of humour'.

The singer's distrust of the press apparently stemmed from criticism he'd received after playing Elvis on stage. He not only rationed interviews carefully, but admitted that he and Freya had developed a system that would help them determine who he was interviewed by in the future. 'We have two boxes,' he revealed in *Record Mirror*, 'a red box and a black box. The ones with the bad interviews go in the black box and we don't do interviews with that person ever again – or even with the paper.'

Back in 1981, Nicholls promptly observed that the star of the show was 'thirty-one, and looks it', describing his face as 'anxious, baggy-eyed and supporting a thick crop of hair slavishly greased into shape'. Offstage photos, he revealed, were *verboten* – 'and no wonder'. It was a fairly damning article, guaranteed to upset both the spin doctor and the singer.

Shaky held the grudge for a full quarter of a century – his anger over the interview re-emerged during a chat to *Record Collector's* Kris Griffiths in 2005: 'He [Nicholls] was so friendly to me, he came to my show, we had breakfast together, chatted amiably for hours and I'll tell you what, in his article he cut me to pieces like a sardine. He was a snake. I'll never understand how anyone can do that.'

Interestingly, *NME* journalist Fred Dellar was on the case in July when *Smash Hits* finally turned. 'The already soured relationship between the music press and Shakin' Stevens's manager Freya Miller took a turn for the worse last week,' he reported, 'when the one-time New Seekers fame-pusher decreed that *Smash Hits* could only interview her would-be superstar if she could vet the article before it went into print' – an invitation the mag greeted with thanks, but no thanks.

'Previously the bulky Miller had roused the ire of journalists by sitting in on Shaky's interviews and interjecting a recurring "no comment" whenever questions involving Stevens's real name, age or marital status were proffered,' Dellar noted. Presumably Dellar was forgiven over the years for his plain-speaking, as he was to be asked to write the sleeve notes to Shaky's 2005 comeback CD. It's notable that Shaky took the opportunity in his *Record Collector* interview with Griffiths to distance himself from Freya Miller's management. 'She upset a few people and had an unhealthy habit of interfering,' he admitted.

Worse than this, though, the *Northamptonshire Evening Telegraph* – Fred Dellar's local newspaper – reported the problems that up-and-coming rockabillies The Jets encountered when touring with the great man. 'The threesome had some fetching pink shirts made specially for the shows, only to have them relegated to the nearest clothes locker after a gig in Corby where Miller decided that such clobber was in danger of upstaging her boy's denim outfits,' the paper revealed.

The article further claimed that The Jets were ordered not to wear anything black or white (because it might clash with the headliner's stage apparel – his favourite colours, apparently, because 'I like the contrast') and were also allegedly told to stay in their dressing room while Shaky was on stage. It was even reported that a tour manager locked them in every night to ensure their compliance!

A July showcase concert at the Apollo Victoria Theatre in central London won over *Melody Maker*'s Patrick Humphries – who, you will remember, had witnessed Shaky supporting the Stones many years previously. He felt that this very different environment was not so much a concert as 'an event, an opportunity to see the vinyl star made mortal, to touch, to lay on hands, to dutifully clutch a handkerchief made moist by the idol, now and for ever'.

While he considered Stevens was 'a little light in the charisma department,' Humphries admitted the star 'looked great as he sauntered out on stage, clad in a vivid pink jacket, and went straight into Conway Twitty's "Mona Lisa".' The show, he said, 'only got going when the hits were produced' – though he felt Shaky's 'tongue-in-drape appeal' filled a gap. 'Audiences need someone like Shaky, a safety valve, someone to scream at.' And that they seemed to be doing, in spades.

Shaky's past caught up with him in August 1981 when a budget album of early material, entitled *Shakin' Stevens*, was released by the Hallmark/Pickwick label. In the throes of Shaky-mania, enough people were curious to give him a third album-chart entry at Number 34. In a later interview Freya Miller appeared to be unamused, while Shaky was at pains to point out 'I didn't receive a penny for stuff I did with The Sunsets, it was all one-shot deals of limited pressings. It was down to management, which I didn't have.'

The release combined the two albums produced by Donny Marchand, who recalls getting a call from Pickwick boss Monty Lewis whose idea it was to re-release them. Polydor and CBS were happy to cash in on the windfall, but Marchand had to give approval. 'I agreed, and Monty Lewis did an incredible job marketing them. Today I get comments from rock 'n' roll fans that they love that more than the new stuff because it sounded more authentic. CBS gave me a £10,000 advance to agree to let them put it out. The deal with CBS was that they would pay Shaky.'

Marchand says he then made a deal with The Sunsets, so that they could benefit from the 1972 album *Rockin' And Shakin'*. 'Once they agreed to do that, I said, "Don't come to me for money with regards to the album [*I'm No JD*], it's an even swap and makes it nice and tidy; no ties, no problems. You guys see what you can get." The percentage in those days was something like twelve per cent and out of that usually you had to pay the act, so this would have been twelve per cent for them.'

As Shaky's money worries had become a thing of the past since his recent chart-topping success 'This Ole House', he decided to celebrate with the purchase of a new Cadillac Deville – 'It's quite flashy, and is a special denim colour. I thought about a Rolls-Royce, but a Cadillac is more like a rock 'n' roll car, so I decided on that!'

'This Ole House' had proved more than a flash in the pan, its stay of seventeen weeks in the charts including four weeks at the top. So 'Green Door' had much to live up to on its July release. Lo and behold, it spent the entire month of August at Number One – higher than any of the three versions of the song that had fought it out for chart honours back in 1956.

Had it not been for competition from the original American version by Jim Lowe (which made Number Eight) and a cover by the lesser-known Glen Mason that reached the Top Thirty, Frankie Vaughan could conceivably have improved on his Number Two showing. But since it was the high-kicking Vaughan's first UK Top Ten entry, he probably wasn't too bothered. And, twenty-five years later, he was generous in his praise of Shaky's effort. 'It proves you can't keep a good song down,' Frankie said, adding, 'I'm also thrilled because his version is similar to mine. When I met Shaky, he told me that he always listened to my records when he was young. I hope he stays in the hit parade as long as I did.'

The idea to cover the song had come not from Stuart Colman, as might have been expected, but from one-time Brinsley Schwarz frontman Nick Lowe, something of a musicologist who'd specialized in picking obscure old songs for his pub-rock outfit to play. Now a well-respected producer, as well as bass player for Dave Edmunds' Rockpile, he shared a beer with Stevens and Colman in a London pub and gave him the idea free, gratis and for nothing. 'Stuart nearly swallowed his beer glass,' said Shaky. 'I thought it was a wacky idea, but it worked.'

Interestingly, the single had entered the chart at Number 22, then leaped an incredible twenty-one places to top spot – a performance last seen when Elvis Presley's 'Surrender' made a similar jump fully twenty years earlier. It was succeeded at the top by the saccharine sound of 'Japanese Boy' by Aneka. It wasn't so much the one-hit wonder Mary Sandeman, a Scottish folk singer turned Oriental, that was noteworthy, but the fact her song was written by one Bobby Heatlie. His was a name that would recur several times in future chapters of the Shakin' Stevens story.

Shaky was now at a peak of popularity few could dream of – and it was all the more remarkable given the state of the charts at the time. The song 'Green Door' knocked off the top spot was The Specials' 'Ghost Town', a dirgeful reflection of recent inner-city riots in Brixton and Toxteth. Heavy metal was enjoying the beginnings of a renaissance, with Motörhead scoring an unlikely Number One album. And with the synthesizer fast rivalling the guitar as the entry-level instrument for would-be pop stars, the success of Marc Almond's electro-pop duo Soft Cell inspired Yazoo and The Pet Shop Boys to follow in their wake.

Escapism was clearly what Shakin' Stevens fans wanted, and their hero was only too willing to supply it. Yet his success was in its own way proving something of a straitjacket. As he travelled the country by Cadillac with an entourage including six bodyguards, he became untouchable and unreachable. A Radio One Roadshow in Chester found him arriving by helicopter, miming to 'Green Door' in front of 40,000 admiring fans and leaving ten minutes later.

Having scored with two architecturally themed rockers, Shaky took the tempo down in October '81 and was rewarded with his fourth hit single of the year. Significantly, however, his revival of 'It's Raining' – a 1962 US success on the Minit label for cult soul singer Irma Thomas – stalled at Number Ten. But maybe his fans had already purchased the album, as *Shaky*, his third long-player of the year – though his first of all-new material – had entered the listings in late September and sold steadily enough to top the UK chart for a single week in November. Despite its short tenure in pole position, due to stiff competition from The Police, The Human League (whose futuristic *Dare* it displaced) and Queen (whose *Greatest Hits* ruled the pre-Christmas marketplace), *Shaky* still remained in the bestselling listings for an impressive twenty-eight weeks.

Recorded once again at Eden Studios, Chiswick, with Stuart Colman at the helm, *Shaky* had featured the standard crew, but the packaging of the album was wildly different from the rockin' and rollin' image of yore: as rockabilly expert Shaun Mather put it, 'The make-up on the cover photo made him look more like Esquerita than Eddie Cochran . . . but the stuff between the grooves was still on the mark.' For the record, Shaky was seen caught in the spotlight and pointing with his right hand on the cover.

It was certainly the case that the steel-guitar work of the now-departed B. J. Cole was less in evidence, Micky Gee taking up the slack on numbers like the opener, 'Mona Lisa', a song previously associated with Carl Mann and Conway Twitty. 'You Drive Me Crazy' was a known quantity, as was 'It's Raining' (his first ballad single) and 'Green Door'.

'Don't Tell Me Your Troubles' was written by Don Gibson and again gave Micky Gee the chance to shine, as he did on the rocking album closer, 'Let Me Show You How I'm Lookin''. 'This Time' was written by Chips Moman, a one-time Phil Spector session guitarist who had produced Elvis, while 'I'm Gonna Sit Right Down And Write Myself A Letter' covered a hit song from 1957 by little-known Billy Williams. Curiously, Barry Manilow would record the song in 1982 – though whether he covered the cover or the original is unclear.

Despite his relatively subdued role, B. J. Cole felt that it was permissible to make hay while the sun shone and capitalize on the successful formula. 'Once Shaky started having hits, it was logical to carry on recording albums, and we did three in two years, plus we went on the road. With those albums, the inspired song selection was a part of what made it happen, picking obscure songs from the rockabilly genre – and for that, I give Stuart [Colman] a lot of credit,' he later reflected.

Not only was *Shaky* a chart-topper, but an online poll nearly twenty-five years later saw it come out a clear winner in the fans' affections, its 30 per cent of the votes were double those of the next challenger.

The November/December 1981 tour saw a sudden change of personnel when drummer Howard Tibble bowed out to be with his wife, who was seriously ill. The new boy in the band was Chris Wyles. 'I got this phone call out the blue from Stuart, who said they were starting a UK tour in three days' time and would I like to do it? I sort of went, "Ummm yeah, okay." I had one rehearsal and went straight in the gig at the De Montfort Hall in Leicester.'

Wyles, whom Colman had produced when he was with a little-known band called Brian Copsey and the Commotions (Geraint Watkins also played on their never-released album), would find himself in situ for some seven years . . . but that hectic first gig will live in his memory for ever. Not least the attention he received from musical director Micky Gee.

'I hadn't really enough time to learn everything,' he admits, 'so it was a bit nerve-racking. I'd not played a lot of rock 'n' roll at that point, and Micky was quite particular about what the drum parts were and so on. He gave me quite a hard time at the outset, but it settled down after a few gigs. He can be quite cantankerous – "Okay, you're the new boy, let's put you through the mill a little bit" – but we jumped on a bus and did something like twenty gigs straight off.'

Chris Wyles was immediately surprised by the youth of the audience to whom he found himself playing. 'They were mainly youngsters, a lot too young to go to concerts on their own – which was good for Shaky because, if Junior wanted to go along, then Mum and Dad would go along as well! You end up selling more tickets. It becomes a family-orientated thing, particularly in Europe where you got whole families coming along to the shows.' But not all the fans who'd followed him since The Sunsets were happy being part of this new, wider audience. 'I think when he started to get the hit records the die-hard rock 'n' rollers didn't like it that much. It was an inverted snobbery thing. "Green Door" wasn't really a rock 'n' roll song, I guess, so though the crowd was wildly enthusiastic, it wasn't a pure rock 'n' roll crowd.'

One such disaffected fan was old friend Richard Williams, formerly of *Melody Maker* and Island Records but now reviewing for *The Times*, who attended Shaky's December '81 show at the Hammersmith Odeon. A big fan of The Sunsets during his time at *Melody Maker*, he drew unfavourable comparisons between that band's version of 'Train Kept A-Rollin'', which he believed to be 'perhaps the most spectacularly intense British interpretation of the rockabilly style', and the recent Stuart Colman productions. 'This process of taming,' he continued, 'was reflected in a show in which Stevens presented all his hits, moving very cutely in a manner combining the young Presley's provocative convulsions with the more stylized choreography of *West Side Story*.'

The talents of Geraint Watkins and Micky Gee were, claimed Williams, 'largely wasted, and Stevens' flirtations with the girls who bombarded him with roses and kisses seemed depressingly parodistic.' In summary, Williams saw Shakin' Stevens as 'a rockabilly Action Man' who 'on the road to *Top of the Pops*, appears to have been cured of the restricted vision which once made him convincing and even interesting'. The fact was, though, that Shakin' Stevens had traded his cult stardom for a wider audience. The genie was out of the bottle, and would not go back. But Shaky – and, of course, Freya – was laughing all the way to the bank.

The year of 1982 proved that, despite a hugely successful twelve months, there were still plenty of landmarks to be passed. One such occurred in late January when the Stuart

Colman-produced 'Oh Julie' became Shaky's first ever self-penned hit. It topped the UK chart for one week but, in what would be a tumultuous year for the man and his band with personnel changes seemingly every few weeks, would not appear on an album until the October release of *Give Me Your Heart Tonight*.

'Oh Julie' was nominated for a prestigious Ivor Novello songwriting award, but was far from Shaky's first attempt at writing: album tracks such as 'Baby If We Touch' and 'Make It Right Tonight' from *Marie Marie/This Ole House* had introduced the public gently to the man's own songs. 'Yes, I'm writing more of my own songs now,' he commented in *Look In* magazine. 'Like any other writer I hope that one of my songs will live on after I'm gone!' Barry Manilow went on to record 'Oh Julie' and put it on the B-side of a hit across the Atlantic, which must have been good for Shaky's bank balance.

Interestingly, Mike Hurst's one-time protégés Showaddy-waddy had their last hits in 1982, and relatively minor ones at that. It was as if their fall from Top Twenty grace, which happened at just about the same time that Shaky was scoring his first hits, had seen the torch pass to the newer act.

Brian Hodgson's relatively mature Matchbox, which had taken its name from a Carl Perkins song, had maintained a chart presence from late 1979 through to mid-1982 without really cracking it – though there was one glorious exception in 1980's Top Five single 'When You Think About Love'. Shaky's support acts on tour had included younger bands eager to gain a head start on the competition: these included the previously mentioned Jets, while the most recent tour had introduced The Shakin' Pyramids, whose *Skin 'Em Up* album skimmed the Top Fifty in 1981.

Paul Barrett, Shaky's former manager, had left life on the road at the age of thirty-seven and, while considering how to make a living, became the agent for bands including Matchbox and The Jets. 'Being on the road for ten years, I'd met everybody on the

1950s rock 'n' roll scene. And at that time there was an upsurge in interest, so I started bringing in American stars because I knew everybody. I knew every club, be it in Copenhagen or Cardiff. And for ten, fifteen years I was the man.'

Of the new bands on the scene, The Stray Cats had the advantage of being American, while the services of Dave Edmunds, The Sunsets' first producer, helped them hit their studio stride quickly. The move to Britain from their native land (where the trio could barely get a gig) paid off as they shot from the London pub circuit to *Top of the Pops* in record time. Their commercial peak was the UK Top Three album *Built For Speed*. The Blue Cats were fairly authentic in sound, while The Polecats were clever enough to attempt a broader appeal: their first album included a cover of David Bowie's 'John I'm Only Dancing'. On the other side of the tracks, The Meteors and Cramps were kingpins of a scene named psychobilly that mixed new-wave shock value with stripped-back rock 'n' roll/rockabilly ingredients.

In a press interview at the time, Shaky grouped himself with The Stray Cats and groups like short-lived two-hit wonders Roman Holliday as representing a new wave of rock 'n' roll. 'That's a particularly good development, because it's a bit of variation on the standard rock 'n' roll. I think it's fantastic that my music can be in the charts alongside groups like Culture Club and Duran Duran. It proves that the whole pop scene at the moment is very open-minded, which can only do everybody a lot of good.'

The Stargazers were Epic labelmates discovered by Muff Winwood who, despite much hard roadwork, registered only one hit – 'Groove', a Number 56 in 1982 – during eighteen months with the label. They were young but authentic rock 'n' rollers and, as their Danny Brittain remembers, were delighted to secure a support slot on Shakin' Stevens' September/ October 1982 tour. But they soon realized there were rules to be obeyed – the chief one being: 'Anyone who laughs at Shaky is off the tour.' Stevens was big enough to play two consecutive nights at the Southampton Gaumont (plus another at neighbouring Portsmouth, a nearly unheard-of event) – the location of an amusing event of almost *Spinal Tap*-esque proportions. Brittain: 'We soundchecked for the show and of course Shaky would run though his own thing, including coming in through the "Green Door". One of the road crew nailed the door shut, and eventually Shaky shoulder-charged the jammed door [completely unaware that it had been nailed down]. Of course it fell flat on the stage. Needless to say everyone desperately tried to keep a straight face . . .' What happened to the guilty road-crew member remains unrecorded – but, as Brittain explains, the star of the show was already living a separate existence from the rest of the band. 'He wouldn't come to dinner with us, but would be in his own dressing room with a crate of Kestrel lager. I thought he was actually a very nervous guy, but could be very civil.'

Whether it was nervousness that led to Shaky crossing swords with a young Richard Madeley who, in the early 1980s, was working on the Yorkshire TV show *Calendar Goes Pop*, it may never be known, but the incident made such a mark that, years later, Madeley initially vetoed the singer's appearance on *Richard and Judy*, stating he wasn't having 'that man' on his show. But Shaky insists the full story has rarely, if ever, been told.

'It was very early on in the career,' he says. 'We got there about eight in the morning into this very small dressing room. It seemed like ages before I went onto the floor to do my interview; Status Quo were there as well. So I finally got on about three o'clock and was getting asked the questions I'd just answered, so I jumped on him – a bit of fun, you know – and broke his watch! After the show I said I'd repair it, but he was in a bit of a strop.'

In many respects, this story vindicates the Freya Miller tactic of taking extra care to look after her star, and keeping interviews and other public appearances firmly scripted. 'With the best will in the world Shaky is not the most vocally eloquent of people,' one band member ventures, 'which is what happened with that interview. I think Madeley said something which Shaky took the wrong way and didn't really have a verbal answer for. I think that he felt Madeley was taking the piss out of him and, rather than come back with a quick, witty remark, jumped on him because he couldn't think of anything.' Since the incident, however, Shaky and Madeley have patched up their differences. The former explains: 'Only recently [April 2005] we went on the show and told the same story and we're fine.'

Two sold-out nights at the Liverpool Empire were typical of the time in 1982. 'The manager of the theatre told us that we were the first act to fill the place for nineteen months,' said a justifiably proud Shaky in *Record Mirror*, adding that, 'They had to get police dogs out to control the crowds. At the moment nobody's doing any business except us. We're not leaving places half empty, we're getting, "Why don't you play here again tomorrow?" People come along to my concerts in family groups, they're looking for a good time.'

Changes were afoot in Shaky's backing group, though. Micky Gee gave way to Billy Bremner, a Scots guitarist who'd made his name in Dave Edmunds' Rockpile, who shared six-string duties with the faithful Roger McKew. Moreover, a four-man horn section had been recruited for the 1982 tour. Dick Hanson (trumpet), John 'Irish' Earle (baritone and tenor saxes), Ray Beavis (tenor sax) and Chris Gower (trombone) were known as the Rumour Brass, due to their work with Graham Parker's band, and proved a crowd-pleasing spectacle.

Geraint Watkins was the last of the original session veterans to leave Stevens' employ: he had enjoyed it while it lasted. In 2005, the genial Welshman explained how things had changed over the last couple of years. 'It was mostly good fun on the road at the start, if a bit fraught at times. Shaky was still young and he wanted this and that, and we were not a cool bunch of musos. But from time to time he'd have some fun with us.

'I think he was just chuffed to have made it that far, and to be honest we were pleased to be on the end of it, being relatively young, up to that point being paid well, and touring quite a bit. A bit further down the line we all got a bit fed up with it, with the wrangles, the management/star thing . . .

'By this time Freya, his manager, almost made a concerted effort to keep him separate from the band. It was like the Elvis thing . . . "Shaky has left the building" and all that. The moment the show finished, he'd be straight out the door and into a car, and back to the hotel. One night he crashed right around the corner from the theatre – I think it was in Nottingham – and there he was in this wreck complete in his theatrical make-up!'

There was a pre-gig ritual in which a band member would be summoned to Shaky's dressing room to sit down with the star before the show and have a chat. Musical hints and tips could be handed out, or merely a polite conversation about family and friends. Sometimes Shaky, if he was staying in the same hotel as the band, would even come to the bar and hang out with them, though such times were relatively rare.

In Geraint Watkins' view, the fact was that Shaky had started to believe his own (Freya-orchestrated) publicity. 'In some ways I think he believed the whole star trip. He almost expected stardom, got to live the part. But,' he adds, 'it was great fun and we played some great rock 'n' roll.'

Watkins was a hard act to follow. The man given the job was Gavin Povey. He had started his professional career with a drummer called Cliff Davies, before moving on to punk band The Edge, formed by ex-Damned members guitarist Lu Edmunds and Jon Moss (later, of course, of Culture Club). The band were hooked up with Akron songstress Jane Ashley and re-christened Jane Aire and the Belvederes, establishing a connection with Stiff Records that brought the talented young keyboard player work with Tracey Ullman and Lew Lewis.

He then linked with up-and-coming songstress Kirsty MacColl, who wrote much of Ullman's material. They collaborated on many of MacColl's early titles – 'Terry', 'He's On The Beach', 'Other People's Hearts' and 'Roman Gardens' among them – and he played piano on her *Desperate Character* album. In-between, he was resident pianist in a pub in Deptford, south-east London, called the United Friends.

'I think the contact with Shaky came through a guy called Liam Sternberg,' Povey recalls, 'who wrote "Walk Like An Egyptian" for [CBS labelmates] The Bangles. I met Billy Bremner through a session with Jane Aire. I think he had high expectations with his own single at the time, "Loud Music In Cars", but it didn't take off. He knew Stuart, and Geraint had something going (probably Van Morrison, as we followed each other into both bands); The Edge had been a sort of Stranglers-style rock 'n' roll band. But although Shaky was rock 'n' roll too, this was rock 'n' roll in its broadest sense.'

The Shakin' Stevens machine was gearing up for what would be in effect a year of world touring. The loss of people like Lee, Cole and Watkins was made good by younger, arguably hungrier musicians, who would happily tour for most of the year as the bid was made for global stardom. But as Chris Wyles reflects, there was little interaction between the star and his backing band, who were left in no doubt that they should only speak when spoken to. 'Shaky was always in his own dressing room, and sometimes before a show you'd get, "Oh, Shaky wants to talk to Roger, or wants to see somebody or other" and you'd go in and talk about the gig and then go back and pass it on to everyone else. You'd think in a rock 'n' roll environment it'd be all the lads together, but quite often we'd turn up for a soundcheck and be hanging round the place waiting for Shaky to come out of his dressing room. The soundcheck could last twenty minutes, after which he'd go back to his dressing room and you'd not see him then until the show. The band would always start with an instrumental . . .

Shaky made his appearance, finished the show, thanked the audience and would be out of the theatre before you'd left. So in effect, in a ten-day period, you might not actually get to have a conversation with him.'

This tactic, while far from morale-boosting, was in reality a clever one. By keeping Shaky away from temptation, Freya Miller was extending his shelf life and ensuring he fulfilled, if not exceeded, expectations. 'I've never been a party person,' he'd admit in an interview. 'My only magic potion is my nightly eight hours' sleep. As soon as I finish a show I go back to the hotel, have a very light meal and then it's beddybyes . . .' In fact, the most rock 'n' roll thing about Shaky in those days was the dry white wine that his contract stipulated had to be provided for pre-show refreshment.

He'd already achieved staggering international success, having topped the charts in Australia, Belgium, Israel and South Africa, and scored hits in Germany, France and Holland. The month of March saw Shaky and his band venture Down Under for the first time, the tour taking in theatre and town-hall venues in Brisbane, Sydney, Melbourne, Newcastle, Canberra, Adelaide and Perth. Then, after three dates in New Zealand, they played a final date in Hobart, Tasmania, before returning home. It was Shaky's first time in Australia.

Gavin Povey enjoyed the global travelling, but was surprised at the scale of his boss's international success. 'Shaky had already had about five big hits by the time I joined the band, and was playing to big, mixed crowds which ranged from teenyboppers, to quiffs, blue rinses etc. There were rock 'n' rollers in Norway, Sweden and Germany for example. And generally speaking we were doing very big halls and theatres. In Munich there was one huge place that held 10,000 people. At this stage in Germany, Shaky's five hits made him bigger than The Beatles, comparatively speaking.'

The Australian jaunt was put under threat when Billy Bremner quit as second guitarist just before the tour: his relationship with Freya Miller had always been difficult, and had clearly played a part in his decision to leave. The choice of a new guitarist fell on New Yorker Mike Festa, an Italian-American then domiciled in London whose recruitment came on the recommendation of Stuart Colman. His integration into the Shakin' Stevens set-up would prove problematical, however: Festa was dismissed by one of his new bandmates as 'a loud-mouthed American who didn't really fit in with the band'.

Instructed by Shaky that he should look as though he was really into the show, Festa apparently took things a little too far according to one band member: 'The first night as the first guitar solo came up he jumped up from behind his monitors and ran to the front of the stage where Shaky was standing by his microphone and started to lean against him. If you've ever seen a Shakin' Stevens show you'd realize the whole band dress in black and always stay behind the monitors in their positions at the back of the stage. Suddenly this American is up and giving it the whole guitar hero bit and everyone was looking, saying, "What the heck is he up to?"'

Roger McKew – who by now was not only a fixture in the guitar department but, given recent departures, the older head that held the band together – belied his laid-back nature when he decided to take the newcomer down a peg or two. A fellow band member recalls: 'Roger never got his guitar out and showed off, but this American guy's sitting there [in the tour bus] and says, "Hey, Rog, know this one?" and giving it all this supposed rock 'n' roll lip. I could see Roger sitting there thinking, "You're supposed to be the rhythm guitar player and I'm the lead guitar player," so he very quietly picked up his Telecaster, suddenly started playing some real down-home country stuff and wiped the floor with him . . . it had to be done!' Festa enjoyed the tour nevertheless, and later settled in Australia permanently.

Shaky had also become immensely popular in South America and would tour there in 1982. One particular gig in

Chile was performed in front of an audience of 20,000, and televised across the continent! This was a daunting debut gig for Les Davidson, who'd been selected as Billy Bremner's permanent replacement after Mike Festa's departure. A seasoned session guitar player hailing from Edinburgh, Bremner had toured the world with Leo Sayer, but was hardly prepared for what he'd experience with Shaky.

The connection was drummer Chris Wyles, with whom he'd worked on the same session – featuring Brian Copsey and the Commotions – that had brought the drummer to Stuart Colman's attention. 'Chris was already in Shaky's band,' says Davidson, 'and he called me up and said, "The guitar player has just left, we're going out to Chile to do a festival, and could you come down to Nomis rehearsal rooms and see how you get on?" I went down there to find out I was in a full-blown rehearsal! I think they'd already made the decision that, if Chris was right and I was capable of doing it, I had the job and I was in. We actually left for Chile about four days after I stepped into the rehearsal studios.'

The Falklands War had ended only a year earlier, and with relations between Britain and Argentina still far from friendly it was, in retrospect, a risk for the band to have been booked on the Argentine national airline. They touched down in Buenos Aires to catch the connecting flight to Santiago, but made it no further than the airport. 'We were actually prisoners of war for about eight or nine hours, under armed guard,' Davidson recalls, still wide-eyed at the ordeal.

Shaky, fortunately for him, had travelled direct ('CBS Records probably sent us on a cheaper flight,' jokes Les), but, being petrified of aeroplanes, probably suffered in his own way. Nevertheless, he was spared the ordeal of being deported to Brazil, the only place that would accept British nationals at that time. Only sax player John Earle, who was travelling on a southern Irish passport, was allowed to take the Swiss connecting flight to Santiago.

So Les and his new bandmates spent an unscheduled night in Rio. 'I hadn't even played a note with the band apart from rehearsals, and then we went to Santiago the next day,' he remembered. 'All unshaven, all feeling dreadful, I think we all drunk our duty frees because we thought we were going to be locked up for ever! And then I did the first gig with the band. It was tremendous fun, it was in a open-air theatre and we were there with Bucks Fizz and a few other bands. I only really remember Bucks Fizz because Felix Krish, the bass player, is an old buddy of mine. There were Argentinean bands, Brazilian bands, I think the two of us were the only British bands.

'Just to show you how unrehearsed that was, there were a couple of songs where Roger, who stood side by side with me on stage, had to shout out some of the chords for me! I'd had to learn so many songs in such a short period of time, and one of the problems with rock 'n' roll songs is they seem to be similar, but not quite. It's actually slightly more difficult to remember them until you get used to them.'

Les, who hadn't seen Shaky perform before, was to receive something of a surprise during the gig. 'I'd never seen anything like it [when] he cartwheeled across the stage. He tried to jump on my shoulders from this ramp, as part of his act, and of course I went straight down on the floor. Shaky, live, always did what he felt like doing, which, of course, created a fantastic show. That was my first show, we did one or two nights there, and I was a band member from that point on.'

Shaky managed to top up his tan in Rio de Janeiro, but rather overdid it and ended up with a bad case of sunstroke. 'Copacabana Beach in Rio is a fantastic place to relax, but a lot of British, myself included, underestimated the strength of the sun. Though I was able to continue my appearances, I spent several days lying in a darkened room drinking gallons of water!' he reflected ruefully, during a 1982 interview.

According to a Shaky interview with *Look In* magazine, there were also plans to go to Mexico at the end of the year, and Canada in 1983. But these never actually came off, and 1982 would remain his world tour year.

Gavin Povey made his recording debut on 'Shirley', a revival of an obscure 1960s John Fred and his Playboy Band track, which hit Number Six in May 1982, and continued the singer's apparent fixation with female names. It was Shaky's fourth record to be titled in that way, though he denied any underlying plan to *Look In* magazine: 'It's just coincidence. They're not long-forgotten loves or anything like that! They just happened to be songs I liked, felt happy about doing and thought people wanted to hear.' Interestingly, the lyrics were reproduced courtesy of Red Stick Music and Shaky Music, suggesting that the singer also had some kind of interest in the publishing rights. Well, Elvis Presley insisted on songwriters signing over their copyright to Hill and Range Music, his publishing company, so if that was the case, at least Shaky had a famous precedent.

Povey was under no illusions as to his own role. 'We were basically just the musos for hire, there wasn't a lot of social interaction, Shaky would do a lot of his stuff [in the studio] after we'd done our parts.' But onstage was where it really came alive. 'He really got into it, he'd throw himself around, which was quite funny as the rest of the band were to all intents and purposes experienced pros who would really not do that sort of thing. But Shaky did have his own brand of showmanship, it was a case of different strokes for different folks.'

'By the time I joined, things were already polarized. Shaky would generally be in his Cadillac and we, being the band, were on the tour bus. Sometimes we would be in the same hotel, but he'd generally speaking be off to do TV and radio interviews. So we didn't socialize much – but that was okay, we were all doing a job. He was a big success before I joined, so I obviously didn't want to impose.'

Povey found this resulted in a communication gap in the studio, which had to be overcome. 'He would be rehearsing with us sometimes, when Stuart Colman called a session, but it could be difficult,' he recalls. 'He'd often know what was required, but not being a musician he didn't have the means to communicate that. Maybe there was a bit of frustration there because of that. He had a lot of pressure on him at the time, I think. It's one thing to be successful, and another to keep it going. And in spite of sometimes being very brusque in his manner – especially when trying to put a point across – he was a gentleman and never bore a grudge.'

This was also the year The Sunsets' Paul Barrett came back into Shaky's life. He collaborated with Hilary Hayward to produce a book which, until this publication, was the only full-length Shakin' Stevens biography on the market. 'Hilary ran a magazine called *Circuit*, which was the bible of the college circuit, with her husband,' Paul explains. 'I just told anecdotes on tape. But unfortunately the book fell between two things. It wasn't in-depth enough to be in-depth and it wasn't superficial enough to be a pop book. There was nothing in the book that was wrong or incorrect or slanderous. It was pretty gentle. We called it *Shakin' Stevens*, but I wanted to call it *Rocky Road Blues*. We had a thousand pound advance, which we split, and that was it.'

The month of August put the seal on Shaky as an all-round entertainer, when he accepted the gilt-edged invitation to the Children's Royal Variety Performance. He was introduced to guest of honour Princess Margaret, certainly the most rock 'n' roll of the royals prior to Diana's ascendancy, and Margaret certainly lived up to her reputation. For one thing, she told Shaky how happy she was that somebody had come in denims!

It was something of a trip down memory lane for Shaky – who performed recent chart-topper 'Oh Julie' on the night – as the Dominion Theatre was just down the road from the Astoria, where he'd held court as Elvis for so many months.

Les Davidson had come across adulation playing with the likes of Leo Sayer, but even he was surprised enough by what he was now witnessing to discuss the Shaky phenomenon with the man himself. 'He and I had our own theories on this,' Les remembers. 'He hit the mark with teenage girls and then their mums; they liked him because he was a loveable character, tall, dark and handsome. His persona came across in interviews and his smile was one of warmth. He genuinely enjoyed the shows.

'The audience was predominantly female. In fact, on the first proper tour I did, the curtains opened to this huge scream that The Beatles must have had. I've never experienced that before. I'd also been in a band called Sniff 'n' the Tears, with a "blokey" audience who knew all your tracks inside out and were interested in how well you played.

'With Shaky, it was more based on teenage adoration, lust, whatever you wanna say. His music, I suppose, was danceable as well; it crossed the barriers. I've learned over the years that if someone genuinely loves it, and they mean it, that emotion will go across to the audience and they will believe him. If you are a parody of it, they won't. And Shaky's never been a parody; he is the genuine article, the real deal.'

Shaky's private life was still being kept under wraps, but in a rare interview at the time he confessed that he saw his Surrey base as a sanctuary. 'There's a room in the house that's a part of the business. That's my study, where I listen to songs I'm considering, where I write and where I talk on the phone. In many ways it's my favourite room. I always wanted something like that, where it's very quiet and I can lock myself away and shut the door when I come out. We all need somewhere like that. The only problem is, it's always in a mess and it's me who's got to clear it up!'

Such time as he was able to spend at home was, he maintained, essential to his sanity. 'If I lived life as Shakin' Stevens all the time and started believing all this showbiz stuff, I could quickly end up going down the wrong path. Right now I'm working, doing my job, but when I get home to my family I close the door and all this is outside. That's done a lot to keep me going this long.

'But it's not quite as clear-cut as being two different people. I've been Shakin' Stevens too long for that. I don't have to pretend to be him – I record what I want to and wear what I like on and offstage, and it's all me. I don't feel obliged to spend four hours in front of a mirror before I come down for a cup of coffee. Once you start doing that you know something's wrong.'

The fourth Shakin' Stevens solo album on Epic was *Give Me Your Heart Tonight*. The uptempo title track, penned by Billy Livsey – an American keyboardist who'd played with Les Davidson in Leo Sayer's band – was completed just before Shaky broke for his summer holidays, and apparently involved much overtime in the studio to get the exact sound he wanted. Its Number Eleven success as a single heralded even greater success for the album, which peaked at Number Three in October 1982. Combined with the Number Ten single showing of 'I'll Be Satisfied', a retread of one of Jackie Wilson's early R&B rockers, all looked rosy. But in fact, the album was a glued-together mixture of sessions comprising a number of different band line-ups. Penny Reel in *New Musical Express* saw it as a 'slick, but ultimately empty performance', exempting only the title track with its 'Crescent City second-line piano' and 'I'll Be Satisfied', which in his view 'works surprisingly well'.

The track that ended the album was probably the oldest – a version of the Doris Day standard 'Que Sera Sera', which had a singalong finale reminiscent of The Beatles' 'Hey Jude'. (Sunsets fans would see this as a nod back to the pre-fame days, or perhaps it was down to a lack of new material . . .)

With Geraint Watkins calling it a day, and, prior to Gavin Povey's arrival, ace rock 'n' roll pianist Pete Wingfield had been brought in early in the year to play a session for the album. Wingfield felt that interaction with the star was limited: 'Shaky seemed a nice enough bloke, but we didn't have all that much contact with him.'

Before his departure, Wingfield recalls producer Colman as being a stickler for detail: 'I particularly remember "Sapphire", if only for the fact that we must have played it about five hundred times before Stuart was satisfied. We laid down the tracks in advance, and in the case of "Sapphire", we played it again and again, as Stuart was very pernickety about the end product. I think as a band we were all happy with the first take! I didn't really want to play it to the point of my hands bleeding, but we got paid and it ended up on the album. It was also good to play rock 'n' roll again, and I think a lot of the guys thought that. But really I was there by default.'

The fact that Geraint Watkins, Billy Bremner and Howard Tibble also appear on the album, credited alongside Pete Wingfield under the 'guest musician' heading, is explained by B. J. Cole who says it's difficult, if not impossible, to recall specific albums: 'We were just recording tracks, not albums. The albums weren't separate projects; we just went in to record, and someone else decided which tracks would appear on an album.'

With declining singles-chart positions it appeared that Shaky-mania might finally be abating. But any such thoughts were washed away in an excess of seasonal enthusiasm as *The Shakin' Stevens EP* gave him his second biggest hit of the year at Christmas. Renée and Renato's 'Save Your Love' stubbornly refused to give way, but Shaky's revival of Elvis Presley's 'Blue Christmas', the lead track of a four-song disc that also included live versions of 'Josephine', 'Lawdy Miss Clawdy' and 'Que Sera Sera', was approved of by purists and teenage fans alike.

Strangely, there wasn't a video to publicize the release and Shaky had to depend on personal appearances to promote it. He was well aware of the growing importance of the medium, though: 'I think videos are very important. Particularly for the overseas market. I like to keep my videos quite simple and basic. I'm very much a live performer and I like that to come across. I do get quite involved in the videos. I sit down with the director and the other people involved and we all come up with ideas. I enjoy making them, too. It's hard work but a lot of fun.'

As it turned out, this album was to be the swansong of Stuart Colman, who revealed in the early 1990s that his sudden departure was due to pressure of work very nearly causing a breakdown: 'My doctor told me I was suffering from stress, which I refused to believe – but that's what it was and it took about three years to go away. Between 1983 and 1984 I took almost a full sabbatical for a year. I kept the radio shows going, did a bit of producing but not much, and felt better for it.'

After long holidays in the United States and the Bahamas, paid for by the hard work that had seen him voted *Music Week* and the BPI's Top Producer of 1982, Colman would eventually continue in production with great success. Cliff Richard was the first artist to get past the answerphone message, and his chart-topping remake of 1962 hit 'The Young Ones' with the comedy group of the same name was one notable result. Stuart had been working with a true rock 'n' roll survivor in Billy Fury alongside his commitments with Shaky, but that association was cut short when the Liverpudlian legend died suddenly early in 1983. Not, however, before the single 'Love Or Money' had returned Fury to the UK singles chart after sixteen years' absence, peaking at Number 57. More happily, in 1986 Colman would achieve a lifetime's ambition by producing *Lifetime Friend*, the comeback album of one of his all-time heroes, Little Richard. Not bad for someone who'd been painting and decorating at the time of his first Shakin' Stevens session . . .

He would be succeeded in the production hot seat by Christopher Neil, a man whose track record included Dollar, Sheena Easton, David Essex and Gerry Rafferty. Admittedly, that was hardly a credible rock 'n' roll CV. But he'd just helmed Hank Marvin's *All Alone With Friends*, a connection that must have held some weight with Shaky. And August 1983 saw the first fruit of the switch in producers, when Shaky's revival of

Ricky Nelson's 1959 hit 'It's Late', climbed to UK Number Eleven. The song had lingered long in his memory, even though Nelson was something of an Elvis follower who had flourished in the years when the King had been serving his country and was therefore out of the spotlight. 'I was just eleven or twelve when "It's Late" was a first hit, in the days when singles had triangular shapes punched out in the middle,' Shaky explained at the time in *Look In* magazine. 'I think the song's just as fresh today as when it was released in '59 – I don't agree with those who say the lyrics are dead.' And just in case anyone was in doubt, while he was into 'music from the 1930s and 1940s as well – and I also like what's happening today – 1950s songs have the ability to make people happy. It was a very optimistic era!'

Guitarist Les Davidson recalls the band 'did it very much like the original. I think I actually sang on that live because I have a deep voice, but not on the record. Roger [McKew] played the solo on that. In the studio, with Roger and myself, it was like, "Who wants to take the solo?" and whoever was feeling up for it took the solo that day.'

Three months later Shaky enjoyed his second and biggest hit of what had been a quiet year with 'Cry Just A Little Bit', an original composition by 'Japanese Girl' songsmith Bob Heatlie. Shaky was justifiably proud of the production. 'Even now, the feel of my music is from the 1950s – but the twist is to make it 1980s. I've basically carried it on, but changing with the times. You must move forward.

'You always say "rock 'n' roll revival", but you can't put a date on it. I don't try to recreate a certain guitar solo from the 1950s. There's machines on "Cry Just A Little Bit", and why not? It's wrong to smother it. I don't really feel obligated or responsible to keep the faith with rock 'n' roll. It's just that I get a feel from it and if I do, I'm sure the people out there do.'

It was perhaps a surprising comment from a one-time rock 'n' roll purist. Les Davidson reveals a little bit more about the use of 'machines': 'We triggered the guitars to get them to sequence in a shuffle beat which was six-eight, which was quite unusual for Shaky. Not the rhythm, but the way Chris Neil recorded it. Shaky was fascinated by this, because one thing he always did was to attend the recording sessions. He was very much hands-on in the sense that he would like to say, "I like that" or "I don't like that."

'When we heard that song, we all had the feeling it was going to be a hit because of his profile. You can hardly hear the guitars on it because, as I said, they were used as triggers. In the finished mix I couldn't even tell you if they were there or not. It was a slightly different approach to recording and, to his credit, Shaky embraced that. He was quite open to that style because, if you think about it, a style like that is a natural progression to a more pop-orientated rock 'n' roll song. "Cry" was a bit more poppy, but I think he had to go in that direction – and, of course, it was a massive hit.'

This all chimed in with Freya Miller's masterplan to expose Shaky to the pop marketplace. 'There was no strategy,' she revealed in a rare interview quote, 'it was just a matter of working together and putting out the right thing at the right time. The talent's always been there. It was just a matter of getting the right format – which we evidently did!' Yet Chris Wyles recalls the singer initially bridling at some of Chris Neil's suggestions. 'Shaky was particular about what songs he recorded, and Chris was trying some different ideas, having come from a more pop background. I think it worked out fine in the end, but I think there were a few days when they worked [together] that they didn't hit it off.'

Apart from the sampler and loop effect Les Davidson talks about, he highlights another facet of Shaky's recording that people probably don't realize. 'Eden Studios was using SSL [Solid State Logic] desks and was going to digital tape, so the recording quality of Shaky's records during that period were of the very highest standard. Not only did we have a great studio and great musicians, but also the best recording equipment. I think in some ways that's probably why his records stand the test of time.'

Chris Wyles sheds light on how Shaky chose the songs to record – something that now fell to him after Stuart Colman's departure. 'He used to carry around cassettes of songs that had been sent in to him. He quite often had the songs two or three years until we got round to recording it, so by the time we got to record it he'd lived with the demo for quite a long time.' But there's no doubt Chris Neil started to exert an influence. 'One or two of the more ballady-type songs with Chris veered off the rock 'n' roll path – "Cry Just A Little Bit", for instance, was effectively not a rock 'n' roll song. But there always had to be something in the song that appealed to him in a rock 'n' roll sense.'

As revealed in a 1983 magazine interview, Shaky's ultimate aim was to write more of the music himself, time and inspiration permitting: 'I enjoy writing very much, but often it's quite difficult to write rock 'n' roll songs, as the music's been around for such a long time that most of it's been done before. I find that I have to spend a great deal of time working on the structure of a song to make it sound new and fresh. That makes me feel great when it does eventually work out right, but it can be too time-consuming sometimes.

'As I can't write enough myself, what I try to do is use as many songs as possible by new and unknown writers. I get a lot of rock 'n' roll songs sent to me by people like that, and I think it's important that they're given a chance. Firstly, for the sake of their careers, and then because the best way to keep rock 'n' roll music going is to bring in as much new blood and ideas as possible.'

Rock, pop or whatever, 'Cry Just A Little Bit' found a wide market, and reached Number Three in the UK in 1983. Its success papered over a few cracks that had been visible when Chris Neil had arrived at the studios with three studio musicians in tow. 'They were used to programming machines, this that and the other,' recalls Chris Wyles who, with the rest of the road band were left standing round, thinking 'What are we supposed to do?' Whereas the recording technique since the very beginning had been to lay a song down 'live' as a band before working on it, 'Cry Just A Little Bit' had been built up in layers. 'The band never played it as a backing track,' explains the drummer, 'which was a problem when we had to play it live because it stood out as a very different song from anything else that we were doing.'

Wyles doesn't agree with Davidson that Shaky was happy with the approach: 'As the session went on it became apparent that Shaky wanted to record in the way he wanted to record, which is backing tracks with the band, so then a lot of the album was done in the traditional way. So yes, Shaky got his way and Chris Neil backed off.'

However, the failure of his new album, *The Bop Won't Stop*, to rise higher than Number 21 – the poorest chart showing from an original album since *Take One!* – was perhaps the first real cause for concern in the Shaky camp. Entering the chart on 26 November, it perished in the pre-Christmas rush. The implication was that, while teen music fans would buy singles on their merits, the more mature album-buying public had moved on. Significantly, the next Shakin' Stevens album, released almost exactly a year later, would be a 'greatest hits' compilation.

The album featured a detour into authentic rock 'n' roll territory with Jerry Lee Lewis's 'Livin' Lovin' Wreck', but in the most part rode on the four tracks that would be successful as singles – but since only 'Cry Just A Little Bit' and 'It's Late' had already been released, they could hardly be blamed for a disappointing chart position. Michael Jackson had started the trend of 'mining' his albums for singles, so it wasn't unusual for so many tracks to be extracted without detrimentally affecting LP sales.

The music was significantly poppier than previously, but Shaky retained the rock 'n' roll feel he knew was crucial to his success. Les Davidson gives the singer credit for 'knowing what his faults were as well as his good points. I think he was aware of that. You must remember that Shaky had been performing for a long time before he had massive success, so he'd had a long and tough and difficult road to that success. That mere fact teaches somebody their strengths and weaknesses, so he never suddenly came and said, "I wanna do a jazz number" or if he did it would be a big joke and everybody would go, "Oh, really?" and then he'd go, "No, no, don't be stupid!" So he was quite aware of his strengths and weaknesses, and was a very focused artist.

'When I was with him he didn't veer away from anything I thought was musically inappropriate for him. And I don't think we recorded anything that wasn't used in some shape or form.'

Quite why *New Musical Express* were still bothering to review Shaky albums only they knew, but under the title 'Shaky – not Stirred', cartoonist and confirmed rock traditionalist Ray Lowry complained that 'I'll probably never commit it to the turntable again as long as I live.' Lowry was undoubtedly in a minority, but the failure of *The Bop Won't Stop* was something of a sign of things to come. That said, Shaky had a suitable riposte to those who had been predicting the end of his career was nigh, revealing in *Look In* magazine that he'd recently enlarged his home at Woking, Surrey – to make room to hang up his trophies! 'Though I live in a large house, every room gets used and I've never had a proper room in which to hang my silver and gold discs, and the various awards I've collected over the years,' he explained at the time. 'Up to now they've all been crammed in a cupboard doing nothing but collecting dust. So I decided that I would have a special trophy room, and that's what the extension is all about.'

6

THE GOLDEN ERA, PART TWO: 1984–5

By now, Shakin' Stevens had become one of CBS's hottest properties. By pure coincidence, another Welsh-born singer, Bonnie Tyler, had achieved a similar status among female artists. More than that, she'd broken the States, something Shaky would have given his right suede shoe to do. Her 1983 album *Faster Than The Speed Of Night* benefited from Jim Steinman's songs and production skills during a period when he was estranged from Meat Loaf, and entered the UK listings at Number One – the first album by a female singer ever to do so. Having established herself as Wales's answer to Tina Turner, Bonnie would go on to gather a worldwide fan following that continues today.

Yet her upbringing – back when she was known as plain Gaynor Hopkins – had seen her reared on more basic musical fare. Born in 1953, five years after Shaky, the very first record she bought, at age thirteen, was 'Hippy Hippy Shake' by The

Swinging Blue Jeans. 'I used to watch *Top of the Pops* all the time,' she recalled. 'I'll never forget watching Joe Cocker and thinking, "My God, he's got a brilliant voice, but what a strange look on his face!" I used to think I'd love to be on there. Then there's Tina Turner, Janis Joplin: I was always singing songs like "Piece Of My Heart" and "River Deep Mountain High" in my bedroom.'

The idea to team up Shaky and Bonnie together came in 1983 from producer Chris Neil. Amazingly, the recording session at Eden Studios marked the first time their paths had ever crossed. 'We got on straight away,' said Bonnie, who found the singer 'very professional'. She was surprised to find he had a ready wit. 'I thought maybe he'd be a bit shy, you know, but he's not really when you get to talk to him.'

For Shaky, the attraction was that Ms Tyler was 'basically down to earth, like myself. She was obviously nervous about the record, which was fair enough as we hadn't met or performed together before.' Nevertheless, the concept of a duet was fairly familiar to Bonnie, since she'd recently recorded separate songs with Scots vocalist Frankie Miller and American singer/guitarist Rick Derringer.

The duo were to work together on 'A Rockin' Good Way (To Mess Around And Fall In Love)', a US Top Ten smash in 1960 for Brook Benton and Dinah Washington. 'The song had always been a favourite of mine,' Shaky revealed, 'and I knew it would make an ideal duet. First it was find the girl, and Bonnie was the obvious choice. She's on the same record label and from the same neck of the woods.'

When Bonnie's management was approached, she reserved judgement and said she wanted to listen to the song first. 'I did, and I quite liked it. I thought it would be a nice, happy song for Christmas.' That would indeed have been the obvious time to release the song, but the scale of the success of 'Cry Just A Little Bit', which had hit the Top Three in November, caused a rethink. 'We had to wait for that to start dropping down the chart before we could release the duet,' explained Bonnie later.

Credited to Shaky and Bonnie, the long-awaited single graced the first chart of the new year at a modest Number 57, but rose rapidly to hit the UK Number Five spot on 21 January 1984. On its way up it passed the descending 'Islands In The Stream' by another promising double act, Dolly Parton and Kenny Rogers, while Frankie Goes To Hollywood were also on the rise with their first hit single, 'Relax'.

This success might have presented Stevens and Tyler with the challenge of performing together – 'I've done duets before but never on stage,' admitted Bonnie at the time – but there's no record of the pair ever performing the song live. The video, shot in sultry monochrome, had them descending separate staircases to meet in the middle – though, both being happily married performers, they drew the line at acting out the 'hugging and kissing' sentiments of the lyrics. 'I don't think you should take the words too seriously,' cautioned Shaky.

Guitarist Les Davidson recalls 'A Rockin' Good Way' as 'one of the easiest records to make, a straightforward twelve-bar blues. And the band was well oiled, we played very well together by that time. When you do lots of live gigs and then go into the studio, the band look at each other and know what's going to go on.

'I remember Bonnie being at Eden Studios and sitting talking to her in the little café area outside. I think both of them can be fiery characters. They're Welsh, they're Celts. I don't think there's anything strange in that.' And was all smooth between the two singers? 'I wasn't aware of them not getting along, but I'd heard that they didn't,' Davidson revealed. 'They were certainly laying down the track around the same time, but I don't think they laid them down at [exactly] the same time. Whatever, they made quite a good record, I thought.'

The single that followed this into the chart, 'A Love Worth Waiting For', had actually been the first track cut without

Stuart Colman's reassuring hand. In fact, as drummer Chris Wyles remembers it, the first the band knew about it was when they turned up to cut the song and found no sign of the producer to whom Shaky owed so much. 'There was a six-piece band in the studio, so Shaky said, "We're all here, we've rehearsed the material. Let's just do it."' His insistence on pushing ahead with the recording was vindicated when 'A Love Worth Waiting For' climbed to Number Two in the spring of 1984, to give him his third Top Five success in a row. It was notable too as the first session in which the vocal team of Tony Rivers, John Perry and Stuart Calver assembled – a triumvirate of talented singers whose blend would become a distinctive part of the Shaky sound. They would enjoy a run of hit records with Shaky, which lasted throughout the 1980s even though the singers accompanying Rivers would come and go.

A contemporary interview reveals Shaky's understandable pride at his achievement. 'I've got into record production lately. I co-produced the current single, and it's something I'd like to do more of in the future. Maybe even with other bands. I'd also like to try my hand at acting, although nothing's really come my way as yet. Nothing really since I did *Elvis* in the West End.'

In Les Davidson's opinion, 'A Love Worth Waiting For' was nothing special, 'a standard mid-tempo rock 'n' roll song, very much in the late-1950s style. It was easy to record because it fell under the fingers for all of us and, because we understood the genre, there wasn't a problem.' Its success proved that while album sales had slipped, Shaky still retained the hit-single touch.

He was unlucky to find Lionel Richie's maudlin (but commercially triumphant) ballad 'Hello' in residence at the top, as this meant that 'A Love Worth Waiting For' was forced to spend two weeks in its shadow. In an era where few artists were entering the chart at peak position, Shaky's singles seemed to describe a graceful parabola: this one entered at 22 in late March, climbing first to 7 and then 3 before falling away down to 6, 15, 27, 39 and 57. Quite a contrast to today's 'straight in, straight out' chart hits. Shaky's main method of promotion came via appearances on variety TV showcases like *The Russell Harty Show*. The video of 'A Love Worth Waiting For', which was filmed over two days, at Farnham and Chiddingfold, Surrey, featured Jason, Shaky's son, playing Shaky as a child.

Shaky made his one and only foray into the US singles chart during May, when 'Cry Just A Little Bit' made it to Number 67. He'd never really take off there, despite the Jack Good TV exposure several years earlier. This 1981 review from *The Washington Post* of a North American album release, *Get Shakin'*, indicates that they were not about to let this Welshman sell them their own music without a fight: 'Stevens has had considerable success as a neo-rockabilly cat on the British charts in recent years. Early on he was produced by Dave Edmunds, who also appreciates the exuberant pulse of the original Sun recordings. Unfortunately, Stevens's latest release comes up short in that department. The album, which includes several of Stevens's British hits, suffers from a shallow mix, some disposable songs and a lack of focus.'

By April 1983, the same paper had changed its tune somewhat: 'Much like Cliff Richard, another British superstar sprung whole from Elvis Presley's swivelling hips, Stevens has enjoyed massive hits everywhere but America. His latest release, *Give Me Your Heart Tonight*, is an impressive collection of polished rockers that draw equally on rockabilly and Louisiana rock 'n' roll. If Stevens has escaped popularity in America, it's probably because his easy-going adult image and joyful classicism don't strike as deeply with young rock fans as the rebellious narcissism and primitivism more typical of American rockabilly.'

Back in mid-1981, Shaky had said that while some of the singles were being released in America, he'd 'no plans to tour just yet. Strangely enough, American performers like Gene Vincent, Buddy Holly and Eddie Cochran were far more popular in Britain before they won over American audiences. And at the moment there is no one in America singing in the same style as me.' By 1983 he'd grown more ambitious: 'Further afield, I've had several gold records in Canada. The United States will be next, I think, because I'm having success just above and just below their borders so it looks like I'll be closing in on them very shortly.' For whatever reason, though, it never happened.

His next British single, 'A Letter To You', was written by Texan Dennis Linde – best known in rock 'n' roll circles as the songwriter of Elvis Presley's 'Burnin' Love', though eagle-eyed Shaky fans would have spotted him as co-writer (with Billy Swan) of 'Vanessa'. Stevens's version made it to Number Ten in the UK in September '84, though female songstress Eddy Raven would take the song to Number One in the US country chart five years later. 'It was virtually the same arrangement, in fact it was a straight nick,' grumbled Shaky. Ah well, maybe the singer was just ahead of his time . . .

In 1984, he explained the philosophy he had adopted when picking songs by outside songwriters (a task that had fallen to him due to Stuart Colman's absence). 'It's a bit like sticking your hand into a bag and hoping you come out with a hit!' he admitted. 'There are so many talented songwriters working away out there that you get hundreds submitted to you, so you need as much time as possible to consider them all properly.'

November brought the first 'greatest hits' compilation of Shaky's career, anthologizing eighteen singles from 'Hot Dog' onwards. This made Number Eight in a very competitive UK chart. The self-penned 'Teardrops' was extracted in December as Shaky's now customary Christmas release – though not, of course, seasonally themed this time. It hit UK Number Five and featured the great Hank Marvin on lead guitar. The connection, of course, was Christopher Neil, who'd produced the ex-Shadow, then taking a break from his legendary instrumental group.

Unfortunately, the 'guest appearance' was at the expense of band guitarist Les Davidson, who'd actually devised the solo. 'And the weird thing was that they said do a solo like Hank

Marvin, so I did . . . then they got Hank in to play my solo.' Fortunately, the Scotsman, a lifelong Shadows fan, took his ousting in good part. 'For me it was great because he was, you know, Hank Marvin. I'd grown up with The Shadows and the background of my music . . . I got to meet him very briefly, and he's a very nice guy.' While Hank overdubbed his contribution to the track separately, he turned up when a version of it had to be recorded for TV, allowing the band to meet a legend.

Chris Wyles hazards a guess that Shaky may have had some technical assistance in writing 'Teardrops' from Roger McKew: 'Roger used to go round to Shaky's house and, if Shaky had an idea for the melody, Roger would quite often work out where the chords were.' Certainly, the collaboration gave Shaky more satisfaction than any duet: 'I've had the pleasure of Hank Marvin playing lead guitar on one of my tracks, one I wrote as well. That's a great feeling. Not everyone likes Hank, but there are millions that do. He's a legend, he's fantastic. He influenced lots of people from Eric Clapton, right across the board.'

Shaky clearly got a big kick out of songwriting, even if the pace of life limited his opportunities. 'When you begin, a song is just a collection of individual lines jotted down on scraps of paper that could be all over your house. Then, as you link those up, the ideas for a melody will come to you and you start to turn it into a song. After the musicians are rehearsed and the number is recorded in the way you imagined it, the final mixing is something you just have to be involved in, because a song can come out of that sounding completely different.'

The track was credited to a three-way production team of Chris Neil, Rod Hewson and Shaky himself. Tony Rivers's backing trio of vocalists were now something of a fixture, but were able to juggle dates and, for at least a year, serve both Cliff and Shaky – until the former went into Dave Clark's West End musical *Time* for a spell in April 1986.

While Rivers and company had been fairly stationary when performing with Cliff, so as not to distract people from the star of the show, Shaky wanted them to dance, handclap and generally be a part of the entertainment. This, Rivers admitted, was 'an eye opener'. Not only did they have to reproduce the harmonies on existing records, but new arrangements were also required as well as dance routines and clapping. 'We came to a compromise,' said the singer, 'but it's always been a bit volatile.'

Rivers, a hardened showbiz professional, had seen stars come and go, but admitted that his first experience of Shaky live blew him away. 'I've never seen anyone move as well as him, or have the ability to whip up so much excitement in the audience with just a bend of his knee or something similar. Cliff is great on stage, but so was Shaky, and I never got that "buzz" watching Cliff move like I did with Shaky.' High praise indeed!

Chris Wyles viewed the situation from behind the drum kit with some amusement: 'It was quite funny really, it never went down very well with Tony and his guys, all this jumping up and down. Shaky basically didn't want them to stop moving from the word go on the stage shows, so if they didn't have anything to sing they had to clap their hands or whatever, and I know they didn't like it, having to do physical things. Having been "heard and not seen," suddenly they've got to put on a show as well.'

Touring continued apace. Wyles recalls the younger band members gathering together on the road – 'Gavin and I were roommates and about the same age.' A piano bar called The Home of the Boogie Woogie Piano in Munich would give Povey his chance to shine in an incident all the band still recall with amusement. Chris Wyles tells the story: 'Boogie-woogie pianists would come from all over the world to play at this bar, and we went in there with our tour jackets on and they started taking the piss because they thought Shaky was rubbish. I was with Irish [sax player John Earle] and a couple of others. The next night we did our gig in Munich and went to the piano bar afterwards with Gavin.

'Now, Gavin is the most fantastic piano player and at a gig

you could rely on his left hand like you wouldn't believe, it's so strong. He pounds away throughout the whole gig and you'd never see him break sweat. So he got onto the piano and started playing. It was like a boogie-woogie competition, he did a few of his best tricks and you could see they were quite impressed. Then a German got on the piano and joined in. Gavin looked at him and modulated the key, so the guy was getting a bit lost as to where he'd gone. He'd find it and then Gavin would modulate it again. This carried on for twenty-five minutes, at the end of which he was dripping with sweat. He finished, got up and got a round of applause – and had free drinks for the rest of the evening!'

Elder statesmen Les Davidson and Roger McKew also roomed together. 'Roger first and foremost is a fantastic guy, a fantastic guitar player and very capable of playing many more styles than he played with Shaky,' Davidson reveals. 'He's a great country player, but he's also able to mix in blues and rock and a bit of jazz as well. And rather like me he listened and listened to a lot of different players so we could find common ground – people like Jimmy Reed, and he would enjoy Hendrix as I did as well. And in return he would introduce me to lots of country players, Jimmy Bryant and people like that, whom I'd never really heard of. Roger was a mainstay of the band, the glue that held it together and a real calming influence. A very gifted musician.' And there now was plenty to hold together. The band that had started out as guitars, bass, drums and piano had added first a brass section and then backing singers.

Another *Greatest Hits* cut – 'Breaking Up My Heart', a song by Bobby Heatlie – was extracted in the spring of 1985 and reached Number 14 in the UK charts. But Chris Wyles found recording this an unsatisfying experience: '"Breaking Up My Heart" was a bloody difficult track, one of those hybrid ones where we used a bit of drum machine and what have you, and mixed it in with the live players.' The song was promoted on TV chart show *Top of the Pops* – the fiftieth time Shaky had appeared. But that would be the last the world heard from Shakin' Stevens until the end of the year.

Don Reedman – CBS Records Director of Concept and Marketing – was the man charged with coordinating the release of TV-advertised albums, and Shaky's *Greatest Hits* was one of the first albums he tackled after joining the company earlier in 1984. 'We came up with the idea of doing it with an upbeat feel,' he says. 'It was a feel-good, fun, party record. We were releasing the album in November and it was a perfect concept to take it through to Christmas. We sold well over platinum, nearly half a million, and I worked with him on the whole creative process.

'Shaky had a very clear perception of what he was about – he understood himself very well, and so did his manager. Freya was a very intelligent woman who understood him well. He always had good ideas for himself and was very good to work with, was always very professional and he delivered.' Given the bad press that Miller sometimes attracted, it's perhaps refreshing to hear Reedman speak so supportively of her: he found her 'demanding, but always in the best professional interest of the artist. I didn't find her unreasonable, I got on very well with her. She was very sympathetic to what I needed and she also demanded I was sympathetic to him; she was very good indeed.'

Don Reedman's vision for the campaign, with which Shaky concurred, was to sell records beyond his usual fan base. 'His music was very upbeat, with a party atmosphere and I wanted to convey that, not just to Shakin' Stevens fans [but people] who would buy a feel-good Christmas party album,' he later explained. 'He agreed with that, he understood what it was that made people like him, and worked well on it – it wasn't difficult at all.'

Reedman, who would go on to invent the concept for Tom Jones's career-reviving *Reload* album of duets in 1999, remained part of a fast-changing scenario at CBS/Epic. In mid-'85, Maurice Oberstein – responsible for signing Stevens to the label – moved to Polygram, and the resultant staff changes did our man few favours. Newcomers were more interested in picking up new projects than a known quantity, and it was inevitable that Shaky's battle to cling on to his status would become more difficult.

However, the one thing he still had on his side was Freya Miller. 'Lots of things could be said about Freya,' admits guitarist Les Davidson, 'but the one thing that is quite clear about her, she was a very good manager. A manager's job is to further the artist's career both artistically and financially, and she did both of those. She certainly did it financially. What cut she was getting, I have no idea, but I'm sure it wasn't a small percentage. Knowing Freya, it was probably a very healthy one. But she did what she was supposed to do and ran a tight ship. I personally got on with her quite well. With most people in showbiz I've always used the attitude they are just another human being. If you look through the bullshit you just find another person.

'With Freya you knew exactly where you stood and if you were straight with her she was straight with you. I think she also liked the fact she was in command of a team of men, she was the boss – she liked that . . . I never had any quarrels with her and one thing I will say is that I don't remember any of the band ever complaining about money. It was always there when it was supposed to be paid.'

It's a common theme among the people who worked with Shaky and Miller at the time. Chris Wyles found Freya 'very tough [when] dealing with money or financial stuff, but I got on with her at times . . . if her shoulders were dropped down you could have a normal chat with her, but if you did business with her she was tough. She had the odd shout at roadies and people, but very rarely did she interfere in the band itself.'

Peter Collins had replaced Chris Neil as producer of the *Greatest Hits* bonus tracks and singles: 'Chris was very, very busy,' recalls Davidson, 'and I think he probably wasn't available to do something, so they got someone in – and if it was any good they hung onto it. That's very much what Shaky's camp was like.' But 1985 would see the surprise reappearance of Dave Edmunds as producer, whose expertise had last been employed on the first Sunsets album. Edmunds' career had seen its ups and downs – the ups including a spell with Nick Lowe, Terry Williams and Billy Bremner as Rockpile, which brought a string of hits between 1979 and 1981. Since then, he'd been moving gradually back into studio work, his most high-profile clients in 1983 being the reunited Everly Brothers, whose comeback single 'On The Wings Of A Nightingale' was an Edmunds production.

Shaky's band now consisted of Dick Bland, Chris Wyles, Gavin Povey, Roger McKew and new boy Ian Aitken, who took over lead guitar duties from Les Davidson in 1985. It must have been difficult for the relatively inexperienced Scot playing lead guitar in the presence of such an able axeman as Edmunds, and some fans made the obvious but unfair comparison. Les Davidson had received three offers to work with three major artists: Joan Armatrading, Meat Loaf and Paul Young. 'They all came in at once,' he smiles, 'and they were all desperate to have me in their band. It was a very difficult situation for me, but then it got solved in my own mind because Ian Aitken who comes from Edinburgh, where I'm from, was introduced to me through a mutual friend. He said he was thinking of coming down to London and looking for a gig, so I thought it was the perfect situation.

'I decided to go with the Joan Armatrading tour, and felt the cleanest way to do it was to get somebody lined up. So I introduced Ian to the band. Because I knew he was a great player there was going to be no problem. He was the perfect replacement.'

November's album release, *Lipstick, Powder And Paint*, saw Shaky return to his rock 'n' roll roots, and as such was ecstatically received by long-time fans. (Shaun Mather's Rock 'n' Roll Hall of Fame website, which had stopped listing Shaky albums after *Give Me Your Heart Tonight*, was particularly impressed.) Gavin Povey contributed the exceptional ballad 'I'm Leaving You', but there were plenty of rock 'n' roll classics to keep the purists happy in the shape of Johnny Restivo's 'The Shape I'm In' and Billy Fury's 'Don't Knock'. The Blasters songbook, which had yielded 'Marie Marie', was revisited for the Dave Alvin composition 'So Long Baby, Goodbye'.

Chris Wyles detected a considerable relaxation in the studio atmosphere with Edmunds' arrival, particularly compared with the Chris Neil era. 'While Chris had been kind of particular about things, Dave Edmunds was very laid-back,' Wyles remarked. 'It all went very, very smoothly with Dave. It was quite tempestuous with Chris in the beginning, and I think Shaky was quite relieved. Whereas he and Chris came from completely different musical backgrounds, Edmunds came from a background of rock 'n' roll. He had a huge selection of guitars and that was more his focus.' Micky Gee would also return to the ranks in place of Ian Aitken.

Aitken was a very good reader of music and used his talents wisely, going on to play in a number of West End shows including *Blood Brothers*, and he later worked with Kirsty MacColl. His history also includes spells with The Wigsville Spliffs – a young rockabilly trio who never actually made an album but who were regulars at the Klub Foot, London's premier venue for such acts – and The Bus Stop Boys, a swing/jazz-type band. He then appeared on some recordings by Scottish folk group New Celeste, whose former guitarist Graeme Duffin had, ironically, made the reverse journey to the charts with Wet Wet Wet.

Sadly, Ian suffered from diabetes and died around 1997. 'We used to call him "Stomach,"' says New Celeste's Iain Fergus. 'He was jovial, liked to live life to the full and was very amusing. Shakin' Stevens was his first major band, though he was well known on the Edinburgh scene. A very adaptable player who could play classical guitar very well. Jazz, rock, all styles. With us he played everything from banjo to guitar synthesizer.'

The *Lipstick, Powder And Paint* album would reach Number 37 in the UK, while its title track, a revival of a mid-1950s US R&B hit for Shaky's favourite bluesman, Big Joe Turner, made Number Eleven in its respective chart. The song had been in his pocket for several years, having been suggested by B. J. Cole. During the filming of the 'Lipstick, Powder And Paint' video at the Duke of York Theatre in London's West End, the singer almost injured himself when he flew off the stage after an ill-judged cartwheel. This mishap was edited from the final cut, but was later aired on kids' TV programme *Swap Shop*.

It was to be a non-album track, 'Merry Christmas Everyone', that would make 1985 a memorable year for Shaky, by becoming the singer's fourth Number One and set a pattern for future releases. Penned by Bobby Heatlie, it topped the UK chart in the Christmas week of 1985. The song had been one of the first tracks laid down with Dave Edmunds and had originally been due for release the previous year, but was sensibly canned so as not to clash with the release of Band Aid's charity single 'Do They Know It's Christmas?', which swept all before it on the charts. Amazingly, Shaky's hit would be Wales's last UK single chart-topper until the Manic Street Preachers ascended the summit in 1998 with 'If You Tolerate This Your Children Will Be Next'.

'He didn't ask for a Christmas song,' remembered songwriter Heatlie, 'but I'd always wanted to write one, and it seemed a good time to do it. Christmas singles are the ones that will get played again and again if they are popular, so it seemed to make commercial sense. I always remember writing it because I did it during July, when there was a massive heatwave. It seemed a little ironic to be sitting in my little studio in Edinburgh in my shorts, sweating profusely, and writing about Christmas and jingle bells.'

Heatlie knew from the minute he wrote the song that it would be a hit, and it has since become one of the most played records each December, earning its writer about £8,000 a year in royalties: 'I had a real spark when I finished it – it just had that factor that makes something a success.' Released on 7 December 1985, it broke the record for the most singles sold within ten hours (a staggering 152,000 copies). It also achieved the notable feat of knocking Whitney Houston's debut hit 'Saving All My Love For You' off top spot.

The song was, amazingly, the first and only time backing singer Tony Rivers, in any of his many incarnations, ever made Number One in the UK charts, and he proudly recalls sitting in the dressing room at the NEC in Birmingham watching Shaky on *Top of the Pops* with his trio on backing vocals . . . while waiting to go on stage with Cliff Richard! And on his website he jokingly claims never to have received the gold disc he was promised by Freya Miller.

Shaky and Cliff made a joint appearance at the Brighton Centre on 21 December 1985 when, along with Hank Marvin, Mike Read and Annabel Croft, they participated in the annual Christmas Celebrity Tennis Tournament. Shaky had been coached by ex-pro Onny Parun and played well. He even stuck around to join in a post-match performance of festive carols.

Stories abounded as to the extent of Shaky's fame. One fan letter from Holland addressed simply to 'Shakin' Stevens, England' – still reached its destination, and another girl tried to bribe a hotel porter with £50 to find out her idol's room number. Whether or not they knew he was a happily married man was an open question, due to Freya Miller's habit of deflecting personal questions during interviews. If she was at pains to conceal her charge's private life from public gaze, then so did the man himself. He was even rumoured to be registered on the electoral roll as Clark Kent (some would have it he'd changed his name by deed poll, though it seemed unlikely).

Shaky's wife Carole had kept in the background before their marriage was made public, and few were aware that the singer was a father of three children (Jason, Paula and Dean). Many pop stars have kept their private lives private, but Shaky certainly went to great lengths to achieve this end. In a rare interview with *Smash Hits* that touched on his offstage life and suggested a new, more relaxed attitude towards the press, he revealed that his children had realized his was no ordinary job fairly early on in the proceedings: 'It's just something they've grown up with and accepted. Obviously they're pleased I'm doing well, but whether they particularly like my music or not I'm not sure! When I want to watch my new video on television it's very difficult to keep them quiet. I say, "Please can I just watch this?" and they say, "Aw . . . if you must."

'It's good like that, it's down to earth. Much better than if they all sat down watching every time I came on. In fact, when I'm singing around the house they are always telling me, "Give it a rest, Dad, will you?"'

As a parent himself, Shaky was happy to help when an SOS went out to him in 1985 after eleven-year-old Wendy Downham suffered serious head injuries in a road accident. After two weeks in a coma, Wendy returned to consciousness after her parents played tapes of all her favourite Shakin' Stevens songs. And when the singer heard what had happened, he made a special visit to the hospital. 'Wendy was so surprised when Shaky walked in and went straight to her bedside that she could hardly speak,' said her father Richard. 'Shaky's her whole life. She's filled the house with his photographs and posters – now *I* think he's a wonderful guy, too!'

But whether or not it was the fact that chart fortunes, particularly on the album front, had started to decline, or whether it was simply a general sense of world-weariness, Shakin' Stevens was beginning to feel things were getting out of his control. 'I was really naive in the early days. I trusted everyone around me and focused on the music,' he mused later. 'There was no time to get involved in the marketing or anything else. For five years I did too much and didn't stop at all. We should've stood back, taken a break and then moved on to the next stage. But unfortunately, we didn't.'

7

HITS FADE: 1986–93

THE YEAR OF 1985 had ended on a seasonal high for Shaky, but
'86 wouldn't prove quite as rewarding in chart terms – and
there were few signs of him gaining a fifth UK chart-topper.

February found 'Turning Away', the first track on side two
of *Lipstick, Powder And Paint* and written by Tim Krekel, giving
him his first chart entry of the year. But however satisfying the
song was in musical terms, its Number 15 peak was the lowest
for a Shaky single since August 1980 and 'Marie Marie'.
Krekel, incidentally, was a singer-songwriter and one-time
member of the Billy Swan band, and the song had been a
country-chart Number One hit in the States in 1984 in the
hands of long-haired songstress Crystal Gayle.

The video was filmed in front of a live audience at the
Greyhound pub in Fulham, one of the London pub venues
The Sunsets had played a decade earlier. Dave Edmunds, who
produced the song, was prominent on guitar in the video –
though Messrs Aitken and McKew had taken care of the duties
in the studio. The clip was directed by Mike Mansfield, fondly

recalled for his *Supersonic* pop programmes in the 1970s, but also, in the early part of the decade, a man who worked extensively with Adam Ant.

Shaky sadly lost his mother in 1984, his father having passed away ten years previously when Shaky was on the road with The Sunsets. Certainly, the fact that neither of his parents were now around may have persuaded him to slow down the pace and enjoy life, in its broadest sense, a little more. He appears to have taken a break throughout most of 1986, making full use of a set of golf clubs his wife had given him as a birthday present. 'Although I'd never really had an interest in the game before,' he told *Look In* magazine, 'I can honestly say that I've been bitten with the bug! My best score is ninety-four, which isn't really that fantastic, but isn't too bad for the amount of time I've been playing. When you hit the ball right and you hear that crack, it's a terrific feeling.'

His home in Woking, Surrey, was ideally situated for access to some of the country's top golf courses, and in the years to come he would make a point of playing on as many foreign fields as he could – the United Arab Emirates Golf Club in Dubai, apparently one of the world's best courses, a treasured example. Partners included Tony Rivers and his son, and the trio once took on Epic Records supremo Paul Russell, together with a couple of other CBS executives at St Pierre Golf Club in Chepstow – and beat them! Given that his answer to a questionnaire poser asking how he relaxed was 'to get out and walk in the fresh, country air,' it seemed the ideal hobby, and one that put him on a par with such well-known rock golfers as Alice Cooper and Mötley Crüe's Vince Neil.

It was in a restaurant in Wentworth, one of Shaky's golfing haunts, that he ran into ex-manager/producer Mike Hurst for the first time in about five years. 'I'll always remember the waiter kept referring to him as Mr Shaky!' Hurst recalls with amusement. 'I still like Shaky, and even though I heard he became a bit aggressive, that wasn't how I knew him at all. He came across as gentle, not the brightest guy, maybe a bit immature, but a great performer who believed in what he did.'

Dave Edmunds had, it seemed, only been engaged for a single album, for by the time Shaky featured again in the singles charts, in November 1986 with 'Because I Love You', he had reverted to Chris Neil as producer. This single climbed one rung higher than its predecessor and its Number 14 success made history for the singer. '"Because I Love You" is my twenty-second chart hit in a row,' he noted. The video, incidentally, was shot not far from Shaky's home at picturesque Leith Hill, Surrey.

That wasn't the only chart action he'd enjoy. When 'Merry Christmas Everyone' re-charted the following month, making the UK Top Sixty, it was clear it was on the way to achieving the iconic status of . . . well, if not Bing Crosby's 'White Christmas', then perhaps Slade's 'Merry Christmas Everybody'. 'It's a traditional Christmas record, so why not?' said its singer, comparing it with Band Aid and Wham!'s 'Last Christmas'.

Album-wise, however, the rot had clearly set in. Released in October, the album *Let's Boogie* didn't do nearly as well as had the single, reaching only Number 59. There had been an unusually long two-year break between albums, and its failure to dent the Top Forty looked ominous. In truth it was a real grab-bag of an effort, with a second vinyl side that contained a live medley of hits recorded at the London Palladium in December 1986. Side one consisted of a new album track, the three previous singles, and a cover of the Emile Ford and the Checkmates' 1959 chart-topper 'What Do You Want To Make Those Eyes At Me For?'

Chris Wyles reveals that, after the Dave Edmunds connection ended, Shaky had tried to return to Stuart Colman 'to try to get back to where he'd been six or seven years previously . . . and it just didn't seem to happen'. The nearest thing to a title track on the album was 'A Little Boogie Woogie (In The Back Of My Mind)', a minor hit in 1977 for Gary Glitter and a curious choice for a cover, let alone identifying an album. It also led to a brief liaison with Glitter's producer and co-writer, Mike Leander. 'If I remember rightly that was one of the things Shaky had kicking around that he wanted to do, and someone put two and two together and must have said, "How about getting Mike Leander to do the production?"' Wyles remembers. 'So that was the only thing we did with him; it was back to the Chris Neil kind of approach.

'He booked us into Mayfair Studios and got me and the bass player to go in at 9 o'clock in the morning. We recorded the backing track of just bass and drums, no chord information, no guide vocals, nothing, and my contribution was finished by 10.15 a.m. We were out the door! He didn't hang about, Mike Leander, and the record was finished by the next day.'

The session was closely followed by a reunion with Stuart Colman, which yielded future single 'Come See About Me'. This revival of the Supremes' 1964 million-selling Motown oldie reached Number 24, and was a bizarre choice given Colman's encyclopaedic knowledge of rock 'n' roll.

Although Colman had produced the album version of 'What Do You Want To Make Those Eyes At Me For?', Shaky re-entered the studio to cut a new take for single release. 'The second version was produced by Carey Taylor, who was Dave Edmunds's engineer and who I believe was a partner in the setting-up of Metropolis Studios,' says Chris Wyles. 'I know that Shaky wasn't happy with the first version, I don't think anybody was really, so he went back to Carey Taylor who engineered the album with Dave Edmunds and got him to do the production, and it became a Top Five hit single.' The track was, indeed, a success, with a then unknown Vic Reeves starring in the video.

The Colman-produced tracks had been cut in one lengthy session at Marcus Studios, but in Wyles's view 'the magic between Stuart and Shaky wasn't quite there. It was quite a painful experience, actually. I think we were doing backing tracks and spending ages and ages fixing little bits here and there.'

The album's side-long live medley, entitled 'The Hits Keep Coming', was from a show at the London Palladium. Chris Wyles recalls it as 'quite a difficult thing to play'. Although some people have assumed it's a studio creation, it was a genuine live recording which, says the drummer, 'is a measure of how good the band was'. Gavin Povey felt Shaky 'almost ran out of people to produce him, and he ended up producing himself which I think was a mistake. You needed someone of a certain stature at that point, as he's had the hits, and in a way was too big for some producers. Shaky was best just being the artist and the performer. I don't think he thought he was the latest Elvis, in fact I think he was wise to that pitfall, and in a sense he ran away from all that. Really simply, Shakin' Stevens was/is Shakin' Stevens. It was a case of "This is what I do"!'

But all was not lost – far from it. While the record scene was looking anything but promising, Shaky's live reputation was as hot as ever. A tour of the Eastern Bloc in 1987 (two years before the Berlin Wall came down) took in Poland, Hungary, Czechoslovakia and East Berlin. On arrival in Warsaw, the band were bussed to Gdansk, five hours distant, to find that Shaky had already arrived following a TV appearance in Germany – this was par for the course. One of the gigs in East Germany was filmed and put out on television.

Shaky celebrated his thirty-ninth birthday in Warsaw, which provoked a rare evening of togetherness among the touring party: 'They set something up at the show that night. Somebody walked on the side of the stage and presented me with some flowers, and then the band played "Happy Birthday". After that, everybody had a meal. The road crew, sound men, lighting engineers, lorry drivers; we all went back to our hotel, where there was a lovely cake for me. We all had a sing-song! It was marvellous: a night I won't forget, and a total surprise.'

Tabloid reporter Rick Sky accompanied the band behind the Iron Curtain, and was astounded at what he saw.

'Throughout the show Shaky, who puts in as many of his twenty-two smash hits as he can, was bombarded with cuddly toys and flowers. Proud dads even held up their tiny daughters to get a kiss from the singer. The fans' devotion is even more amazing when you realize that a ticket cost about one tenth of an average Polish worker's monthly salary. The people have had to scrimp and save hard for their seat in this sell-out show, just like they do for other Western goods. Says Shaky: "It's incredibly flattering. It really inspires me to put on a good show."'

Shaky told Sky he couldn't help noticing the difference between his UK tours and the East-European equivalent: 'Things that we take for granted as necessities, they often don't have. One countryside hotel didn't have any milk or proper toilet paper. But I don't mind. For one thing it keeps you firmly down to earth.' After the show, some of his Polish fans, determined to meet their idol, fearlessly ran the Freya gauntlet . . . without conspicuous success. 'My manager caught a couple of them lurking along the corridor in our hotel. And a number of times when they spotted me leaving the hotel they even tried to bundle their way into the car with me. But I think really all they want is my autograph – once they get that they're quite happy.'

Chris Wyles certainly enjoyed the experience of touring with Shaky in such places: 'At that point western bands weren't really going there that much, but the government knew there was a lot of unrest with the youths and so started to bring people through and have western pop music. Interesting trip really, especially one place called Bialystok, which is right up on the coast, and was amazing.'

It wasn't so much a case of Shaky's popularity waning at home but of his genuine popularity in Europe that saw him playing at venues recently populated by the likes of The Rolling Stones and Spandau Ballet. Norway, Sweden, Denmark, Holland and Germany all saw the Welshman play at big indoor gigs – in Gothenburg, for instance, he attracted an audience of

The classic Shaky look (*left*): Posing in his characteristic denims in April 1981, Shaky adapts to the rigours of regular photo shoots and public appearances as his career in the music business takes off.

Fame and fortune beckons (*below*): In May 1981 Shaky performed 'You Drive Me Crazy' on BBC TV's *Top of the Pops*. The single peaked at Number Two in the charts, unable to match the success of 'This Ole House', which had become Shaky's first Number One hit earlier in the year.

With his boyish good looks and unique dance moves Shaky was soon wowing audiences of all ages. By the end of 1982 he had secured three Number One singles, two Number Two singles and three bestselling albums.

Above: Anyone for tennis? In December 1985 Shaky took part in a tennis fundraising event in Brighton, alongside the Shadows' Hank Marvin (*left*), Cliff Richard (*right*) and DJ Mike Read (*far right*).

Right: Seven years after his first appearance on *Top of the Pops*, Shaky returns in July 1988 with a performance of 'Feel The Need In Me'.

Left: At the end of a highly successful decade in the music business Shaky sings at the Children's Royal Variety Performance in April 1990.

In September 1992 Shaky joins forces with Queen drummer Roger Taylor on the single 'Radio' (*pictured below during the filming of the video*). The song debuted in the UK Top Forty, but rose no higher than thirty-seventh position in the charts.

Above: After a New Year's Eve drink-driving incident in January 2002, Shaky attends Coleford Magistrates Court where he is issued with a two-year driving ban.

Shaky appears at the launch of the Fifteenth Edition of *The Guinness World Records Book of British Hit Singles* in May 2002 (*right*), where he is presented with a Number One Gold Award, in recognition of his many hit singles throughout the 1980s.

Living legend (*left*): Shakin' Stevens performs his chart-topping hits on the German TV show *Fifty Years of Rock* in Hanover in April 2004.

In the spotlight again: A year later Shaky takes to the stage in the second heat of ITV's music show *Hit Me Baby One More Time*. After renditions of 'This Ole House' and a cover version of 'Trouble', Shaky receives most votes from the viewing public to win a place in the final, beating fellow contenders (*below from second left to far right*) Belinda Carlisle, Clive Jackson (lead singer of Doctor and the Medics), Jaki Graham and Haddaway. In May 2005 he is declared the winner of the entire competition.

Back on top: Shaky performs 'Trouble' on *Top of the Pops* in June 2005 (*right*). The double-A-side release of 'This Ole House' and 'Trouble' peaked at Number Twenty in the UK charts.

To promote his greatest-hits album *The Collection*, Shaky holds a one-off show at Shepherd's Bush Empire in London in spring 2005 (*left*), a precursor to his much anticipated autumn tour.

That old Welsh magic: After a career in the music business spanning almost forty years, fifty-seven-year-old Shakin' Stevens continues to produce quality rock 'n' roll performances that succeed in appealing to old and new fans alike.

8,000 people. And Freya Miller was proud of the fact that, in Germany, Shaky had created history by dominating the singles chart with no fewer than four simultaneous hits.

'It was hard work, but in fact I quite liked it,' says Les Davidson, a veteran of earlier tours. 'There'd only be a couple of ballads in the show, when all the lighters and candles would come out, and the rest of the time it was rock 'n' roll, it was straight down the line.' The guitarist, who now owns a recording studio in London, considered these 'proper rock 'n' roll tours – two coaches, one for the band, one for the crew and a separate arrangement for the artist, who's flying or chauffeur-driven. A couple of pantechnicon lorries, taking your own lighting rig, taking your own catering, so everything was taken care of. Adidas gave us outfits, tracksuit and shoes, and we stayed at the Adidas hotel . . . it was big stuff.'

While Scandinavia and Germany were major Shaky strongholds, he didn't do quite so well in France. Davidson remembers playing at 'a venue that probably held about 2,000 people in Paris . . . I think we went to Spain as well, but I think the Paris gig was thrown in to keep the band and the trucks moving. Having a day off is financially very restricting so you wanna keep everybody working. So I think France wasn't full of fans, but virtually everywhere else the shows were huge. Holland, Sweden, Denmark, Norway, Switzerland, Austria – and, of course, enormous in Germany. Here [in London] we would do a couple of nights at Hammersmith.'

A spring '89 tour of Britain saw Howard Tibble back behind the traps, Chris Wyles having moved from the sublime to the ridiculous and taken up a gig with Dame Edna Everage: 'The show was on for six weeks in the West End, so off I went – but *Back With A Vengeance* ran for nine months and paid very well!

'Suddenly, in the middle of all this, another European tour came up with Shaky. I was recording with a band called Red Box during the day and doing Edna at night, so I had to make a choice between the West End show or going back to Shaky. I said I couldn't do the tour, they got back in touch with Howard [Tibble] and, bless him, he's been there ever since.'

Les Davidson recalls Chris Wyles having to play like a big-band drummer – in effect, leading the band by reacting to the singer's movements. 'Shaky would come out on stage and whip up not only the crowd but the band. Chris, as the drummer, had one of the hardest jobs because Shaky would do the whole dancing thing . . . he would be singing a song and would do this and do that and Chris had to hit cymbals and accents accordingly. He had a tough job, but did it formidably well – he was excellent at it.' When Chris had joined the band, he had had to learn certain things his predecessor had played. Now, with another forty-odd songs that could go in a set, his successor faced an even greater challenge.

Having covered the Supremes, Shaky next turned his attention to the Detroit Emeralds' mid-1970s soul hit, 'Feel The Need In Me', which reached Number 26 in the UK in August 1988. (The wife of Adam Ant appears as one of the dancers in the video.) Chris Wyles, now on the outside looking in after seven years on the team, was not impressed. 'I thought "Feel The Need In Me" was absolutely atrocious!' he says. 'I remember seeing it on TV and feeling quite glad I wasn't there.'

Shaky himself would admit in a 1992 interview that straying onto the other side of the musical tracks had been an error of judgement: 'Reviving songs like "Come See About Me" and "Feel The Need In Me" didn't work because they're the kind of songs best performed by black artists. "What Do You Want To Make Those Eyes At Me For?" was a good record, though, because we gave it a New Orleans-type soul approach, with plenty of brass. I don't think reviving old songs is a bad thing, but you do need to take the song forward somewhat.'

The B-side, 'If I Can't Have You Baby', was a co-write between Shaky and Tony Rivers that had begun life in a Gdansk hotel room. Unluckily for Rivers, it had been bumped from its promised place on the flip-side of "What Do You Want To Make Those Eyes At Me For?', the previous single release and a much bigger seller. 'Freya Miller decided to put something else on that B-side . . . just my luck!' Rivers admits. Nevertheless, he was still pleased to have written a song with Shaky and to have had it recorded. 'I'd never got that lucky with Cliff . . .'

Without a doubt, Shaky's single-chart fortunes were now on the slide too, and when 'How Many Tears Can You Hide?' only made Number 47 in the UK charts in October, it was clear that a change of tack was necessary. It came in December in the shape of a rare ballad hit. Reviving the Bing Crosby/Grace Kelly oldie 'True Love' was a calculated risk, but one that paid off (relative to his recent chart success): it crept into the Top Forty at Number 36. The accompanying album, *A Whole Lotta Shaky*, peaked six places lower in its respective chart.

Having been patronized by Adidas, Shaky found himself selling Heineken lager when ad agency Lowe Howard-Spink signed him up to feature in a poster campaign. The photographs were to be taken by top society snapper Terry O'Neill. 'It was the first advertising job I did,' the latter recalls. 'It was interesting to be asked to shoot many images. Then they put it on a computer. Shakin' Stevens was very easy-going and very patient. It looks quite simple, but it took all day. I think he was a bit nervous about being dishevelled, because he normally looks so immaculate. But once he understood the idea he was quite relaxed. I took a couple of hundred shots, and the art director then selected the shots he wanted to use.'

The year of 1988 ended on an upbeat note when, on New Year's Eve, Shaky was invited to reprise his first chart-topper, 'This Ole House', on BBC TV's *Top of the Pops* as one of the programme's most successful performers. That hit, however, had happened seven long years ago – what could he do to revive his fortunes?

Shaky's next attempt to find a foothold in the charts came in 1989. Here was a step into the unknown – his cover of

Marty Wilde's 'Jezebel' was produced by J. J. Jeczalik, guitarist with avant-garde trio the Art Of Noise. It was probably no coincidence that the band had, just months earlier, collaborated with Tom Jones to return him to the Top Five for only the second time since 1971. But Jones's choice of cover, Prince's 'Kiss', was infinitely more promising than Shaky's version of a 1962 hit, and the disparity in chart position confirmed this: 'Jezebel' peaked at Number 58.

But the man who during the past decade had accumulated no less than twenty-seven Top Thirty hits, unsurpassed by any other act, wasn't finished yet. 'Love Attack' restored him to the UK Top Thirty in May, albeit at Number 28. *Smash Hits* were so impressed that they granted him some eighteen column inches, headed – rather sarcastically – 'The Legend Breaks His Silence'. The accompanying picture showed him in a buttoned-to-the-brim trenchcoat, with turned-up jeans poking out from underneath the hem incongruously. 'I think I've gone off the rails a bit,' Shaky honestly revealed. 'You know, I've sort of fallen off the beaten tracks, and I wake up in the middle of the night and I think, "Aaah my God, what's happened? Jesus Christ, what's going on here?"' It was 'A Little Boogie Woogie' that had inspired the outburst, the song being a departure from the traditional Shaky style and consequently less popular with the fans. Needless to say, he felt the current release 'Love Attack' was the song to bring him back on track. 'It's proper rock 'n' roll and it comes straight from the heart. I'm back with my first love and the white boots are back – and that's what it's all about, you know?' he babbled to an obviously confused *Smash Hits* reporter.

Interestingly, the song's writers, Steve and Heather Taylor, had originally penned 'Love Attack' with Buddy Holly in mind. At the time, Paul McCartney was running a competition to write a song the late bespectacled guitarist might have sung – so, having got in to the final ten, the duo decided they were going to try to get Shakin' Stevens to do it.

'We re-demoed it and sent it to CBS/Epic and a couple of music publishers who all returned standard rejection notes,' Steve explains. 'So Heather decided, out of desperation, to send it to the fan club, to see if anyone would pass it on to Shaky, because we felt he'd like it if he'd actually heard it. She did that in mid-1988 and we heard absolutely nothing.

'Then at the end of '88, Heather decided to ring the fan club and Freya herself answered the phone. "I don't believe this," Freya said. "I rang you yesterday and didn't get a reply. You're on the list to ring today. Shaky loves the song and wants to record it as a single." Next thing we knew, there was a message on the answerphone from Shaky, saying, "We're recording the song in CBS's Whitfield Street Studios, and I'd like to have a talk to you about the arrangement. I love the song and I don't understand why no one's played any of your material to me before."

'He then said, "Do you fancy coming to London, to sit in on the production, just to be there? I can produce it and you can help me." So next day we met Shaky and got involved with the arrangements, which was great. We spent a few days there and I ended up singing backing vocals on the track. He said, "You sound like Buddy Holly, which I'm not going to, so it will be different."

'The song ended up having the Shaky hallmarks all over it, the cymbal smashes and things he puts in, and the band, particularly thanks to Micky Gee, made it sound like a Shaky song. It got released in May that year and we were invited to some of the shows. We couldn't believe it 'cos we got to the first one and fans were running up and down singing "Love Attack" before the show had even started . . . he'd already been doing it live, which was great!'

The Taylors had more luck than Ian Gomm, the Brinsley Schwarz guitarist-turned-piano tuner. 'I tried getting some rock 'n' roll songs I'd written to Shaky,' he remembered. 'I called up Epic Records, and they said, "He's got his own publishing company, Shaky Songs, you're too late." He was good at picking songs – that was his secret. I think [writing his own songs] is where he went wrong – what would you rather have, twenty per cent of something or one hundred per cent of nothing, which is what it dwindled to?'

In 1989, Shaky missed out on some exposure that could well have helped rejuvenate his career when Cliff Richard invited him to appear at 'The Event', a two-day residency to be held at Wembley Stadium on 16 and 17 June. The object was to showcase Cliff in his various modes, including a rock 'n' roll segment. Tony Rivers, who'd served as one of Cliff's backing singers for many a year, was charged with putting together a seventeen-piece outfit christened the 'Oh Boy! Band'.

In the spirit of sharing the spotlight, there were to be guest appearances by The Dallas Boys, The Vernons Girls and The Kalin Twins. Cliff asked Tony, who was on tour at the time with Shaky, to pass on the invitation to do a duet with him: Little Richard's 'Tutti Frutti' was suggested as a possible song for the collaboration. Rivers believed the feeling in the Shaky camp was that the singer's presence was only required to help boost ticket sales – when in fact the Friday show had already sold out without his help, and the Saturday gig soon followed suit – and so the invitation was ultimately declined.

Despite this missed opportunity, Shakin' Stevens ended the 1980s as Britain's biggest singles artist – a fact since confirmed by *Guinness World Records British Hit Singles & Albums*. He followed The Beatles and Elton John in the 1960s and 1970s respectively as the most successful UK singles chart performer of a decade. By 1990 Stevens had thirty hit singles to his name, not to mention a dozen hit albums.

Yet to many people his career could be reduced to the shorthand of three chart-toppers – the 'Christmas Green House Trilogy', as *Record Collector* magazine rather cheekily called it. This would still rile Stevens years later: 'Just because they were Number One doesn't mean they were the best ones,' he fumed. 'I've done far better tunes than "Green Door" or

"This Ole House", but it's a vicious circle because you only hear those two on compilation CDs, and "Merry Christmas Everyone" – people may think I'm a three-hit wonder.'

Keyboardist Gavin Povey left Shaky's employ in late 1989, when a November tour of the Far East that took in Bangkok, Kuala Lumpur and Singapore caused dissension in the ranks: 'Freya Miller had doubled up the shows on each night and so I left about the time we were to tour Thailand.' He formed a band, The Good Rockin' Daddys, playing rock 'n' roll and R&B, before moving to Ireland, where he recorded and/or performed with the likes of Dolores Keane, John Faulkner, Dave Spillane and Finbar Furey. In 1998 he formed his own record label, Stompin' Records, which released a compilation of Irish rock 'n' roll bands, and he has since gigged with several bands, including that of Van Morrison.

Povey briefly rejoined Shaky's band in the 1990s, after Freya Miller had departed the scene, and observed a downturn in fortunes: 'I don't think he was as successful as before, but he had consolidated his audience who were especially loyal in the UK. We were still playing 1,500-seaters.'

As a new decade dawned, March 1990 saw Shaky's run of success continue – against all odds – as 'I Might' reached Number 18 in the UK charts. This track employed the talents of yet another new producer, Pete Hammond, whose background included working with the hottest hit team in the land, Stock, Aitken & Waterman, and whose recent credits included Sinitta and Tina Turner. The single also cemented an unlikely alliance with the country's rudest comic, *Viz*. They had 'adopted' Shaky as a kind of anti-hero, and he had appeared as the centre-forward for Fulchester FC in their 'Billy the Fish' strip (other guest stars had included religious leaders Cardinal Basil Hume and Archbishop Robert Runcie). Shaky returned the compliment by personally commissioning *Viz* artists to show him relaxing with the likes of Roger Mellie, the Fat Slags and Postman Plod.

As a postscript, Graham Dury's painting of Shakin' Stevens surrounded by musical notes was a highlight of an exhibition of the magazine's art later that year. 'It has a Mona Lisa quality, I feel,' reckoned editor Chris Donald, with only part of his tongue in his cheek. 'His eyes follow you around the room.'

Pete Hammond and Shaky would collaborate for three further singles during the year – 'Yes I Do' (Number 60), 'Pink Champagne' (Number 59) and 'My Cutie Cutie' (Number 75). As the chart positions would suggest, 'I Might' received the most radio play, some stations featuring the track as often as four times a day, but there were reports of lack of product in the shops, which instilled no great confidence in the CBS/Epic machine. Indeed, many of those acts that had been with the label since Shaky's arrival had already left or were leaving. And while the singles for 1990 continued to be released on the Epic label, they also appeared on *There's Two Kinds Of Music: Rock And Roll*, a Shaky album released on the TV-advertised Telstar label, in conjunction with Epic, later that same year.

This project reunited Shaky with Don Reedman, the CBS executive who'd helped steer his *Greatest Hits* into so many record collections some six years previously. He concedes it was an attempt by Sony to use TV again to give Stevens a bit of a boost, while avoiding putting significant promotional spend behind what looked like an ailing act. 'Sony didn't believe, and didn't want to put money into TV advertising again, and so turned to Telstar. It was the sort of thing Telstar was doing, venturing into artist projects, but it didn't set the world on fire.' Indeed, with a Number 65 showing in October 1990, with just two weeks in the Top Seventy-Five, this was to mark Shaky's album-chart low-point.

It was, Reedman admits, a more difficult sell than *Greatest Hits*. 'You're never going to do as well as putting them altogether onto one album. It wasn't fresh enough.' But in his view the Freya and Shaky team was still very much functioning. 'They always believed in his ability – Shaky has always believed in himself, and that's a big part of his success, he's never ever doubted he's always going to be a "star". That's the reason these people are successful and become successful again – they're driven by their passion, and that's what makes them as they are.'

'Love Attack' writers Steve and Heather Taylor had another couple of songs on the *There's Two Kinds Of Music* album – 'Pink Champagne' and 'Tell Me', the second of which was covered by another artist in Denmark after Shaky had a hit with it there. Steve Taylor claims that the approach was the same as the one the duo had adopted for 'Love Attack': 'We were obviously more aware of the man's style, but we were trying to bring rock 'n' roll into the modern era – one foot in the 1950s and one foot in the 1990s.'

In terms of songwriting, Shaky's one-time guitarist Les Davidson believes the singer missed out by not realizing the abilities of the people in his band: 'I think sometimes record companies because they're large organizations don't see what they have right in front of their noses. I think Roger McKew was starting to write, and Gavin Povey, the keyboard player, was a good writer as well.' Les has since pitched songs to Shaky's management, but as yet without result. 'He did a song called "Blue Christmas" . . . but not my one!'

Happily the year ended as it had begun, with a Top Twenty single. The success of 'The Best Christmas Of Them All' (pushed by a video shot at Blackpool's Opera House) clearly hit a switch in the Shakin' Stevens machine, as would become clear the following year.

It's a bizarre fact that Christmas records tend to be recorded in the height of summer. So it was that, in August 1991, Shakin' Stevens entered Westside Studios in London to record a festive-flavoured album. It was something of a surprise that he hadn't tried this tack before; no surprise, however, that it took *Merry Christmas Everyone* as its title.

Producer John David, real name John Williams (he changed it to avoid confusion with the classical guitarist), was another Welshman who was well known for his work with Dave Edmunds, teaming up with him in the band Love Sculpture and working with him on his later post-Rockpile career as bassist. As a songwriter, he'd penned 'She Means Nothing To Me', a Top Ten hit for Cliff Richard and Phil Everly in 1983. David collaborated with Shaky on writing 'Merry Christmas Pretty Baby' and an arrangement of the traditional 'Silent Night'. Ronnie Harwood, of 'You Drive Me Crazy' fame, co-wrote three numbers with Stevens, while Gavin Povey chipped in with the closing 'So Long Christmas'. Last but not least, the most successful seasonal song of all time, Irving Berlin's 'White Christmas', also received a Shaky makeover.

The new single from the album, the Stevens/Harwood-penned 'I'll Be Home This Christmas', performed disappointingly: it took until three days after the festivities to reach its peak of Number 34 in the UK charts. This, even though it was promoted 'live' on *TV AM*, and backed by two tracks recorded live at the London Palladium, 'Dizzy Miss Lizzy' and 'With My Heart'.

Shaky's partnership with Freya Miller ended at around this time. She had clearly, and deservedly, prospered from the association, the *Financial Times* of 16 September 1989 reporting that the former rectory in Suffolk she shared with husband John Hart had been put on the market for a cool million pounds. Miller would prove a hard act to follow.

Her replacement was Roy Massey, whose previous management charges had included Alvin Stardust and Gilbert O'Sullivan. He would only remain in place for around three years, but several significant changes were made during his tenure.

Though it wasn't then apparent, the year of 1992 would see Shakin' Stevens bow out of the recording scene. With Epic/CBS the owners of his biggest hits, it was inevitable that another compilation would hit the racks to follow up 1984's *Greatest Hits*, a Number Eight success and Shaky's last UK Top Ten album. It was decided, too, that a bonus single would be recorded in order to stimulate sales, and the production of this was entrusted to the pairing of Rod Argent and Peter Van Hooke.

Argent and Van Hooke had met in the pit orchestra while performing in an Andrew Lloyd Webber show. They had hit it off immediately and developed into a hot late-'80s production duo. What was more, you may remember, the former's progressive band Argent had reportedly been blown off stage by Shaky and the Sunsets back in August 1973 in Emmen, Holland. Van Hooke, for his part, was one of Chris Neil's 'supporting musicians' who had showed up at the producer's first Shaky session nearly a decade previously.

The introduction was made by Roy Massey, whom Rod had known when Massey worked for Astra Agency, then representatives of Argent: 'Peter and I only produced that one single, "Radio", for Shaky, and that was the result of Roy hearing some of the other stuff we did, like Tanita Tikaram's first two albums, the debut album by an American singer/songwriter named Joshua Kadison – which sold two million copies in the US and included three US hit singles – and Nanci Griffith's *Late Night Grande Hotel*, and liking it.'

'Radio' was written by Bob Heatlie and Gordon Campbell, both of whom had previously written for Shaky with 'Breaking Up My Heart' and 'Merry Christmas Everyone' (both Heatlie), and 'Because I Love You' (Campbell). Heatlie had endured 'a bad period for a few years, with divorce and things,' after his Christmas Number One, and wrote relatively few pop songs thereafter, but has since made a second career in music, writing incidental material for children's television shows.

New manager Massey was a great admirer of Queen and, Argent feels, 'wanted to change Shaky's direction – I think that was why [Queen drummer] Roger Taylor played on the record.

What happened was that we were given a demo, which had a few rough edges, and we had to improve it. I played keyboards on it, but Peter Van Hooke isn't on the final thing; he played the drum parts while we were layering the track at my studio, then we hired a bigger London studio where Roger overdubbed his part, because my studio wasn't really big enough.'

Argent and Van Hooke added 'a slightly different approach from Shaky's previous records. I think he wanted to move away from his rockabilly groove a bit . . . We had to recreate that demo that was given to us, and some things on the final record are very different from the demo . . .' As for the singer himself, 'He was well-prepared and just got on with it . . . I thought he was a very sweet guy, very unpretentious.'

At the time, Shaky told *Gold* magazine that he was 'excited about the new record, as I feel it marks a new phase in my career. To have thirty hits in a ten-year span was a great thrill, but it has also been a difficult achievement to emulate. Now though, I feel I'm ready for new challenges, and I'm looking to the future.' He praised Argent and Van Hooke, saying they 'had a great time in the studio because they're both rock 'n' rollers at heart'.

'Radio', unusually credited to 'Shaky featuring Roger Taylor' and with Argent on keyboards, achieved the desired Top Forty placing, but only just, debuting at its Number 37 peak in early October 1992. The video was shot in dramatic black and white; appropriately, the visuals emerged from the speaker of an old-fashioned radio. The clip succeeded in becoming the first by Shaky to be played on MTV, probably due to Taylor's participation.

Argent, who, having been born in 1945 was three years older than Shaky, had grown up listening to the same music and had been 'captivated by rock 'n' roll when I first heard it'; the first single he ever bought was 'Lawdy Miss Clawdy' by Elvis. He puts Shaky's success squarely down to good song choices, 'mainly vintage rock 'n' roll songs. Some of them were even pre-rock 'n' roll songs, like "Green Door", which I remember by Frankie Vaughan, who certainly wasn't a rock 'n' roller.'

Rod, who stayed on Christmas card terms with Shaky for several years and was even invited to his house, was surprised that any musical change had been deemed necessary. 'He's got an excellent voice for rock 'n' roll, which is the music he loves, and he's stayed with that style for most of his career.' He and Van Hooke appeared with Shaky just once, promoting the record on a TV show in Ireland. 'And I think my cousin, Jim Rodford, who's a bass player and played with Argent, and is now in The Zombies, was approached to play with Shaky at one time . . .'

Despite being digitally remastered and featuring no fewer than twenty-five hits, the new greatest-hits album *The Epic Years*, suffered from lack of promotion and could only struggle to Number 57. This would be Shaky's last UK hit album for well over a decade, and it's salutary to think that the far more successful *Greatest Hits* featured more or less the same track listing. The title of the album appeared to mark the end of his association with the label and, though no announcement was made, Epic were not to release any further Shakin' Stevens material with the exception of hits compilations.

Meanwhile, a twenty-two-date UK tour had been set up, kicking off at Croydon's Fairfield Hall on 15 November and climaxing at London's Dominion Theatre, scene of so many past triumphs, on 9 December. Despite his fluctuating fortunes in the charts, Shaky continued to sell out venues. Stage sets and lighting rigs varied year on year, but the level of performance remained of the highest quality. The end of each tour would be marked by a party with his loyal fans, many of whom had travelled the length and breadth of the country to see his shows.

Shaky was used to being told by critics that he lived in the past . . . but a section of his past came back to haunt him in February 1993 when four former members of The Sunsets – Carl Peterson, Steve Percy, Rockin' Louie and Paul 'Duane'

Dolan – sued for alleged non-payment of royalties from the 1970 album *A Legend*. Thus it was that the singer found himself standing alongside producer Dave Edmunds at Cardiff's High Court – though there was little love lost between the two. The Sunsets' argument was that, when *A Legend* was reissued, Shaky and his management had received the royalties of which former manager Paul Barrett insisted that the rest of the band were due a share. 'All he did . . . "Green Door" . . . all those are his,' Barrett confirmed, 'but the records he made with the group belong to the group. And that's what we had to sue him for.' According to newspaper reports, Judge John Weeks, QC, evidently agreed, and the judgement in The Sunsets' favour was handed down on 16 February. While the royalties themselves were modest, costs were estimated at more than £500,000.

'I think the judge thought it was tacky,' says Paul Barrett now, 'but we got every penny that was due to us. It wasn't a fortune. Was it worth about twenty years? It was about seventy grand shared between us. But it cost them half a million. That's the great satisfaction. Not the seventy grand. It cost them half a million and they didn't get away with it. People ask if I'm bitter. Hurt, really. What an unnecessary thing to have done. All they had to do was pay the guys. There was no problem. Just like Cliff did with The Shadows. What's Cliff's is Cliff's and anything they make is theirs.'

Rockin' Louie admits the whole process of taking Shaky to court embittered him. 'It was so unnecessary, paying all those lawyers for all those years. I'll never understand why they did that. They didn't do it together. Edmunds won't talk to Shaky now, and Shaky won't talk to Edmunds. In court they were a separate item totally. Well away from each other. They didn't want to know each other.'

It was Louie's detailed diary from the time that appears to have clinched the verdict. 'The judge called them the *Llewellyn Diaries*. My real name is Robert Llewellyn, and when the judge called them the *Llewellyn Diaries*, it cracked me up. They were trying to say that there was never a contract signed between Edmunds and us. But in my five-year diary I put, "Went down Dinas Powys to see Edmunds to sign the contract with Parlophone." And that was it.

Shaky's manager at the time, Roy Massey, tried his best to avert disaster. 'He realized how ludicrous the situation was,' says Barrett, 'and phoned me when the court case was going on saying, "We've got to stop this," but he arrived too late in the day to save it. It was so stupid. Half a million for seventy grand. It doesn't make sense, does it? I think Shaky hoped that Edmunds would carry the can, and Edmunds expected Shaky to. They were blaming each other.'

As Barrett recalls, however, there was a postscript to the case 'which showed a lot of courage from Shaky. When the whole thing with *A Legend* was coming to a close, he came down to see us with his friend Adrian Owlett, and faced us . . . all the guys on *Legend* . . . me, Louie, Carl, Percy and Duane. So there was five of us and two of them. And they had the balls to face us. And it was great to see them. Shaky was saying, "It's all over now. It's all finished." And we went for a drink in Penarth, and it was great, because we were pals, and he wanted it to be all over. And he invited us to a couple of shows and we had dinner.'

And that was that. Or was it? Barrett again: 'When I spoke to him he would repeat, "It's all over." And I said, "Well, Shaky, how can it be all over because there's *I'm No JD* and *Rockin' And Shakin'*? You know, Steve's a carer, Louie cleans windows, Duane hasn't got a job. You owe these guys and you owe me, just for those records, for nothing else."

'I said, "Send me a cheque for £100,000 and we'll all be pals for ever." And he said he couldn't. And this conversation went on for a while, and in the end I said, "Fuck off." And that's broken the arrow. That's the end of it. Because I can't forgive him for that. I could forgive him if he made it good, but the fact that he won't, I can't forgive him. But, it's not just for me, it's for all of us.

'So, that's the way it remains. It's a shame, because we shared so much. He came to my wedding, and we were on the road when I had the call that his father had died. So I had the terrible decision to make of whether to tell him before the gig or after. I thought there's no point in telling him before. So they did the gig and I actually didn't tell him till the following morning, when I took him to the station and put him on the train to Paddington. So we were close. We shared all that stuff.'

8

FORTUNES ABROAD:
1994–2004

WHEN SHAKIN' STEVENS CELEBRATED his fiftieth birthday in 1998, he did so out of the spotlight.

The touring had continued until 1995, when he took a break to take stock. The 'farewell tour' (though it wasn't billed as such) featured unknown acoustic guitarist Danny Davies in support and kicked off at the Lakeside, in Frimley, Surrey, in late March, running through to the Blackpool Opera House in mid-April. The venues were of sizeable town-hall proportions, the band a mixture of old and new. Faithful retainers Roger McKew and Howard Tibble were still on board, with Tony Rivers's son Anthony Thompson playing guitar, as well as offering backing vocals. Jools Holland's brother Chris played keyboards, with Bob Watkins and Keith Atack on bass and lead guitar respectively. Interestingly, Atack had toured the world with Bonnie Tyler promoting 'Total Eclipse Of The Heart' in 1984, the same year she duetted in the charts with Shaky.

But all good things come to an end, and Shaky came off the road to sort out his business affairs: 'The decade before that it was so heady and manic and come 1984–5 we should have stood back . . . I wanted to see what I had done and what records I had in other territories, just to catch up and look at the whole thing.'

The history books suggest Shakin' Stevens called time on his recording career in 1993, after the release of *The Epic Years*, but that's not quite the whole truth.

Brian Hodgson of Matchbox, who'd written 'Shooting Gallery' on the *This Ole House* album, linked up with Stevens once more in the early 1990s. 'Shaky called me to write some songs with him, but it was like pulling teeth and didn't really work. We subsequently were in Nomis Studio for three to four days working on a number called "Crying Over You", with Howard Tibble, Gerry Hogan and Ian Aitken, but it was never recorded.'

A new single was released in Germany in 1994 – 'I Can Help', Shaky's rendition of the Billy Swan classic from exactly two decades previously. It was a song he'd first heard when The Sunsets were playing the Hope and Anchor pub in London in 1974: 'There was a guy there and he was involved with a group called Brinsley Schwarz. And he came downstairs and said, "You'll appreciate this record" . . . He played it to me and I just thought, "Wow, this is fantastic." I thought it was a terrific record and of course the rest is history because it was a Number One [for Swan] in practically every country.'

Surprisingly, when Shaky first decided to cover a Billy Swan song, originally it was to have been 'Vanessa' on the *Give Me Your Heart Tonight* album, but he'd been inspired to go for 'I Can Help' in the end after seeing Swan at a London show and being invited on stage to sing the song with him. 'When I left that gig I was on a high. I couldn't sleep for the rest of the night, I was so knocked out.' With Epic seemingly out of the picture, the two-track CD single (backed by 'Calling You') on the Arcade label was a Germany-only release – little surprise, given the lingering strength of his support there.

One-off gigs in Denmark and Hungary, and a 1997 support slot to Status Quo at Norwich City's Carrow Road ground were scant fare for his loyal fans to feast on, though when foreign arms of CBS/Epic released compilation albums of old hits, healthy sales suggested a market still existed. In 1999 alone, one went to Number One in Denmark and Number Twelve in Norway.

With a four-year gap in Shaky's touring schedule, some might have wondered whether he was still willing, in his sixth decade, to return to the road. Yet the jaunt that kicked off in April 1999 was fully eighteen months in the making. New manager Sue Davies had fanned a spark of media interest by persuading the *Sun*, Britain's top-selling tabloid, to run a series of articles aimed at encouraging a comeback: the *Daily Star* and *Sunday Times* had also run articles, but at that point Shaky hadn't been ready to step back into the spotlight again.

Twenty dates in April and May took in the same kind of town-hall venues as had the 1995 tour, and, as before, a home-town date at St David's Hall brought Cardiff out in full force. A special support act was selected in the form of Linda Gail Lewis, sister of the iconic rocker Jerry Lee. Using Shaky's band for her backing, she played a set that mixed originals with such 'family jewels' (as she termed them) as 'Great Balls Of Fire'. The partnership was renewed in October at London's Shepherd's Bush Empire, a one-off show preceded the week before by a 'Danse Gala' in Hamar, Norway. The first gig of the new millennium was a corporate event in Cologne, Germany.

Shaky sang two duets with Linda Gail, 'Real Gone Lover' and 'A Rockin' Good Way', while old standard 'This Ole House' saw some welcome new twists in the phrasing. Stalwarts were delighted 'Marie Marie' was still in the set, while the unrecorded, country-styled 'True Love Travels On A Gravel Road' was an absolute delight.

The 1999 band featured exciting newcomer Darrel Higham on guitar alongside the returned Gavin Povey (keyboards) and stalwart Howard Tibble (drums), with Tony Rivers and Anthony Thompson providing the by-now expected vocal backing. But the big news was that Stuart Colman was once again playing bass. He had now become a hotshot producer in Nashville, and it could well be his experience there that led to the tour being billed as 'Hits – Rockin' Country Blues'.

Tony Rivers remembers the 1999 tour as exceptional, especially at the opening show at Ayr, Scotland, on 8 April. 'The audience reaction when Shaky walked on stage [having not toured for some years] was awesome, and he responded to them, whipped them into a frenzy, had them "in his hand" – a great night for all.' When the tour hit the London area at Croydon's Fairfield Hall later in the month the audience was equally responsive, something the veteran singer admitted was rare for capital audiences.

The near sell-out crowd was a mixture of young and old with a surprising number of teenagers, and the tour ended with the Welsh dates including St David's Hall. At this, Shaky asked for the house lights to be turned up and paid tribute to members of The Sunsets in the audience. The encore featured a memorable medley, with plenty of Darrel Higham rockabilly licks including a breathtaking sequence of 'Tear It Up', 'Heebie Jeebies' and 'Rip It Up'.

Press reports during the tour were ecstatic. Scotland's *Daily Record* reported a party atmosphere at Glasgow's Pavilion fostered by groups of fans resplendent in jeans, white T-shirts, denim jackets and plastic 'Elvis' wigs. And audience participation reached an unscheduled peak when, during 'Lipstick, Powder And Paint', 'two lads bounded up on stage to dance alongside him. Shaky took it all in his stride and even stopped mid-song to sign an autograph for one young fan. The only time he almost lost his cool was right at the end, when one woman almost knocked him over in her eagerness to get a kiss from her idol. He may have just turned fifty-one and the trademark jeans and denim jacket might have been replaced by a smart suit, but from the moment he kicked off with "This Ole House", Shaky showed why he was the bestselling singles artist of the 1980s.'

Shortly after the 1999 tour, the band went into the familiar surroundings of Eden Studios and recorded some of the best received songs on the tour, with Stuart Colman as producer. 'How Could You Be Like That?' was a Shakin' Stevens/Ronnie Harwood co-write, while Webb Pierce and Mel Tillis's 'I Ain't Never' has been recorded by both writers as well as Dave Edmunds. Last but far from least was 'True Love Travels On A Gravel Road', a song penned by Dallas Frazier and Al Owens, and originally recorded by the little known Duane Dee in 1968. It was clearly Elvis Presley's version, cut the following year and included on *From Elvis In Memphis*, however, that inspired this performance.

It has been suggested that Darrel Higham was thought 'too rockabilly' to appear on the latter track, and there was certainly some bad blood between him and the Shaky machine that he still feels reluctant to talk about. Higham, who opened the 1999 tour set with a great performance of 'Gone, Gone, Gone', is a hugely respected rockabilly player who now fronts his own band, The Enforcers, and has done session work with the likes of Jeff Beck and Chrissie Hynde.

In 1992, he'd toured the United States with Eddie Cochran's original backing group, The Kelly Four. Yet he is today unwilling to discuss his time with Stevens, even though 'I'd been a fan of Shaky's for many years. I just did one tour with him, and some bits and pieces afterwards. I enjoyed my time with him.'

He was asked to go down and audition by Shaky personally, as they'd met a couple of times before – but he insists 'it wasn't through Stuart Colman', lending credence to the suggestion of musical differences with the producer who calls the studio shots. The problem, insists Higham, wasn't the material – 'It had a lot of the ingredients of rockabilly.' Nor were there problems with the singer himself – 'I like him, he's an okay bloke, but I haven't got good things to say about the experience.' Perhaps a discreet veil should be drawn over the matter.

Whether it was producer or management he fell out with, Higham now plays the low-key European rockabilly circuit, his time with Shaky having failed to provide the leg-up to wider commercial success it had perhaps promised to be. On the plus side, his reputation in his chosen field is second to none, and many of Shaky's fans would welcome him back in the band with open arms.

As a proud Welshman, Shaky was delighted to return to his home city in May 1999 to perform at an all-star one-off show celebrating the launch of the Welsh Assembly. The concert on 26 May was billed as 'Voices Of A Nation' and saw him alongside Tom Jones, Shirley Bassey and Sir Harry Secombe performing in front of the Queen, the Duke of Edinburgh and the Prince of Wales. (The politically driven Manic Street Preachers refused to appear because of the Queen's presence.) He performed the new co-written song, 'How Could You Be Like That?', which had also been featured in the tour set.

The pre-millennium year was certainly offering the opportunity to make up for lost time, and Shaky, his appetite for live performance re-established, simply couldn't keep off the stage. An open-air 'Millennium Street Party' in Cardiff saw him performing to a live audience in excess of 100,000. The event, which also starred The Bootleg Beatles, Brian Connolly's Sweet and 'Voice of an Angel' star Charlotte Church, was broadcast nationally on BBC TV.

This would be no single-song cameo but a full-throttle performance that brought back great memories of the old days. Leaping on stage to the strains of 'This Ole House', Shaky brought down the curtain on the old millennium in fine style with a sixteen-song hit-packed set. 'Hot Dog' and 'Tear It Up' were well-deserved encores earned by a stripped-down band of Micky Gee (once again restored to the ranks as Darrel Higham's replacement), Stuart Colman, Howard Tibble and Gavin Povey, with Tony Rivers and son Anthony Thompson on backing vocals.

Old songwriting pal Brian Hodgson was one of many delighted to see Shaky back in the limelight. 'His strengths are his great moves and grooves on stage. He also has that animal thing on stage. He may have a limited range, but he still has a real feel for what he does.'

In spring 2000, Shakin' Stevens repeated his success with another UK tour, in which he was again advertised as 'performing rock and country blues as well as new arrangements of his hits'. Paul Barrett, who saw Shaky's show at a sold-out St David's Hall, thought the show proved him 'simply the best practitioner of rock 'n' roll since the 1950s. He has proved a lot of critics wrong. He was said to be a 1980s phenomenon, but he is a reminder that rock 'n' roll never went away, and he's surprised a lot of people with his resilience.' High praise indeed!

The support act was Rosie Flores, a girl from Nashville, who 'plays guitar like Chuck Berry and sings like Brenda Lee'. There had been two significant changes in Shaky's own band: Gavin Povey had left for the second and final time, to be replaced by Ben Waters on keyboards and squeezebox, while Martyn Hope from the Elio Pace band was now entrusted with lead guitar duties.

Waters, who would remain in Shaky's employ until 2003, was best known for his musical partnership with Mick Jagger's brother, Chris, as well as playing with his own band. His exciting stride piano style, harking back to the early days of rock 'n' roll, saw him much in demand, and musicians with whom he had shared a stage ranged from Pink Floyd's Dave Gilmour through Rolling Stone Ronnie Wood and The Kinks'

Ray Davies to singer-songwriter (and his cousin) P. J. Harvey. He was arguably the stylistic heir apparent to Geraint Watkins, and was much welcomed by the rock 'n' roll purists among Stevens's fan following.

He had first played piano with Shaky when he was eighteen, briefly taking over from Chris Holland, Jools's brother, in 1993. In 2005, he recalled his spell with Shaky with evident pleasure – and frankness. 'We used to have the old drinking joke on the road about "This Old Souse" [laughs], but I think Shaky really loves the old rock 'n' roll stuff. It always comes across when he's singing it. When he is with the band in the rehearsal room, he would do whatever it takes to get what he had in mind: he knew what was required in a particular situation. The problem often was he didn't have the means to tell you that, but he does have a talent for knowing when something isn't quite in place, or something doesn't quite fit.

'He is a fiery character but sometimes you have to be like that to make things work. I was surprised at how much he knew about the source stuff of rock 'n' roll. Once we did an ITV show and we couldn't quite get what he wanted. He turned round and said, "Try and do it like Huey 'Piano' Smith and the Clowns' 'Hit Me One More Time'." When it all worked well, it was really great to be in the band.'

The Glasgow Pavilion show was particularly hotly anticipated, having proved a highlight for Shaky's Scottish fans the year before. This time, however, the post-gig headlines were of a different nature. Perhaps alarmed by the stage invasions of the year before, Shaky's management insisted a capacity crowd of more than 1,000 fans should not stand in their place or dance in the aisles. Indeed, it was reported that the singer walked off the stage when some fans rose from their seats and warned that the show would not go on unless they sat down again.

The Pavilion management revealed to the *Glasgow Herald* that it acquiesced to the order only to ensure that the show went ahead. Iain Gordon, the theatre's general manager, observed: 'In my twenty-eight years at the Pavilion, I have never encountered anything like this. Fans are here to enjoy themselves and have a bit of a bop in their seats or in the aisles. We never have any trouble with our audiences, who are simply out for a good night's entertainment. I am shocked and surprised by this order. If Shaky and his management insist on this again, they are not welcome back.'

Press officer Brenda Carson revealed the theatre had no idea about the stipulation until the singer arrived. 'He insisted that we put typed notices around the theatre, saying there would be no standing or dancing allowed. We were bemused by it but went along with it just to make sure the show went ahead. Everyone was outraged and there was a lot of grumbling among the audience at the start. Even the bouncers were saying: we're just following orders.

'It was not an overzealous management that was making this order, but [Shaky] himself. He seems to be trying to cultivate a new image, but this was a rock 'n' roll concert, not a poetry reading. And it was an older audience, with most people aged between thirty and fifty, not drug-crazed teenagers ripping up the seats. It put a tremendous damper on the show and the atmosphere was very poor.'

About fifty fans walked out during the two-hour show, one smashing an £800 glass door in disgust as he left the front of the building. 'We are not condoning that sort of behaviour,' stressed Ms Carson, 'but that shows just how upset many people were. There wasn't booing at the end, but I think a few die-hards were waiting outside for him. A lot were wanting to tell him to lighten up and I think he should.' When the *Glasgow Herald* enquired further, Shakin' Stevens and his management were unavailable for comment.

Back in 1984 Shaky had told *Look In* magazine's readers that 'I like to have the lights put on the auditorium so I can get a proper look. It's even better when I can get a few up on stage to sing something with me.' How times had changed . . .

Fortunately there would be happier news in October. The British Academy of Composers and Songwriters presented Shaky with a prestigious Gold Badge Award to celebrate his worth in the world of music. Brian Hodgson of Matchbox, who was on BASCA's Gold Badge Committee, had been the prime mover for the award, as he revealed in 2005: 'I actually nominated Shaky for the Gold Badge Award to commemorate his contribution to the music industry. He won it in 2000, and I think it's a fitting tribute to a guy who worked all through the 1970s before finding success.'

In 2002, the singer was honoured by the *Guinness World Records British Hit Singles & Albums*, when he was awarded a Number One Gold Award to reflect his 1980s success. Further tentative recording sessions took place in 2002–03 at Berry Hill Studios in Coleford, Forest of Dean. The producer was John David, who'd worked on the Christmas album a decade previously.

Shaky's only setback of the year had occurred in the early hours of 1 January, on a ill-fated journey back from New Year's Eve festivities. He and wife Carole had been heading for their Gloucestershire hotel after the evening's celebrations when they were pulled over and the singer, who had been driving, was arrested and held in police custody for several hours. Speaking about his ordeal later, Shaky admitted it was something he never wanted to repeat. 'I wouldn't recommend being arrested and put in the cells to anybody. They take your shoes and belt off and tell you to empty your pockets. It's horrible.'

On 16 January 2002, at Coleford Magistrates Court, it was revealed that Shaky had spent Hogmanay with friends in the village of Clearwell, and when a pre-booked taxi had failed to turn up, leaving him and his wife standing around in sub-zero temperatures, he took the risk of driving the short distance to their hotel. Police officers spotted his slow-moving car weaving from side to side, and the result was an uncomfortable night in the slammer. His punishment was a two-year ban, a £400 fine and he was also ordered to pay £30 costs.

'We've all done it – made those mistakes,' he later lamented, before admitting, 'I had too much. I was over the limit. I was driving the car down this very narrow lane and couldn't have been doing more than twenty-five miles an hour. I was going from the restaurant to the hotel, which was only a five-minute walk, but it was up a lane [that] was dark and a little bit icy. Life isn't always pretty, you get your ups and downs . . .'

Shaky soon bounced back, however, and while live performance had once again been put on the back burner, the chance to perform in front of 200,000 fans at Vienna's Donauinselfest (Danube Festival) in June brought the singer back to the stage in 2003 with the same band he'd used on his last UK tour. And there were eighteen stages to choose from at what is possibly the biggest free admission festival in Europe. The highlight of his first live performance in Vienna since 1994 was a duet of 'I Can Help' with Billy Swan, who was performing in his own right. (Bonnie Tyler was also present, but 'A Rockin' Good Way' remained unperformed!). An Austrian TV special devoted to the festival broadcast about five minutes of Shaky's show, though the whole performance had been recorded and filmed for a possible TV documentary.

That same year saw Shaky and former Sunsets producer Donny Marchand encounter each other for the first time in three decades. The songwriter-producer, now in his sixties but still very much involved in the music business, had called the singer up and arranged a meeting in a restaurant to re-establish contact and maybe pitch a few songs to him. 'We talked, but he didn't talk much; he didn't like to talk about the days of The Sunsets,' Marchand recalls. 'In fact, when I asked if he went home much, he said, "I never go back."' The biggest surprise for Marchand was being instructed that he had to address the singer – whom he'd always called 'Mike' – as 'Shaky': 'Even his manager Sue has to call him that – it's like being called [Adam] Ant,' he laughs. 'I came to the conclusion that he still sees himself as being as hot as he was during the 1970s.'

Marchand had also recently contacted an old friend, Mike Batt of Wombles fame, who was enjoying a renaissance as producer of rising star Katie Melua. 'I went down to his house for the day and we were just bullshitting about things we'd done together in the early days. I kind of figured it would be like that [with Shaky], but he was still playing the "big artist" thing. By the time he left the restaurant he was really cool, it was all friends. He wasn't unfriendly when he came in, but [I] saw suspicion in his eyes as if it were some trap. I had the feeling that the guy, because he was a big star in this country for four years or so, can't take at face value somebody just saying "hi". He always had this thing that someone wants more from him.

'I booked a table at a very good Greek restaurant, and as we walked down there [we saw] it was crowded. He said, "I can't go in there, everyone will bother me." I said, "It's a family place, the kids won't know who the hell you are." There was another a few blocks down which was empty, and so he was happy to go in there. Within half an hour that place was packed, but no one bothered him or said a word. I'd forgotten my lighter and when I went back the next day to pick it up I asked if the staff knew the guy – nobody even knew who he was!'

Not that this mattered to manager Sue Davies, a former radio plugger, who was busily promoting the interests of her charge. When approached in 2004 about an interview for a proposed *Legends Of Welsh Rock* book, she insisted on ultimate copy approval and that the photograph used must also be of her choosing. Likewise, David Roberts at the *Guinness World Records British Hit Singles & Albums* has been in receipt of near-annual missives instructing that the three-line biographical information on Shaky should be changed to make him look more contemporary: 'She was unhappy about the lack of mentions about stuff he'd done that was not just rock 'n' roll. I think he was also very keen to put forward that he wrote his stuff as well. He did actually write one Number One, but I wouldn't peg him down as a sensitive singer-songwriter or anything.'

9

THE COMEBACK: 2005

So why the sudden Shakin' Stevens renaissance? In producer Stuart Colman's wise words, 'Everything eventually comes full circle, including the cycle of cool and uncool.'

The revival had its roots in Denmark, where a greatest hits album, entitled *Collectable*, was released on Epic on 26 July 2004. To coincide with the release date, Shaky made a TV appearance on public broadcast channel TV2 at the Langelands Festival in front of 25,000 people.

Campers were woken at 8 a.m. to Shaky's soundcheck, which lasted for two hours – evidence that he wanted to put on the perfect performance. The seventy-five-minute show kicked off at 7.30 p.m. Shaky played eighteen numbers during the concert, while the band was the same as 2003 with Elio Pace replacing Ben Waters and the addition of a two-man brass section. His shows were now such rare events that fans travelled from as far afield as Germany, Switzerland, Poland and the UK.

While there, Shaky and his band did a live-in-the-studio performance on Denmark's national TV 2 station's breakfast TV show, *Go' Morgen Danmark*. The unplugged-style performance featured Shaky, Elio Pace on piano, Martyn Hope on acoustic guitar and Bjorn Jonsson on drums, who Sony Records had provided. 'Marie Marie' and 'Oh Julie' were performed in down-home, foot-stomping style . . . some achievement, at 7 o'clock in the morning!

Elio Pace had been a long-time Shaky fan who'd seen him in concert many times in the 1980s and longed for the chance to get up there and play the songs he knew by heart. As well as old friend Martyn Hope, who'd played with Pace since 1993 and had suggested him as replacement for the in-demand Ben Waters, two more members of Pace's band were co-opted in the form of saxophonist Peter Effamy and trumpeter Paul Newton.

Six more concerts around the country – all sell-outs – followed in November, by which time the title had sold 40,000 units, enough to turn platinum in the Danish market. Around 18,000 people attended a free celebration concert in the capital's Tivoli Gardens on 29 April when Shaky was presented with his platinum disc. In the concert the previous day Shaky had performed 'Trouble' – the Pink track he had chosen to cover for *Hit Me Baby* – for the first time live.

Steve Tallamy, strategic marketing director at Sony/BMG Denmark, was involved in the making of the album: 'My view was that people in the UK regarded Shaky as an Eighties' artist. True, he had his hits in the Eighties, but his music was as far from the Eighties as you can get. A large group of people in Denmark showed they are more interested in the fact that it's good music, than they are in just what's fashionable.'

The Danish product was a CD/DVD set, the latter format containing, according to Tallamy, 'cleaned-up versions of what Shaky thought were his best videos'. Spotting a success story in the making that could run outside Scandinavia, Sony's international department quickly extended rights to include the whole world, so the set would be released in additional territories. Some were slightly different; for instance the UK version, while identical content-wise, had different artwork. 'We had to change the cover image,' Shaky explained, 'because apparently it didn't look like me. The words "Shakin' Stevens" at the top kind of gave it away, though! As far as the tunes go, the remastering made them kind of shinier, made them kick ass a lot more.'

The success of *The Collection* CD/DVD package, with its twelve video clips hand-picked by the artist, persuaded Sony BMG to release a longer, stand-alone DVD that would feature thirty-four of Shaky's promo videos – notable inclusions were those for the less successful singles 'Feel The Need In Me', 'Jezebel', 'Pink Champagne' and 'My Cutie Cutie', while further selections never before available on DVD were promised. Confusingly this was also to be called *The Collection*, but unfortunately the release was shelved.

Celebrity fans were coming out of the woodwork – coming out literally, in the case of Boy George, whose Culture Club group had once been a last-minute replacement for Shaky on *Top of the Pops* when he fell ill. George had apparently had a crush on him back then. *Pop Idol* winner Will Young was also keen to be photographed with Shaky at a Guinness awards ceremony. Could it be that our man has become something of a surprise icon to the gay community?

Comedian Rob Brydon of *The Keith Barrett Show* fame confessed he'd been a Shaky fan in his schooldays and been bullied as a result – the pair were due to be united at last on his Christmas 2004 TV special. (Note the near-coincidence of surnames!) Unfortunately, the appearance didn't happen, leading to all kinds of rumours about Shaky's health. 'In the green room at the show I had a glass of wine and went gaga and was taken in to hospital,' he revealed. The problem turned out to be a chest infection he'd contracted in Denmark when he'd played his recent series of shows.

'I had been asked to appear on Rob Brydon's Christmas special, so when I got back from Denmark I went for a check-up and my chest and nose were inflamed. I was given steroid tablets which were put in me internally to quicken the process.' But the steroids reacted with the wine, and erroneous reports of heart problems immediately hit the headlines.

There was, however, another unexpected side effect to his hospitalization that was positive. 'I'm fine now and I didn't smoke for three days in hospital, so I thought why not stop for good now? So I kept going. It's tough, because I started smoking behind the bicycle sheds at school.'

As well as Boy George and Rob Brydon, other well-known fans included *Little Britain*'s David Walliams and Matt Lucas, while Bolton's Peter Kay confirmed his membership of the fan club by inviting Shaky to appear in the video for 2005's Comic Relief single, '(Is This The Way To) Amarillo'. What most viewers didn't realize was that 'Green Door' had made the shortlist for the Comic Relief single, and that Peter Kay and Shaky had even made a video together before the final choice was made.

In a precursor to the 2012 Olympic selection process, the decision went to the wire and it wasn't until the videos were actually being edited that '(Is This The Way To) Amarillo' finally won the vote. 'It was a toss-up between "Green Door" and "Amarillo",' the ever-ebullient Kay revealed, 'and we filmed "Green Door" with Shaky and "Amarillo", and we didn't know until we got to edit. We decided [to go for] "Amarillo", and since then it's just grown and grown and grown.' The choice, of course, had the effect of reviving the career of 1970s hitmaker Tony Christie, but Stevens got a consolation prize. While most of the featured stars appeared two by two at the comic's shoulder, Shaky shared the spotlight with Kay alone.

In early 2005, ITV's *Hit Me Baby One More Time* was broadcast to British TV audiences, borrowing its title from teen queen Britney Spears' debut hit. In a series of seven heats the studio-based reality-TV programme would pit five former popstars against one another, in a 'battle of the bands' scenario, with the winner of each heat (voted for by the viewing public) going through to a grand final. The acts were asked to choose a new song to perform as well as an old, signature hit. In Shaky's case he paired his Number One song 'This Ole House', with 'Trouble', first recorded by punky female singer Pink. 'We were sent a list of two hundred songs to choose from,' Shaky explained, 'and I saw this track by Pink. The whole idea was to do your [own] arrangement. It was quite different for me to do – a male voice doing a female song – but a lot of people said it suits my voice, and it seems to work.'

In fact, Shaky was already aware of the song, which was just as well, since no CDs were supplied with the list. Some months earlier while on a long motorway drive, he had pulled into a service area and decided to purchase some new in-car entertainment. 'I looked at the rack of CDs and Pink had a new one out. I thought, "Hmm, okay I'll have a listen to that," played it in the car and liked it. It's weird that, [two] years later, I looked down the list they gave me and saw a Pink track – I thought, "Let's do that one."'

Hosted by Bolton-born Vernon Kay, the format of *Hit Me Baby* was exported to the States immediately after its UK run and, in Stateside form, enjoyed the best debut audience among the 18–49 demographic of any programme for two years. Stars over there included the likes of Arrested Development and Vanilla Ice. Yet in Britain the show billed as 'the battle that has the nation on the edge of their seats' was in reality far from the ratings success ITV had hoped for. Having crammed their Saturday-night schedules with celebrity-based shows, *Hit Me Baby* only managed to pull in around 2.4 million viewers for much of the series, a relatively poor showing in the ratings war. The final show on 21 May managed to squeeze itself into a very small space between the FA Cup Final and the *50th Eurovision Song Contest* in Kiev.

The seven acts involved in the final – Chesney Hawkes, Tiffany, Shalamar, Hue and Cry, 911 and T'Pau's Carol Decker were the others – had all enjoyed hits during the 1980s and early 1990s, when Top Ten singles sold in their hundreds of thousands. The question was, how would they fare in the download era, when little more than 20,000 singles sold would ensure a chart-topper?

Prior to his *Hit Me Baby* appearances, Shaky played a one-off concert at Shepherd's Bush Empire in April 2005, performing two sets of forty-five minutes each to a sell-out crowd. (A sign at the door stated the show was being recorded for possible future commercial release.) Backstage, Chris Wyles renewed old acquaintances. It seemed a happy ship, but in musical terms he wasn't as impressed as he'd expected to be: 'What I will say is the new band isn't a patch on the old band. Shaky was full of, "Oh, we've got some really good guys" and what have you, but I personally felt that, particularly in the guitar-playing front and the brass, it wasn't a patch on what it was twenty years ago. The piano player, Ben Waters, was very, very good, but the funny thing was it was almost the identical show I played in back in 1989. All the songs I used to play are in there, there's very little new material – there were maybe two songs that I didn't recognize.'

It was Wyles' first meeting with manager Sue Davies and, having been involved in the Freya era, he had his opinion: 'I can only think that perhaps Shaky attracts strong-willed women! I think he responds better with a woman as a manager.'

He also noted that the age range of the fans was, as would have been expected, considerably older than when he left the band some seventeen years earlier – the kids that had come to see Shaky in his golden years had grown up. 'There were a lot more people there in traditional rock 'n' roll gear who ranged from mid-twenties up to mid-forties really. It did get to a point where a lot of shows we did had youngsters, kids basically, and Shaky, as a lot of top artists do, attracts an awful lot of people in wheelchairs. He always used to have people going backstage, three or four kids who weren't well going in to see him. The gig at the Empire leaned towards older people, but then I spoke to one of the backing singers who is twenty-five or twenty-six. When he was having his hits she was six or seven years old, but she was going "I love Shakin' Stevens."'

Former guitarist Les Davidson saw the timing as perfect: 'Unlike so many records that are basically just a drum group with a bass and someone rapping over them, [he's] an artist who wants to sing you a song. The one thing you get with Shaky is you get a song. And a lot of people like songs. They call it branding, don't they? He's very much branded. You don't have to reinvent, the brand is there. He's branded and he's singing songs. These are two things that people want to buy.'

But brands can be compromised, and an interview with *The Sun* published on 16 April 2005 showed Shaky following a risky strategy when the paper's showbiz reporter Sean Hamilton, in the words of his feature's headline, 'met his childhood hero . . . and got a slap'.

'WHHHAAACCK!' it continued. 'Rocker Shakin' Stevens has just slapped me across the face. I am reeling in shock. I have just been hit by a showbiz legend . . . and I'm not even sure why. My cheek is stinging and Shaky is plonking himself down in his seat like nothing has happened. He's shakin' and I'm just quakin'. As tolerant as I am, I'm tempted to show Shaky the old "Green Door" – right now.'

It seemed a curious time for Shaky to repeat his Richard Madeley gaffe of two decades previously. This kind of thing really shouldn't happen – and, to be fair, it rarely did. Radio interviewers learned to cope with Shaky bringing his manager in on live interviews, even if this could result in occasional awkward silences as notes were slipped across the table.

On this particular occasion Shaky had just been voted into *Hit Me Baby One More Time*'s grand final and his new album was about to make its Top Ten debut. So what went wrong? Or maybe the question should be, what went right? Instead of a couple of columns devoted to Shaky's latest venture, the details surrounding the slap – which Hamilton revealed had been prompted after the singer became convinced that the 'series of opening questions about his comeback were not reverent enough' – gave him a whole page in Britain's top-selling tabloid.

The first album Hamilton ever bought back in 1981, aged seven, was one of Shaky's: 'I thought he was cool. I've always thought he was a good laugh – those high collars, Elvis moves and heavily-dyed black quiff. It's a great act.' But he was soon to realize that this was no act, as the singer was to confirm: 'In conversation, it's Shaky – that's S-H-A-K-Y, no E. And Shakin' Stevens on the product.'

Hamilton continued: 'Shaky remains exactly the same throughout the interview – aggressive, guarded, difficult and on edge . . . You sense Shaky went through some rough times in the Nineties. It is as though he is blocking out something. His sentences often drift away and I find myself wondering if he is on medication. When I finish the interview and turn my tape recorder off, Shaky realizes he's been out of order. He says, "I hope I haven't f★★★★d it. I know I can be a bit ga-ga." It is the truest thing he has said all morning.'

Having survived ten rounds with Wapping's finest, Shaky's eventual victory on *Hit Me Baby One More Time* was testament to both his performance and the willingness of his fans to vote early and vote often. According to the show's bulletin boards, there were divided families up and down the land, with mum voting for Shaky and daughter for Chesney.

He admitted the process had been an ordeal, even for him: 'When the last artist on the show finished we were all put in a room – it was like being in a dentist's waiting room. Then this guy came in and said who had won. When I came back on stage, it was as if the audience was three miles away – it felt like a hundred steps before I got to the microphone. It was quite nerve-racking, but enjoyable.'

Chesney Hawkes took defeat badly, apparently: 'Everyone got on backstage, but I hardly spoke to Shaky much, even though he was mates with my dad [Chip] years ago. He just kept himself to himself. He had thirty hits in the 1980s so, let's face it, all his old fans would be watching the show at that time of night. Most of my fans would be out clubbing.'

Shaky wasn't impressed by such sour grapes. 'I'm shocked,' he said. 'I thought he'd be man enough to take my win. I know he really wanted to win, too. Maybe it was because one of his friends on the show said he wanted me to win before changing his mind and saying Chesney. He didn't like that much. It's a great shame he's said that.

'We were singing live in the final and, being more experienced than Chesney, I know that you have to rest your voice or you lose it. I wasn't rude to anybody when we heard I'd won. I tried shaking everyone's hands, but I was dragged away as it was a live show. I turned around and looked at everybody and said, "We're all winners. Well done."'

Shaky himself said he would have voted for soul singer Jaki Graham. 'She was a lovely lady and took it very well. There were a lot of people there who were very upset and angry, tears, etc., but she was fantastic, shaking everyone's hand.'

Victory having been ensured, no news outlet was overlooked in an attempt to ensure that 'Trouble' made the highest chart entry possible. Shaky pressed the flesh at numerous record shops, even opening a new HMV Store in Thanet, Kent, and at every one the locals were surprised at the crowd he drew. Despite being late at Thanet due to a TV recording commitment, he stayed and talked to everyone present.

A BBC *Breakfast* interview with Dermot Murnaghan and Sian Williams on 27 June took him to a nationwide audience, but the big news had happened three days earlier when, after a near fifteen-year absence, Shaky made his long-awaited return to *Top of the Pops*. As was the practice, his performance of 'Trouble' had been recorded on the Wednesday before the show's Friday transmission, while he also performed 'This Ole House' for possible transmission at a later date.

Les Davidson had been an interested viewer at breakfast. Now a studio owner and still on the session scene, he was interested to see how his former 'boss' shaped up on the TV Centre couch. The verdict? 'He was most eloquent. He would talk happily about the 1980s, about how it was a great time and all the madness. I think Shaky's essentially sensitive and shy . . . put him on stage and he's a different person.'

'I didn't really fit into the 1980s,' Shaky had told his *Breakfast* inquisitors, 'because I came in on the tail end of punk, with the three chords. It was good that punk came in because it needed a bit of a kick. My music was [called] rock 'n' roll, but it's all types of music in one: it's country blues, it's Cajun, it's traditional rhythm and blues . . . swing. There's all kinds of music for everybody, really.'

Although no one expected 'Trouble' to replicate the Number One achieved by Comic Relief's '(Is This The Way To) Amarillo' anthem, it failed to live up to even lowly expectations, entering the chart on 25 June at Number 20. It was the lowest of six new entries in the Top Twenty, among them rapper Nelly, new punks Green Day and Fightstar, and female singer Jem. One week later, it had disappointingly slipped to Number 37 on its way out of the all-important Top Forty. It won a new lease of life, however, when it was included on *Now 61* – amazingly the first time one of Shaky's tracks had been cleared for inclusion on the top-selling series that began life as *Now That's What I Call Music* back in 1981. Whether overzealous management had kept him off the series or not, he was now making up for lost time.

While the timing of the album was perfect, Guinness's David Roberts didn't feel that the same could be said of the release of 'Trouble': 'Why did they leave it so late before releasing the single, which I don't think got anywhere near the Top Ten? Has that Shaky bubble burst now?'

Sue Carlin, thirty-six, a fan who'd been following Shakin' Stevens since 1981 and travelled as far afield as Vienna and

Denmark to see her idol, was also convinced that promotion was the key: 'I think he could appeal to a new audience, but he needs the right promotion to get him noticed, or else they will never know he has any new material out.' She felt his *Hit Me Baby* win, which she saw in person, was typical of the man: 'Shaky always gives his all in every performance, such a great entertainer, and the audience love to sing and dance along with him.'

Someone who was less than impressed by his *Hit Me Baby* experience was former manager Paul Barrett, who holds a distinctly cool opinion of the singer's present situation: 'I think that was sad. I think the programme was sad. I think his performance was sad. I think what he's doing is sad. He's wasted years.

'He told me in 2000 that Elvis had three stages in his career – rockabilly kid, king of rock 'n' roll, and international superstar. Shaky was the rockabilly kid when he was in The Sunsets, king of rock 'n' roll when he was having all his hits, now he wants to be an international superstar. Why hasn't the Sands Hotel in Vegas phoned him? He can't figure it out. He's a lousy cabaret act. He's a lousy pop singer. He's a great, great rock 'n' roller. And if he just settled back and did rock 'n' roll, he wouldn't have to worry.

'He could wash that dye out of his hair, he doesn't need it . . . he told me he's waiting for that third stage in his career, but it won't happen. If he just relaxed and did what he does well . . . He should've have gone on that bloody silly pop show and cut 'em up great – I thought it was demeaning.'

On the album front, *The Collection* had entered the UK chart in the third week of April, restoring his name to that listing for the first time in twenty years. Its release date, two days after his heat victory on *Hit Me Baby One More Time*, ensured a respectable initial placing at Number Six behind hits collections from Basement Jaxx and Tony Christie, plus new releases from Garbage and Natalie Imbruglia. Among the other new entries he beat was a singles compilation from 1980s chart rivals A-Ha.

The album then moved up two places to Number Four, seeing off Garbage and Imbruglia, being pushed down to fifth spot in its third week by the entry of one of Shaky's favourites, Bruce Springsteen, and his *Devils And Dust.* The slide, when it came, was fairly steep, to 10, 19 and 23. By the start of June, however, the next burst of TV publicity had kicked in, resulting in an upturn to 16 and a gold disc certification for 100,000 copies sold. Next moves were to 28 and 53, before it departed the Top Seventy-Five after a creditable ten-week stay.

Songwriter Steve Taylor: 'When he made the album charts for the first time this year, the DJ who does the chart show on the radio said, "Shakin' Stevens has charted at Number Six," and everyone in the studio applauded, which is great. Then you get the situation where, how far will they let it go with new material and will they play the stuff? I don't think too many people played "Trouble", which worries you a little because it is a good track, it stands up on its own and there's nothing wrong with it. It should have been played on Radio Two because people like Shaky, he has the talent to do it, and he definitely has enough tenacity to do it – it's just whether the media will support him. I think the public would certainly buy the product if they knew it was there.'

Interestingly, Pink wasn't the only female singer Shaky had his professional eye on. K. T. Tunstall's debut hit, 'Black Horse And The Cherry Tree', had been another option for his TV cover version, as, more bizarrely, had an unnamed song by Welsh three-piece noise merchants Feeder. '"Black Horse . . ." would have been great to do,' he confirmed. 'We met K.T. last week and we were chatting. We like her stuff quite a lot.' (Interestingly Tunstall's follow-up, 'The Other Side Of The World', also appeared on *Now 61*.) As for a possible album's worth of contemporary covers performed the Shaky way: 'It's a possibility, but it would be nice to do a newer album as well. It's possible because of the Pink thing . . . maybe there are more surprises. No one would expect me to do a Feeder cover!'

He looked forward to his UK 2005 tour, scheduled as ever for the pre-Christmas period: 'I'm touring with a new band that includes a trumpet, tenor sax, piano, two lead guitarists, a drummer, a bass guitarist and myself. I do quite a few of the hits, a few album tracks, songs I've not done before. There's all kinds of styles within the tracks I've recorded, so there's something there for everybody.' It was clear he'd rediscovered his appetite for touring too: 'It's nice to go on stage and see people enjoying themselves. My songs are feel-good and it's nice to see a reaction. We both get a tonic. You're giving something to the audience.'

So where did Shaky's future lie? While he was assured of a core following in Britain, it seemed the influence of *Hit Me Baby* – certainly on the evidence of 'Trouble' – would prove short-lived. One possible avenue to increase his audience was the US 'new country' scene. There was talk of interest from such influential figures as singer/songwriter Tony Joe White, and Pete Anderson, who has produced country singer Dwight Yoakam. The latter was a particular favourite of Stevens, thanks to the satellite TV channel CMT. That was where, in 1992, he'd been introduced to Yoakam's music by the track 'A Thousand Miles From Nowhere': 'I liked it, it's very hooky and the video was very good. It's one of those things where I bought the CD and it had three tracks on there I liked immensely. "A Thousand Miles From Nowhere" was the one I kept playing and playing, and it sounds great in the car.'

Donny Marchand reveals this rootsy musical direction was in the forefront of Shaky's mind back in 2003: 'If I was him, and he did agree with me on this, I'd be thinking of doing more country-rock. Creedence Clearwater, that's the kind of direction maybe you ought to think of . . . he said that's what he was thinking, and even said something about a bit of blues. Whether he can really do blues, I don't know.'

So could Shakin' Stevens' future see him reborn in the USA? With Stuart Colman batting for him, it's not impossible that Shakin' Stevens could, at long last, carve out the Stateside career he craved back in the mid-1980s, albeit in a much less spectacular fashion. But it would require much financial investment and time away from home, making it less of an attractive option at this time of his life. On the other hand, the billing of his 2005 tour as 'Rock, Rhythm, Hits And Country Blues At Its Best' suggested a continuing wish to diversify musically without alienating his existing fan base.

One thing seemed certain, though: he would carry on. As far back as 1986 he'd insisted, 'I can't see myself stopping, even if I stopped having hits. I did it for so long without them, they're not that important now. It's all I know how to do. As long as I'm enjoying it I could go on for ever.'

So how will Shakin' Stevens be remembered? For his chart achievements? As a rock 'n' roll revivalist? He certainly won't accept that description: 'How can you revive rock 'n' roll? It's never gone away!' Gruff Rhys of Super Furry Animals has stated his belief that Stevens has been an ambassador for his country. Stuart Cable, lately of Welsh three-piece The Stereophonics and now a TV presenter, has argued that a statue of Shaky should be erected on the banks of the River Severn to greet those passing from England to the Principality. 'That's always an amusing thought when I approach the Severn Bridge these days,' laughs Shaky. 'I'm proud to have been flying the flag.'

One last, little-known fact: Shakin' Stevens indirectly helped found the School Disco phenomenon. It's said that Bobby Sanchez, the DJ behind this club event that has been much imitated the world over, was moved to inaugurate it in 2001 after being fired by his last employer for daring to air a Shaky classic.

The story has Sanchez losing his deejaying job at an upmarket house club for playing Shakin' Stevens' 'This Ole House'. Depressed, he drove to the gates of his former school in Dulwich, South London, and thought, 'What is it about society that means they don't like Shakin' Stevens? It's a good song, we used to listen to it when we were kids. Can't we go back to our youth?' Sanchez put his school tie around his neck 'and something came over me. I had this creative phase. You can't create a time machine, but you can go back in time through music and dressing up.'

Much, of course, as Shakin' Stevens has been doing for nearly four decades . . .

DISCOGRAPHY
AND VIDEOS

1970 The Spirit Of Woodstock; Down On The Farm: 7-inch single

1972 Honey Don't; That Is Rock 'N' Roll: Sweden 7-inch single

1972 Sea Cruise; Honey Don't: Netherlands 7-inch single

1972 Sweet Little Rock 'N' Roller; White Lightning: 7-inch single

1973 Honey Honey; Return Of The Superstar: Netherlands 7-inch single

1973 The Spirit Of Woodstock; Holy Moley: Netherlands 7-inch single

1974 Honey Honey; Holy Moley: Germany 7-inch single

1974 It Came Out Of The Sky; Riot In Cellblock No. 9: Netherlands and Germany 7-inch single; first solo single

1974 Lonesome Town; Don't Jive Me No More: Netherlands 7-inch single; solo recording with session musicians

1975 Jungle Rock; Girl In Red: UK and Europe 7-inch single; reissued 1985

1975 Ready Teddy; Tear It Up; Monkey's Uncle; Frantic; My Baby Died: EP; 1982 reissued

1976 Sexy Ways: Sexy Ways; Evil Hearted Ada; Blue Swingin' Mama; Rock Around with Ollie Vee: EP

1976 You Mostest Girl; Rock-A-Billy Earthquake: Netherlands 7-inch single

c.1977 Donna; Sugaree: Germany 7-inch single

1977 Never; You Always Hurt The One You Love: 7-inch single

1977 Somebody Touched Me; Way Down Yonder In New Orleans: 7-inch single

1978 Justine; Wait And See: 7-inch single; also released with B side: I'm Ready

1978 Treat Her Right; I Don't Want No Other Baby: 7-inch single

1979 Endless Sleep; Fire: 7-inch single

1979 Spooky; I Don't Want No Other Baby: 7-inch single

1980 Hey Mae; I Guess I Was A Fool: 7-inch single

1980 Hot Dog; Apron Strings: 7-inch single

1980 Marie, Marie; Baby If We Touch: 7-inch single

1980 Memphis Earthquake: Memphis Earthquake; You Mostest Girl; Evil Hearted Ada; My Bucket's Got A Hole In It: EP; picture sleeve

1980 Shakin' Stevens: Marie Marie; Hey Mae; Is A Bluebird Blue?; Baby If We Touch: US 10-inch single; picture sleeve

1980   Shooting Gallery; Make It Right
        Tonight: 7-inch single
1980   You Mostest Girl; Memphis
        Earthquake; Evil Hearted; My Bucket's
        Got A Hole In It: EP
1981   Green Door; Don't Turn Your Back:
        7-inch single
1981   It Came Out Of The Sky; Return Of
        The Superstar: Germany 7-inch single
1981   It's Raining; You And I Were Meant To
        Be: 7-inch single; limited edition
        picture Disc
1981   No Other Baby; Manhattan
        Melodrama: 7-inch single
1981   Shaky Sings Elvis: Dixieland Rock;
        Got A Lot Of Living To Do; Wear My
        Ring; Ready Teddy; Trying To Get To
        You; My Baby Left Me; Mean Woman
        Blues; Jailhouse Rock: US 7-inch single
1981   Shaky Sings Elvis: Blue Suede Shoes;
        King Creole; Dixieland Rock; Got A
        Lot Of Living To Do; Wear My Ring;
        Ready Teddy; Trying To Get To You;
        My Baby Left Me; Mean Woman Blues;
        Jailhouse Rock: Germany 12-inch single
1981   This Ole House; Let Me Show You
        How: 7-inch single
1981   You Drive Me Crazy; Baby You're A
        Child: 7-inch single
1982   Blue Christmas; Josephine (Live);
        Lawdy Miss Clawdy (Live); Que Sera
        Sera (Live): EP
1982   Donna; Outlaw Man: Spain 7-inch
        single
1982   Get Back John; Outlaw Man: Italy
        7-inch single
1982   Give Me Your Heart Tonight; Thinkin'
        Of You: 7-inch single; limited edition
        picture disc
1982   Greatest Original Hits: This Ole House;
        You Drive Me Crazy; Green Door;
        Oh Julie: EP and cassette; released in
        Australia as Four Play
1982   I'll Be Satisfied; Don't Be Late Miss
        Kate: 7-inch single
1982   It's Rock 'N' Roll (Signature Tune);
        I Told You So; Sexy Ways: Germany
        7-inch single
1982   Oh Julie; Don't Tell Me We're Through;
        Give Me Your Heart Tonight; Boppity
        Bop: promotional EP

1982   Oh Julie; I'm Knockin': 7-inch single
1982   Shirley; I'm For You: 7-inch single
1982   Special Edition: Blue Christmas (Studio
        Recording); Josephine (live); Lawdy
        Miss Clawdy (live); Que Sera Sera
        (live): EP, gatefold picture sleeve,
        recorded on British tour 10-11-82
1982   Tiger; Give Me A Break: 7-inch single
1983   A Rockin' Good Way; Why Do You
        Treat Me This Way? (Live): 7-inch
        single; duet with Bonnie Tyler; limited
        edition picture disc; 1987 reissued on
        cassette with lyrics
1983   A Rockin' Good Way; Why Do You
        Treat Me This Way? (Live), The Bop
        Won't Stop (Live): 12-inch single; duet
        with Bonnie Tyler; picture sleeve
1983   Cry Just A Little Bit; Love Me Tonight:
        7-inch single; limited edition picture
        disc
1983   Cry Just A Little Bit (Longer Version);
        Love Me Tonight; Your Ma Said You
        Cried In Your Sleep Last Night: 12-inch
        single
1983   Cry Just A Little Bit; Cry Just A Little
        Bit (Instrumental): US 12-inch single
1983   It's Late; It's Good For You Baby: 7-inch
        single; limited edition shaped picture
        disc
1983   Justine; Jungle Rock; Story Of The
        Rockers; My Baby Died: EP
1983   Reet Petite; Jungle Rock: Germany
        7-inch single
1983   Sweet Little Sixteen; Girl In Red:
        Germany 7-inch single
1983   Tiger; Sweet Little Sixteen; Give Me
        A Break: 7-inch single; picture disc
1983   Two Hearts, Two Kisses; Nut Rocker:
        Sweden 7-inch single; coloured vinyl
1983   Your Ma Said You Cried In Your Sleep
        Last Night; It's Good For You Baby:
        Netherlands 7-inch single
1984   A Letter To You; Come Back And Love
        Me: 7-inch single; picture sleeve with
        lyrics; limited edition with fold-out
        'Shake 'n' Roll' game and picture sleeve
1984   A Letter To You; Come Back And Love
        Me; Cry Just A Little Bit (Luongo's
        Remix): Netherlands 12-inch single
1984   A Love Worth Waiting For; As Long
        As (Live): 7-inch single; picture sleeve

1984 A Love Worth Waiting For; Don't Tell Me We're Through (Live); As Long As I Have You (Live): 12-inch single; picture sleeve

1984 Draggin' & Shakin'; Cry Just A Little Bit (mixed with Draggin' The Line by Invisible College): US 12-inch single; DJ use only; 8:05 mix feature

1984 Oh Julie (Shaky); I Have A Dream (Abba): 7-inch single; Kelloggs Rice Crispies mail-order offer

1984 Party Mix: 7-inch single; limited edition (Megamixofhits) free in double pack with Teardrops single

1984 Teardrops; You Shake Me Up: 7-inch single; featuring Hank Marvin

1984 Teardrops; You Shake Me Up; Mega Mix Of Hits: Cry Just A Little Bit; You Drive Me Crazy; A Rockin' Good Way; Give Me Your Heart Tonight; A Love Worth Waiting For; Green Door; I'll Be Satisfied; A Letter To You; I'll Be Satisfied (Reprise); Shirley; Oh Julie; It's Late; Marie, Marie; Hot Dog; This Ole House: 12-inch single; featuring Hank Marvin

1984 Tiger; Do The Bop: Germany 7-inch single; Shaky sings on A-side only

1985 Breaking Up My Heart; I'll Give You My Heart: 7-inch single; also in a pop-up gatefold sleeve

1985 Breaking Up My Heart (Extended Remix); I'll Give You My Heart: 12-inch single

1985 Lipstick, Powder And Paint; I'll Give You My Heart (Remix): 7-inch single

1985 Lipstick, Powder And Paint; As Long As I Have You; I'll Give You My Heart (Remix): 12inch single

1985 Merry Christmas Everyone; With My Heart: 7-inch single; 1986 Reissued as limited edition with gatefold sleeve and advent calendar

1985 Merry Christmas Everyone; Blue Christmas; With My Heart: UK and Europe 12-inch single; European issue had different cover; limited edition with Advent calendar

1986 Because I Love You; Tell Me One More Time: 7-inch single; picture sleeve; limited edition with autograph; limited

edition tour souvenir pack, gatefold picture sleeve

1986 Because I Love You (Extended Version); Because I Love You (7-inch Version); Tell Me One More Time: 12-inch single; Netherlands EP; picture sleeve

1986 Turning Away; Diddle I: 7-inch single

1986 Turning Away (Extended Remix); Diddle I: 12-inch single

1987 A Little Boogie Woogie; If You're Gonna Cry: 7-inch single; picture sleeve

1987 A Little Boogie Woogie (In The Back Of My Mind) (Boogie Mix); A Little Boogie Woogie; If You're Gonna Cry: 12-inch single and cassette; limited edition

1987 Come See About Me; Boppity Bop: 7-inch single

1987 Come See About Me (Extended Remix); Come See About Me; Boppity Bop: 12-inch single; limited edition with sew-on patch

1987 What Do You Want To Make Those Eyes At Me For?; (Yeah) You're Evil: 7-inch single; three limited editions: (1) with jigsaw; (2) picture disc 25 hits commemorative; (3) competition pack

1987 What Do You Want To Make Those Eyes At Me For?; (Yeah) You're Evil; Merry Christmas Everyone; Blue Christmas: limited edition EP

1988 Feel The Need In Me; If I Can't Have You: 7-inch single

1988 Feel The Need In Me; Tiffany Interview: promotional cassette

1988 Feel The Need In Me (Dance Mix); If I Can't Have You: 12-inch single

1988 How Many Tears Can You Hide?; If I Really Knew: 7-inch single; limited edition with pin-on badge

1988 How Many Tears Can You Hide? (Dance Mix); If I Really Knew: 12-inch single

1988 True Love; Come On Little Girl: 7-inch single

1988 True Love (Extended Version); Come On Little Girl; Merry Christmas Everyone (Extended Version); Blue Christmas: 12-inch single

1989 Jezebel (Remix); As Long As I Have

You: 7-inch single; limited edition competition pack

1989 Jezebel (Monster Mix); As Long As I Have You (Live On Tour): 12-inch single

1989 Love Attack; As Long As I Have You: 7-inch single and cassette; also limited edition cassette with free Love Attack patch offer

1989 Love Attack (Extended Version); As Long As I Have You: 12-inch single

1990 I Might; Love Won't Stop: 7-inch single and cassette

1990 I Might (Extended Version); Love Won't Stop: 12-inch single; limited edition with picture disc

1990 My Cutie Cutie; If I Lose You: 7-inch single and cassette; also limited edition cassette with two bonus tracks: This Ole House; You Drive Me Crazy

1990 Pink Champagne; Rockin' The Night Away: 7-inch single, cassette and CD single; limited edition shaped picture disc

1990 Pink Champagne; Rockin' The Night Away; If I Lose You: Netherlands 12-inch single

1990 The Best Christmas Of Them All; Que Sera Sera (Live): 7-inch single and cassette; recorded at Southampton Gaumont

1990 Yes I Do; You Shake Me Up (Remix): cassette & CD single

1990 Yes I Do (Extended Version); Yes I Do; You Shake Me Up (Remix): 12-inch single; limited edition with picture disc

1991 I'll Be Home This Christmas; With My Heart: 7-inch single and cassette

1991 I'll Be Home This Christmas; I'll Be Home This Christmas (Instrumental Karaoke Version), White Christmas (Instrumental Karaoke Version), Merry Christmas Everyone (Instrumental Karaoke Version): 7-inch single and cassette; picture sleeve with lyrics; limited edition with Shaky Christmas card

1992 Radio; Oh Baby Don't: 7-inch single and cassette; featuring Queen drummer Roger Taylor

1992 Radio (Acoustic Version); Hey Mae;

Shooting Gallery: limited edition CD single; featuring Queen drummer Roger Taylor

1992 Radio; Oh Baby Don't; Shooting Gallery; Hey Mae; + three other tracks: Austria 2-CD single set, featuring Queen drummer Roger Taylor

1994 I Can Help; Calling You: Germany CD single

1999 Rock 'n' Roll Hitmix '99 (Radio Version); Rock 'n' Roll Hitmix '99 (Maxi Version): Germany CD single

2005 Trouble; This Ole House: UK CD single; tracks remastered in 2004

VINYL, CASSETTE AND CD ALBUMS CHRONOLOGICALLY

1970 *A Legend*: Shaky does not sing on: Down On The Farm, I Hear You Knockin', Down Yonder We Go Balling; flipback sleeve; 1979 reissued; 1981 reissued as *Rock On With Shakin' Stevens And The Sunsets*: A Legend. Cast Iron Arm; Leroy; Flying Saucers; Please Mr Mayne; Lights Out; I'll Try; Down Yonder We Go Balling; Hawkins' Mood; Down On The Farm; Lonesome Train; I Believe What You Say; The Train Kept On Rollin'; The Spirit Of Woodstock; I Hear You Knockin'; Thirty Days; Schooldays (Anthem)

1971 *I'm No JD*: Debut LP; 1973 issued in the Netherlands as *The Best Of Shakin' Stevens And The Sunsets* with same tracks, but different cover; 1981 reissued as *That is Rock and Roll* and on cassette as *Shakin' Stevens*.
That Is Rock 'N' Roll; Right String Baby; I Fell Apart; Super Star; Sea Cruise; Little Queenie; Come Along With Me; Rock 'N' Roll Swinger; I'm Not A Juvenile Delinquent; Honey Don't; Girl Please Stay; Sea Of Heartbreak

1972 *Rockin' And Shakin' With Shakin' Stevens*: LP; 1984 reissued in UK and Sweden.
Roll Over Beethoven; White Lightning; One Night With You;

Hi Heel Sneakers; Tallahassee Lassie; Yakety Yak; Maybelline; Heart Of Stone; Good Rockin' Tonight; At The Top; Walk On The Water; Rip It Up

1973 ***Shakin' Stevens And The Sunsets***: LP; issued in Europe as *The Spirit Of Woodstock*; 1981 generally reissued; later reissued on CD with bonus tracks: Sweet Little Sixteen and Reet Petite. The Spirit Of Woodstock; It Came Out Of The Sky; Blue Moon Of Kentucky; Big River Boogie; Me And Bobby McGee; Tallahassee Lassie; Honey Honey; That's Rock 'N' Roll; Buzz, Buzz, Buzz; Don't Jive Me No More; Train Kept On Rollin'; Return Of The Superstar; Holy Moley; Riot In Cell Block No. 9

*c.*1975 ***Live England 1975***: Probably a pirate recording; available on CD. Don't Lie To Me; Great Balls Of Fire; Honey Hush; Baby I Don't Care; Tear It Up; Jungle Rock; Like A Teenager; Sweet Little Rock 'N' Roller; Red Light; Shake Baby Shake; Punk; Monkey's Uncle; Wasted Days And Nights; Get Back John; C'mon Everybody; Tallahassee Lassie; Hey Yeah Medley; Blue Suede Shoes; Que Sera Sera; Hound Dog Medley

1975 ***Manhattan Melodrama***: LP and cassette; 1980 reissued in UK and Germany with bonus tracks: Blue Moon Of Kentucky; Riot In Cell Block No. 9; Tallahassee Lassie; Don't Jive Me No More. Manhattan Melodrama; Alan Freed; California Cowboy; Lady Lizzard; Punk; Outlaw Man; I Told You So; Longer Stronger Love; Like A Teenager; Holy Roller; No Other Baby; Get Back John

*c.*1975 ***Story Of The Rockers***: LP. Frantic; Baby Blue; Ready Teddy; Tear It Up; Justine; Oakie Boogie; Drinkin' Wine Spo-Dee-O-Dee; Blue Swingin' Mama; Here Comes My Baby; Memphis Earthquake; Blue Suede Shoes; Going Down Town

1976 ***C'mon Memphis***: 10-inch LP; live performances; 1979 reissued as 12-inch LP in the Netherlands, in France as

Shake Baby Shake, in Germany as *Sexy Ways* (German & French LPs omit My Bucket's Got A Hole In It and Oakie Boogie) and in Sweden as *Come On Memphis* with bonus tracks: Ready Teddy and Tear It Up; 1981 reissued in UK as *At The Rockhouse* with two different sleeves. Honey Hush; My Bucket's Got A Hole In It; Evil Hearted Ada; Wine, Wine, Wine; Blue Swingin' Mama; Oakie Boogie; Reet Petite; Baby Blue; Rock Around With Ollie Vee; You Mostest Girl; Sexy Ways; Rock-A-Billy Earthquake

1978 ***Shakin' Stevens***: LP; issued with two different sleeves; insert sheet; featuring false starts and studio chit chat; 1981 reissued as *Play Loud*. You Can't Sit Down; I'm Ready; So Glad You're Mine; Let's Dance; Till I Waltz Again With You; Such A Night; Justine; Baby Blue; Wait And See; Can't Believe You Wanna Leave; Medley: Whole Lotta Shakin' Goin' On/Jenny Jenny/Tutti Frutti

1979 ***Take One!***: LP and cassette; 1982 reissued as *Hot Dog*. Lovestruck; Hot Dog; Is A Blue Bird Blue?; That's All Right; Without A Love; Shame, Shame, Shame; Shotgun Boogie; I Got Burned; I Guess I Was A Fool; Ah, Poor Little Baby; Little Pigeon; Do What You Did

1980 ***Marie, Marie***: LP; picture sleeve; 1981 reissued on LP and cassette with same cover as *This Ole House*. Hey Mae; Baby If We Touch; Marie, Marie; Lonely Blue Boy; Make It Right Tonight; Move; Slipping And Sliding; Shooting Gallery; Revenue Man; Make Me Know You're Mine; Two Hearts; Nobody

1981 ***Collection, The***: Germany LP; picture sleeve. 12 tracks

1981 ***Get Shakin'***: Canada LP and cassette; picture sleeve; cassette had different track order. You Drive Me Crazy; This Ole House; Revenue Man; Marie, Marie; Let Me

Show You How; Shooting Gallery;
Hot Dog; Shotgun Boogie; Baby You're
A Child; Is A Blue Bird Blue?; Hey
Mae; Make It Right Tonight

1981 *Rockin' On*: Australia double LP;
Volume 1 issued in New Zealand as
single LP.
VOLUME 1: That Is Rock 'N' Roll;
Buzz, Buzz, Buzz; The Train Kept On
Rolling; Holy Moley; Riot In Cell
Block No. 9; Manhattan Melodrama;
I Told You So; Longer Stronger Love;
Like A Teenager; Holy Roller; No
Other Baby; Get Back John.
VOLUME 2: Shaky Sings Elvis Medley:
Dixieland Rock/Got A Lot Of Living
To Do/Wear My Ring/Ready
Teddy/Trying To Get To You/My Baby
Left Me/Mean Woman Blues/Jailhouse
Rock; It Came Out Of The Sky; Blue
Moon Of Kentucky; Me And Bobby
McGee; Alan Freed; The Spirit Of
Woodstock; Lady Lizzard; Punk;
Outlaw Man; Tallahassee Lassie; Honey
Honey

1981 *Shaky*: LP and cassette; issued in
Australia as *Green Door* with bonus
track: Hot Dog; 1990 released on CD.
Mona Lisa; You Drive Me Crazy; I'm
Knockin'; It's Raining; Don't She Look
Good; Green Door; Don't Bug Me
Baby; Don't Tell Me Your Troubles; I'm
Gonna Sit Right Down And Write
Myself A Letter; This Time; Baby You're
A Child; Don't Turn Your Back; Let Me
Show You How; I'm Lookin'

1982 *Baby Blue*: Denmark LP; limited
edition; picture disc; 1984 reissued in
Germany.
Baby Blue; Sexy Ways; Rock Around
With Ollie Vee; Rock-A-Billy
Earthquake; Drinking Wine Spo-Dee-
O-Dee; Honey Hush; Tear It Up;
Justine; Ready Teddy; Frantic; Oakie
Boogie; My Baby Died

1982 *Die Weisse Serie*: Germany LP; picture
sleeve.
Blue Moon Of Kentucky; Outlaw
Man; I Told You So; Buzz, Buzz, Buzz;
The Train Kept On Rollin'; The Spirit
Of Woodstock; Tallahassee Lassie; Alan

Freed; Riot In Cell Block No. 9; Like
A Teenager; Manhattan Melodrama;
Me And Bobby McGee

1982 *Early Days, The: Shakin' Stevens And
The Sunsets*: US LP; issued in Europe
as *Silver Wings*; on German picture disc
LP, the numbers Outlaw Man,
Manhattan Melodrama and Get Back
John are different from those on the
Dutch LP.
Tiger; Don't Rip Me Off; Give Me A
Break; Girl In Red; Outlaw Man;
Manhattan Melodrama; Sugaree; Sweet
Little Sixteen; Silver Wings; Donna;
Get Back John; Jungle Rock; Red Flag
Rock

1982 *From Memphis To New Orleans*:
Germany LP; featuring 'Rockin'
Louie'.
Tiger; The Georgia Peach; Punk; Jump,
Jump, Jump; Lady Lizzard; Nightrider;
Shake The Hand Of A Fool (Serre La
Main D'un Grand Fou); My Girl; Hop,
Rock And Bop; Nut Rocker;
California Cowboy; Lonesome Town

1982 *Jungle Rock*: Netherlands LP .
12 tracks

1982 *Profile*: Germany LP.
It Came Out Of The Sky; Tallahassee
Lassie; Buzz, Buzz, Buzz; Riot In Cell
Block No. 9; Don't Jive Me No More;
and seven more tracks

1982 *Shake It Up*: Germany LP.
Frantic; Monkey's Uncle; Tear It Up;
Justine; Ready Teddy; Reet Petite; Story
Of The Rockers; Oakie Boogie; Jungle
Rock; My Baby Died

1982 *Shakin' Stevens And The Sunsets*: UK
and Europe box set with two LPs and
poster; recorded circa 1974; later
reissued in UK as double cassette
album.
DISC 1: Sweet Little Rock 'N' Roll;
Too Many Stars; The Georgia Peach;
Shake The Hand Of A Fool (Serre La
Main D'un Grand Fou); Hop, Rock
And Bop; Silver Wings; She Got The
Gimmies; Do The Bop; Tossin' And
Turnin'.
DISC 2: Nut Rocker; Punk; White
Lightning; It Came Out Of The Sky;

Nightrider; Ruby Baby; Jump, Jump, Jump; My Girl, My Girl; You Talk Too Much; I Rocked

1982 *Teenage Idol, The*: Germany double LP set

1982 *You Drive Me Crazy*: US LP.
You Drive Me Crazy; This Ole House; Marie, Marie; Let Me Show You How; Green Door; Hot Dog; Baby You're A Child; It's Raining; Hey Mae; Make It Right Tonight

1982 *Give Me Your Heart Tonight*: LP; later reissued on CD.
Josephine; Give Me Your Heart Tonight; Sapphire; Oh Julie; I'll Be Satisfied; Vanessa; Boppity Bop; Don't Tell Me We're Through; Shirley; You Never Talked About Me; Too Too Much; (Yeah) You're Evil; Que Sera Sera

1983 *Bop Won't Stop, The*: UK LP and cassette; cassette included a Shaky computer game; limited edition box set with LP, cassette and autograph book.
A Love Worth Waiting For; As Long As I Have You; Brand New Man; Cry Just A Little Bit; Diddle I; Don't Be Two Faced; It's Late; Livin' Lovin Wreck; Love Me Tonight; A Rockin' Good Way; The Bop Won't Stop; Why Do You Treat Me This Way?
US LP.
The Bop Won't Stop; Why Do You Treat Me This Way?; Diddle I; Don't Be Two Faced; A Rockin' Good Way (To Mess Around And Fall In Love) – duet with Bonnie Tyler; Brand New Man; I Cry Just A Little Bit; As Long As I Have You; A Love Worth Waiting For; Love Me Tonight

1983 *Classics Collection*: LP and cassette; cassette had two different covers; 1987 reissued on CD as *The Collection*; 1989 reissued in Europe on LP and CD as *Reet Petite*; 1991 reissued in Europe on CD as *Sixteen Rock 'n' Roll Greats* and as *Music Mirror*.
Reet Petite; Monkey's Uncle; Tear It Up; Silver Wings; Ready Teddy; Story Of The Rockers; Sweet Little Sixteen; Lady Lizzard; Queen Of The Hop;

Outlaw Man; Rock Around With Ollie Vee; Blue Swingin' Mama; Jungle Rock; Justine; You Mostest Girl; Girl In Red

1983 *Jetzt Kommt Shaky*: Germany only LP; gatefold picture sleeve in West, East German LP had a single sleeve.
You Drive Me Crazy; Oh Julie; Let Me Show You How; Give Me Your Heart Tonight; Don't Turn Your Back; Shirley; I'm For You; This Ole House; Baby You're A Child; Marie, Marie; Baby If We Touch; Green Door; Don't Be Late; It's Raining; You And I Were Meant To Be; I'll Be Satisfied

1983 *Lonesome Town*: Sweden LP.
14 tracks

1983 *Rockabilly Greatest Hits*: Germany LP and cassette; picture disc.
Justine; Hey Baby; Hydroelectric Dam; Sleep Rock 'N' Roll; Forgive Me; Jungle Rock; Rockabilly Baby; Out Of Sight; The Only Thing; James Dean; My Baby Died; Story Of The Rockers

1983 *Rocker, The*: Germany LP.
Peggy Sue; Tossin' And Turnin'; This Time; She Got The Gimmies; Ruby Baby; Too Many Stars; Queen Of The Hop; Hey Good Looking; Two Hearts Two Kisses; Wee Hours Blues; I Rocked; Baby I Don't Care

1983 *Stars And Music*: Germany LP.
Queen Of The Hop; Tossin' And Turnin'; Two Hearts, Two Kisses; I Rocked; Lonesome Town; Ruby; Tiger; Hey Good Looking; Shake The Hand Of A Fool (Serre La Main D'un Grand Fou); Baby I Don't Care; Hop, Rock And Bop; Peggy Sue

1983 *Track Years, The*: LP and cassette; previously unreleased Track session recordings from 1976–8.
Somebody Touched Me; Just Walking In The Rain; Mountain Of Love; Rebound; You Always Hurt The One You Love; No Other Baby; Way Down Yonder In New Orleans; Keep On Knockin'; Gotta Lotta Livin' To Do; Ruby Baby; Never; Tossin' And Turnin'; Hound Dog

1984 *Greatest Hits*: LP and cassette; issued in

Europe as *The Best of Shakin' Stevens*;
1990 reissued on CD; 2001 reissued in
Germany on CD as *Simply The Best*
without tracks: Blue Christmas and I'll
Be Satisfied.
This Ole House; You Drive Me Crazy;
A Letter To You; It's Raining; Green
Door; Hot Dog; Teardrops; Breaking
Up My Heart; Oh Julie; Marie, Marie;
A Love Worth Waiting For; It's Late;
Give Me Your Heart Tonight; Shirley;
Blue Christmas; Cry Just A Little Bit;
A Rockin' Good Way (To Mess Around
And Fall In Love) – duet with Bonnie
Tyler; I'll Be Satisfied

1984 *Rock'n Shaky, The*: Germany LP;
picture disc with 22 tracks; Denmark
LP; limited edition; picture disc with
12 tracks.

1984 *Shakin' Stevens*: Double LP set in
gatefold cover and double-track cassette
album; 1987 Disc 1 reissued on CD as
Sugaree.
DISC 1: Sugaree; This Time; Baby I
Don't Care; Wee Wee Hours; Hey
Good Lookin; Lonesome Town; Peggy
Sue; Two Hearts Two Kisses; Queen Of
The Hop; Nut Rocker; Californian
Cowboy; Lady Lizzard; .
DISC 2: Tiger; Girl In Red; Guitar
Man; Manhattan Melodrama; Don't
Rip Me Off; Sweet Little Sixteen;
Jungle Rock; Donna; Red Flag Rock;
Get Back John; Silver Wings; Give Me
A Break

1984 *Story Of The Rockers*: Germany double
LP; 1992 reissued in Europe on CD
under the same title and as *Blue
Swingin' Mama*.
Blue Swingin' Mama; You Mostest
Girl; Sexy Ways; Honey Hush; Evil
Hearted Ada; Jungle Rock; My Baby
Died; Reet Petite; Monkey's Uncle;
Silver Wings; Memphis Earthquake;
Rock Around With Ollie Vee; Story Of
The Rockers; Frantic; Baby Blue;
Ready Teddy; Tear It Up; Justine; Oakie
Boogie; Drinkin' Wine Spo-Dee-O-
Dee

1984 *Tiger*: Germany LP; recorded circa
1974.

Tiger; Shake The Hand Of A Fool
(Serre La Main D'un Grand Fou); This
Time; Too Many Stars; Two Hearts Two
Kisses; Peggy Sue; Baby I Don't Care;
I Rocked; Nut Rocker; Lonesome
Town; Wee Hours Blues; My Girl

1984 *Ultimate Rock 'N' Roller, The*: France
LP.
Ruby Baby; Shake The Shake The
Hand Of A Fool (Serre La Main D'un
Grand Fou); White Lightning; Hey
Good Looking; Nut Rocker;
Lonesome Town; Tiger; Sweet Little
Rock 'N' Roller; This Time; Too Many
Stars (In Rock 'N' Roll Heaven); Peggy
Sue; Wee Wee Hours

1985 *Hop Bop And Rock*: Netherlands LP.
Hop, Rock And Bop; Sweet Little
Rock 'N' Roller; Shake The Hand Of
A Fool (Serre La Main D'un Grand
Fou); Do The Bop; The Georgia Beach;
You Talk Too Much; Punk; Jump, Jump,
Jump; Two Hearts Two Kisses; Wee Wee
Hours; My Girl, My Girl; Lonesome
Town; Nightrider; Tossin' And Turnin';
White Lightning; Silver Wings

1985 *Lipstick, Powder And Paint*: Cassette;
red vinyl.
Lipstick, Powder And Paint; Bad
Reputation; Don't Lie To Me; I'm
Leaving You; The Shape I'm In; Don't
Knock Upon My Door; Turning Away;
Love You Out Loud; As Long As I Have
You; With My Heart; Ain't It A Shame
(You Win Again); So Long Baby
Goodbye

1985 *Original Shakin' Stevens And The
Sunsets, The*: Double cassette album.

1985 *Twenty Rockabilly Classics*: Cassette;
reissued on CD as *Shakin' Stevens And
The Sunsets*; later reissued on CD as *The
Magic Collection*.
You Mostest Girl; Sexy Ways; Honey
Hush; Evil Hearted Ada; Jungle Rock;
My Baby Died; Reet Petite; Monkey's
Uncle; Silver Wings; Memphis
Earthquake; Rock Around With Ollie
Vee; Story Of The Rockers; Frantic;
Baby Blue; Ready Teddy; Tear It Up;
Justine; Oakie Boogie; Wine, Wine,
Wine; Blue Swingin' Mama

1986 **Collection, The:** Cassette; issued in West Germany as double LP in gatefold cover.

Sweet Little Sixteen; Monkey's Uncle; Tear It Up; Silver Wings; Ready Teddy; Reet Petite; Outlaw Man; Queen Of The Hop; Lady Lizzard; Story Of The Rockers; Jungle Rock; Justine; You Mostest Girl; Girl In Red; Rock Around With Ollie Vee; Blue Swingin' Mama; Sugaree; Baby I Don't Care; Tiger; Frantic

1986 **Elvis Presley And Shakin' Stevens, Volume 1:** Italy and the Netherlands cassette; featuring eight songs by each artist; picture sleeve.

Elvis Presley (EP): Blue Suede Shoes; Shakin' Stevens (SS): Sweet Little Rock 'N' Roller; EP: Heartbreak Hotel; SS: Nightrider; EP: Mystery Train; SS: My Girl, My Girl; EP: I'm Left, You're Right...; SS: Shake The Hand Of A Fool (Serre La Main D'un Grand Fou); EP: I Love You Because; SS: Jump, Jump, Jump; EP: I'll Never Let You Go; SS: Hop, Rock And Bop; EP: I Forgot To Remember; SS: Wee Wee Hours; EP: Baby Let's Play House; SS: Tossin' And Turnin'

1986 **Elvis Presley And Shakin' Stevens, Volume 2:** Italy and the Netherlands cassette; featuring eight songs by each artist; picture sleeve.

Elvis Presley (EP): Tutti Frutti; Shakin' Stevens (SS): Two Hearts, Two Kisses; EP: Money Honey; SS: White Lightning; EP: Tryin' To Get To You; SS: Do The Bop; EP: That's All Right (Mama); SS: Silver Wings; EP: Good Rockin' Tonight; SS: You Talk Too Much; EP: I Was The One; SS: The Georgia Peach; EP: I Got A Woman; SS: Punk; EP: Just Because; SS: Lonesome Town

1987 **Good Rockin' Tonight:** CD.

Justine; Tiger; Sugaree; Baby I Don't Care; Sweet Little Sixteen; My Baby Died; Jungle Rock; Frantic; Tear It Up; Ready Teddy; Story Of The Rockers; Monkey's Uncle; Silver Wings; Outlaw Man; Girl In Red; Reet Petite

1987 **Let's Boogie:** LP; partly recorded live at the London Palladium.

Come See About Me; Forever You; A Little Boogie Woogie (In The Back Of My Mind); Because I Love You; What Do You Want To Make Those Eyes At Me For?; The Hits Keep Coming: Cry Just A Little Bit; You Drive Me Crazy; A Rockin' Good Way (To Mess Around And Fall In Love) – duet with Bonnie Tyler; Give Me Your Heart Tonight; A Love Worth Waiting For; Green Door; I'll Be Satisfied; A Letter To You; Shirley; Oh Julie; It's Late; Marie, Marie; It's Raining; Hot Dog; Teardrops; This Ole House

1988 **A Whole Lotta Shaky:** LP; reissued in UK on CD as *A Whole Lotta Hits* (not the same as the Danish item of that name).

What Do You Want To Make Those Eyes At Me For?; How Many Tears Can You Hide?; Jezebel; Sea Of Love; True Love; Just One Look; Oh Julie; Do You Really Love Me Too?; I'm Gonna Sit Right Down And Write Myself A Letter; Josephine; Woman (What Have You Done To Me?); Heartbeat; Tired Of Toein' The Line; Mona Lisa

1988 **Outlaw Man:** CD (but see *c.*1990s CD of the same name).

Tiger; Girl In Red; Outlaw Man; Manhattan Melodrama; Don't Rip Me Off; Sweet Little Sixteen; Jungle Rock; Donna; Red Flag Rock; Get Back John; Silver Wings; Give Me A Break

1980s **Rockin' And Shakin' With Shakin' Stevens:** Cassette.

Jungle Rock; Monkey's Uncle; Tear It Up; Silver Wings; Ready Teddy; Story Of The Rockers; Justine; Frantic; My Baby Died; You Mostest Girl; Reet Petite; Girl In Red

1980s **Roll Over Beethoven:** Double cassette album.

Volume I: Roll Over Beethoven; White Lightning; Hi Heel Sneakers; Manhattan Melodrama; Alan Freed; California Cowboy; Lady Lizzard; Outlaw Man; I Told You So; Longer Stronger; Like A Teenager; Holy Roller;

You Mostest Girl; Sexy Ways; Honey Hush; Evil Hearted Ada.
VOLUME II: Jungle Rock; My Baby Died; Reet Petite; Monkey's Uncle; Silver Wings; Memphis Earthquake; Rock Around With Ollie Vee; Story Of The Rockers; Frantic; Baby Blue; Ready Teddy; Tear It Up; Justine; Oakie Boogie; Wine, Wine, Wine; Blue Swingin' Mama

1980s *Shakin' Stevens And The Sunsets*: Cassette.
That Is Rock 'N' Roll; I'm Not A Juvenile Delinquent; Right String Baby; Come Along With Me; Girl Please Stay; Little Queenie; Lonely Blue Boy; Make It Right; Shooting Gallery; Baby; Sea Cruise; Rock 'N' Roll Singer; I Feel Apart; Super Star; Honey Don't; Sea Of Heartbreak

1980s *Shakin' Stevens And The Sunsets*: Cassette.
Tiger; Wee Hours Blues; My Girl; This Time; Shake The Hand Of A Fool (Serre La Main D'un Grand Fou); Baby I Don't Care; Peggy Sue; Lonesome Town; Tossin' And Turnin'; Jump, Jump, Jump; Two Hearts Two Kisses; Queen Of The Hop

1980s *Shakin' Stevens And The Sunsets*: Cassette.
Maybelline; White Lightning; One Night With You; Hi Heel Sneakers; Tallahassee Lassie; Yakety Yak; Roll Over Beethoven; Hearts Made Of Stone; Good Rockin' Tonight; At The Hop; Walking On The Water; Rip It Up (Saturday Night)

*c.*1980s *Greatest Hits*: Netherlands LP and cassette.
Tossin' And Turnin'; Jump, Jump, Jump; Two Hearts Two Kisses; Nightrider; Lonesome Town; Punk; Do The Bop; Shake The Hand Of A Fool (Serre La Main D'un Grand Fou); Sweet Little Rock 'N' Roller; The Georgia Peach; You Talk Too Much; Hop Rock And Bop; Wee Wee Hours; My Girl My Girl; Silver Wings; White Lightning

*c.*1980s *Very Best Of Shakin' Stevens, The*: Germany cassette.

This Ole House; You Drive Me Crazy; It's Late; Green Door; Teardrops; Oh Julie; Marie, Marie; It's Raining; Give Me Your Heart Tonight; Shirley; Cry Just A Little Bit; A Rockin' Good Way (To Mess Around And Fall In Love) – duet with Bonnie Tyler

*c.*1980s *Starportrait*: Europe cassette.
Cast Iron Arm; Leroy; Flying Saucers; I'll Try; Down Yonder We Go Balling; Hawkins' Mood; Down On The Farm; I Believe What You Say; The Spirit Of Woodstock; I Hear You Knockin'; Thirty Days; Schooldays (Anthem)

*c.*1980s *Super 1*: Europe Cassette.
This Ole House; Hot Dog; You And I Were Meant To Be; Make It Right Tonight; Lonely Blue Boy; Do What You Did; Shotgun Boogie; Revenue Man; I Guess I Was A Fool; Holy Roller; No Other Baby; Get Back John

*c.*1980s *Sweet Little Rock 'N' Roller*: Cassette.
Ruby Baby; Peggy Sue; Hey Good Looking; It Came Out Of The Sky; Shake The Hand Of A Fool (Serre La Main D'un Grand Fou); Lonesome Town; You Talk Too Much; Sweet Little Rock 'N' Roller; Wee Hours Blues; Lady Lizzard; Silver Wings; White Lightning

1990 *Hits Of Shakin' Stevens, The*: CD; 1994 reissued in Denmark as *A Whole Lotta Hits* (but see the *c.*1990s CD of the same name).
This Ole House; You Drive Me Crazy; It's Late; Green Door; Teardrops; Oh Julie; A Love Worth Waiting For; I'll Be Satisfied; Marie, Marie; It's Raining; Give Me Your Heart Tonight; Shirley; Cry Just A Little Bit; A Rockin' Good Way (To Mess Around And Fall In Love) – duet with Bonnie Tyler; A Letter To You; Why Do You Treat Me This Way?

1990 *There's Two Kinds Of Music . . . Rock 'N' Roll*: Netherlands LP and cassette.
Love Attack; I Might; Yes I Do; You Shake Me Up; Tell Me; Tear It Up; My Cutie Cutie; The Night Time Is The Right Time; Pink Champagne; If I Lose You; Queen Of The Hop; Rockin' The Night Away

1991   *Merry Christmas Everyone*: Cassette.
Rockin' Little Christmas; White
Christmas; Sure Won't Seem Like
Christmas; I'll Be Home This
Christmas; Merry Christmas Everyone;
Silent Night; It's Gonna Be A Lonely
Christmas; The Best Christmas Of
Them All; Merry Christmas Pretty
Baby; Christmas Wish; Blue Christmas;
So Long Christmas

*c.*1991   *Hits I, The*: CD.
This Ole House; It's Late; Sea Of Love;
Shirley; Because I Love You; Teardrops;
A Rockin' Good Way; A Love Worth
Waiting For; Shame, Shame, Shame;
Hot Dog; Don't Turn Your Back;
Heartbeat; Tired Of Toein' The Line; A
Little Boogie Woogie (In The Back Of
My Mind)

1992   *Epic Years, The*: Cassette album and
CD; 2004 digitally remastered and
reissued on CD as *Collectable*.
This Ole House; Cry Just A Little Bit;
Lipstick, Powder And Paint; Green
Door; A Love Worth Waiting For; What
Do You Want To Make Those Eyes At
Me For?; A Rockin' Good Way (To
Mess Around And Fall In Love) – duet
with Bonnie Tyler; Marie, Marie;
Teardrops; Turning Away; You Drive Me
Crazy; A Letter To You; Oh Julie;
Because I Love You; I Might; Hot Dog
(featuring Albert Lee on lead guitar);
Breaking Up My Heart; It's Raining;
Love Attack; Shirley; A Little Boogie
Woogie (In The Back Of My Mind);
Give Me Your Heart Tonight; It's Late;
Radio; I'll Be Satisfied

*c.*1992   *Hits II, The*: CD.
Oh Julie; You Drive Me Crazy; This
Time; I'm Knockin'; Give Me Your
Heart Tonight; A Letter To You; Merry
Christmas Everyone; Lawdy Miss
Clawdy; Que Sera Sera; Blue
Christmas; Josephine; What Do You
Want To Make Those Eyes At Me For?;
With My Heart; Endless Sleep

*c.*1992   *Hits III, The*: CD; 1998 reissued on CD
as *The Hits Of Shakin' Stevens Vol. 3*.
Green Door; Cry Just A Little; The
Shape I'm In; Turning Away; I'll Be

Satisfied; Breaking Up My Heart;
Marie Marie; I'm Gonna Sit Right
Down And Write Myself A Letter; Treat
Her Right; Lonely Blue Boy; Your Ma
Said You Cried; Lipstick, Powder And
Paint; It's Raining; Mona Lisa

1993   *All The Hits*: Triple CD or cassette box
set version of The Hits I–III

1994   *Singles Collection, The*: Germany CD.
You Drive Me Crazy; Oh Julie; Green
Door; A Love Worth Waiting For; This
Ole House; Cry Just A Little Bit;
Lipstick, Powder And Paint; A Rockin'
Good Way; Marie, Marie; Teardrops;
Turning Away; A Letter To You; I
Might; Because I Love You; Breaking
Up My Heart; It's Raining; Shirley; A
Little Boogie Woogie (In The Back Of
My Mind); Give Me Your Heart
Tonight; It's Late; I'll Be Satisfied; Your
Ma Said You Cried; Yes I Do; I Can
Help; Merry Christmas Everyone

*c.*1990s   *A Whole Lotta Hits*: The Danish
Collection: Denmark CD; the 1994
Denmark LP of the same name has a
different track listing.
A Rockin' Good Way (To Mess Around
And Fall In Love) – duet with Bonnie
Tyler; Oh Julie; You Drive Me Crazy;
Cry Just A Little Bit; Green Door; Give
Me Your Heart Tonight; Breaking Up
My Heart; Heartbeat; Hello Josephine;
I'll Be Satisfied; It's Late; Marie, Marie;
What Do You Want To Make Those
Eyes At Me For?; This Ole House; A
Letter To You; A Little Boogie Woogie
(In The Back Of My Mind); A Love
Worth Waiting For; Because I Love You;
I Might; It's Raining; Lipstick, Powder
And Paint; Merry Christmas Everyone

*c.*1990s   *Greatest Hits*: CD; 2001 reissued in
Germany as *Best Of The Best Gold:
Greatest Hits*.
Ruby Baby; Queen Of The Hop; Two
Hearts, Two Kisses; Baby I Don't Care;
She Got The Gimmies; This Time;
Peggy Sue; Hey Good Looking; Wee
Hours Blues; I Rocked; Too Many
Stars; Tossin' And Turnin'; Hop, Rock
And Bop; Lady Lizzard; Nut Rocker;
Nightrider

*c.*1990s *Greatest Hits, The*: Poland CD; two
cover versions.
Two Hearts, Two Kisses; White
Lightning; It Came Out Of The Sky;
You Talk Too Much; Sweet Little Rock
'N' Roller; This Time; She's Got The
Gimmes; Ruby Baby; Hey Good
Looking; Wee Hours Blues; I Rocked;
Outlaw Man; Rock Around With Ollie
Vee; Blue Swingin' Mama

*c.*1990s *Manhattan Melodrama*: CD.
Longer Stronger Love; Outlaw Man;
Lady Lizzard; I Told You So; The Spirit
Of Woodstock; It Came Out Of The
Sky; That's Rock 'N' Roll. Numbers
8–13 are performed by The Honolulu
Dance Band (all instrumental): A Love
Worth Waiting For; Cry Just A Little
Bit; A Rockin' Good Way (To Mess
Around And Fall In Love); Give Me
Your Heart Tonight; Shirley; Oh Julie

*c.*1990s *Outlaw Man*: CD (but see 1988 CD of
the same name).
Baby I Don't Care; Queen Of The
Hop; Peggy Sue; Hey Good Lookin';
Two Hearts, Two Kisses; Wee Wee
Hours; This Time; Lady Lizzard;
Sugaree; Lonesome Town; Tiger; Girl In
Red; Outlaw Man; Manhattan
Melodrama; Don't Rip Me Off; Sweet
Little Sixteen; Jungle Rock; Donna

*c.*1990s *Rock 'N' Roll Is Here*: Poland CD; two
cover versions.
Jungle Rock; Tear It Up; Silver Wings;
Ready Teddy; Reet Petite; Sweet Little
Sixteen; Rock Around With Ollie Vee;
Tiger; Lonesome Town; Shake The
Hand Of A Fool (Serre La Main D'un
Grand Fou); Peggy Sue; Queen Of The
Hop; Baby I Don't Care; Two Hearts,
Two Kisses; This Time; Hey, Good
Lookin'; Wee Hours Blues; Outlaw Man

*c.*1990s *Rocker, The*: CD.
Drinkin' Wine Spo-Dee-O-Dee; You
Mostest Girl; Reet Petite; Silver Wings;
Ready Teddy; Frantic; Tear It Up;
Monkey's Uncle; Sexy Ways; Oakie
Boogie; Evil Hearted Ada; My Baby
Died; Baby Blue

*c.*1990s *Sixteen Great Songs*: CD.
Baby Blue; Jungle Rock; Silver Wings;

Rock Around With Ollie Vee; Frantic;
Sexy Ways; Evil Hearted Ada; Wine,
Wine, Wine; Ready Teddy; Reet Petite;
My Baby Died; Honey Hush; Oakie
Boogie; Tear It Up; Monkey's Uncle;
Blue Swingin' Mama; Story Of The
Rockers

*c.*1990s *Sweet Little Sixteen*: CD.
Sweet Little Sixteen; Ready Teddy;
Reet Petite; Queen Of The Hop; Story
Of The Rockers; Jungle Rock; Peggy
Sue; Frantic; Two Hearts, Two Kisses;
Justine; Baby I Don't Care; Shake The
Hand Of A Fool (Serre La Main D'un
Grand Fou); Ruby Baby; Tiger

1998 *Hits Of Shakin' Stevens Vol. 2, The*: CD.
Hot Dog; Lipstick, Powder And Paint;
Turning Away; Because I Love You; A
Little Boogie Woogie (In The Back Of
My Mind); Come See About Me; What
Do You Want To Make Those Eyes At
Me For?; Feel The Need In Me; How
Many Tears Can You Hide?; True Love;
Love Attack; I Might; Radio; Que Sera
Sera; Josephine; Merry Christmas
Everyone

1999 *Very Best Of Shakin' Stevens, The*:
Germany three-LP box set; Norway
CD.
Ruby Baby; Queen Of The Hop; Two
Hearts Two Kisses; Baby I Don't Care;
She Got The Gimmies; This Time;
Peggy Sue; Hey Good Looking; Wee
Hours Blues; I Rocked; Too Many
Stars; Tossin' And Turnin'; Shake The
Hand Of A Fool (Serre La Main D'un
Grand Fou); My Girl; Hop Rock And
Bop; Do The Bop; The Georgia Peach;
Lonesome Town; Jump, Jump, Jump;
Nut Rocker; Lady Lizzard; Night
Rider; Tiger; Don't Rip Me Off; Give
Me A Break; Girl In Red; Outlaw Man;
Manhattan Melodrama; Sugaree; Sweet
Little Sixteen; Silver Wings; Donna; Get
Back John; Jungle Rock; Red Flag
Rock

2003 *Hits And More*: Triple CD box set.
CD 1: This Ole House; It's Late; Sea
Of Love; Shirley; Because I Love You;
Teardrops; A Rockin' Good Way (To
Mess Around And Fall In Love) with

Bonnie Tyler; A Love Worth Waiting
For; Don't She Look Good; Hot Dog;
Don't Turn Your Back; Do You Really
Love Me Too; Tired Of Toein' The
Line; A Little Boogie Woogie (In The
Back Of My Mind).
CD 2: Oh Julie; You Drive Me Crazy;
This Time; I'm Knockin'; Give Me Your
Heart Tonight; A Letter To You; Merry
Christmas Everyone; You And I Were
Meant To Be; Que Sera Sera; Blue
Christmas; Josephine; What Do You
Want To Make Those Eyes At Me For?;
With My Heart; Feel The Need In Me.
CD 3: Green Door; Cry Just A Little
Bit; The Shape I'm In; Turning Away;
I'll Be Satisfied; Breaking Up My
Heart; Marie, Marie; Don't Tell Me
We're Through; Treat Her Right; I
Guess I Was A Fool; Your Ma Said You
Cried In Your Sleep Last Night;
Lipstick, Powder And Paint; It's
Raining; Radio (Acoustic Version)

2004 *Collection, The*: European CD box set
with bonus DVD; digitally remastered.
Reissue of *The Epic Years* with bonus
tracks: I'll Be Satisfied; Feel The Need
In Me; It's Late; Merry Christmas
Everyone.
DISC TWO – DVD: This Ole House;
A Little Boogie Woogie (In The Back
Of My Mind); Come See About Me;
What Do You Want To Make Those
Eyes At Me For?; A Rockin' Good Way
(To Mess Around And Fall In Love) –
duet with Bonnie Tyler; Love Attack;
Teardrops; Turning Away; Green Door;
Radio; My Cutie Cutie; It's Late

VIDEO CASSETTES AND DVDS
CHRONOLOGICALLY

1992 *The Epic Videos*: digitally remastered;
not available as a DVD format.
This Ole House; Cry Just A Little Bit;
Lipstick, Powder And Paint; Green
Door; A Love Worth Waiting For; What
Do You Want To Make Those Eyes At
Me For?; A Rockin' Good Way;
Teardrops; Turning Away; You Drive Me

Crazy; A Letter To You; Oh Julie;
Because I Love You; I Might; Breaking
Up My Heart; It's Raining; Love
Attack; Shirley; A Little Boogie
Woogie; Give Me Your Heart Tonight;
It's Late; Radio

1990s *Shakin' Stevens in 'Oh Boy!'*: DVD;
includes full TV documentary of *Elvis –
The Musical*, plus one full episode of
Oh Boy!

APPEARANCES ON COMPILATIONS

1971 *Battle Of The Bands*: All By Myself;
LP; reissued in 1991 on CD as *The Best
Of Rock 'N' Roll*

1972 *The Great British Rock 'N' Roll –
Rockabilly Album*: Jungle Rock; Girl In
Red;
LP;

1972 *The Rock 'N' Roll Super Show Live*:
Little Queenie (Live);
Germany double LP

*c.*1972 *Platinum High School*: Justine; Jungle
Rock; My Baby Died; Story Of The
Rockers;
LP

1973 *Rockabilly Dynamite*: Sweet Little
Sixteen; Girl In Red;
Germany double LP

1973 *The Best Of Rock 'N' Roll*: Little
Queenie (with live crowd overdub);
LP

1973 *The Great British Rock 'N' Roll –
Rockabilly Album II*: Sweet Little
Sixteen; Silver Wings;
LP

1973 *The Rock 'N' Roll Super Show*: Little
Queenie, Right String Baby, Rock 'N'
Roll Singer, Sea Of Heartbreak, Come
Along With Me (with live crowd
overdub);
Germany LP

*c.*1974 *Rockabilly Dynamite II*: Lady Lizzard;
Outlaw Man;
Germany LP

*c.*1976 *Rockabilly Greatest Hits*: Justine; Jungle
Rock; My Baby Died; Story Of The
Rockers;
LP

Discography and Videos

1977   *It's Rock 'N' Roll*: It's Rock 'N' Roll (Intro); I Told You So; Sexy Ways; LP and cassette; also released as *Make Like Rock 'N' Roll*

1978   *Elvis – Cast Album*: Tupelo Mississippi Flash, Blue Suede Shoes, King Creole, Dixieland Rock/Got A Lot Of Livin' To Do/Wear My Ring/Ready Teddy, Trying To Get To You, Too Much, Such A Night, My Baby Left Me, Treat Me Nice, Mean Woman Blues, Jailhouse Rock; LP and cassette

1979   *Jack Good's Oh Boy!*: Medley: Summertime Blues/C'mon Everybody/Something Else/Twenty Flight Rock (with Fumble); Honey Don't; LP and cassette

1982   *Hit Wave '82*: Oh Julie; LP

1982   *Light Up With Dynamite*: Justine; LP

1983   *Hot Hits 1*: Jungle Rock; Netherlands red vinyl 7-inch promotional EP for Coca-Cola only, picture sleeve

1985   *Rockabilly Rebels*: Girl In Red; Jungle Rock; LP

1980s   *Forever Young*: A-SIDE: Rod Stewart: In A Broken Dream; Why Does It Go On? B-SIDE: Shakin' Stevens: Sweet Little Sixteen; Reet Petite; 7-inch EP

1990s   *Shakin' Stevens & Gene Vincent CD Double Pack*: You Mostest Girl; Sexy Ways; Honey Hush; Evil Hearted; Jungle Rock; My Baby Died; Reet Petite; Monkey's Uncle; Silver Wings; Memphis Earthquake; Rock Around With Ollie Vee; Story Of The Rockers; Frantic; Baby Blue; Ready Teddy; Tear It Up; Justine; Oakie Boogie; Wine, Wine, Wine; Blue Swingin' Mama; One CD for each performer

INDEX

Index